MW01532573

"The text and photos look great!"
— JIMMY CARTER, whitewater paddler, author,
39th President of the United States

"*Wherever Waters Flow*... is a flood-stage read with few eddies."
— JOHN LANE, author of
Chattooga: Descending Into the Myth of Deliverance River

"Doug has led an incredible life, filled with paddling, wilderness
trips, conservation battles, and working with young people.
In *Wherever Waters Flow*, he recounts his own story with great
modesty and graciousness towards his companions."
— PAYSON KENNEDY, founder of Nantahala Outdoor Center,
technical advisor and stunt man for *Deliverance*

"Doug is responsible for many people seeing rivers as paths to
adventure, as our forefathers did. To each of these people,
Wherever Waters Flow is a record and proof, a capsule of
'a time that will not come again.'"
— CLAUDE TERRY, founder of Southeastern Expeditions,
technical advisor and stunt man for *Deliverance*

"Doug Woodward helped me understand a central part of my father's
novel, *Deliverance*, — the river itself. *Wherever Waters Flow* is a
wild rush of experiences around the world, but also a thoughtful,
intimate look at the environment, its future and ours."
— CHRISTOPHER DICKEY, author of *Summer of Deliverance*,
Newsweek's Middle East Regional Editor and Bureau Chief in Paris

WHEREVER WATERS FLOW

A Lifelong Love Affair with Wild Rivers

To Patricia Price,
who was with me
at the start of this story,
companion, sweetheart,
fellow swimming instructor,
practical joker and much more.
Warmest wishes to you and
your beautiful Family.
Love always,
Doug Woodward

by DOUG WOODWARD

HEADWATERS
PUBLISHING

Produced by Headwaters Publishing   SAN: 850-654X
PO Box 494   Franklin, North Carolina 28744   USA
www.headwaterspublishing.com

LIBRARY OF CONGRESS CATALOGING-IN-PUBLICATION DATA

Woodward, Douglas Lamar, 1936 –
Wherever Waters Flow: A Lifelong Love Affair with Wild Rivers /
Doug Woodward
272 p.: photos; 21.5 cm.
Includes bibliographical references and index
ISBN 0-9779314-0-4 (hardcover, alk. paper)
978-0-9779314-0-8
1. Kayaking – North America – History.   2. Canoeists – United
States – Biography.   3. Woodward, Douglas Lamar – Travel.
4. Deliverance   5. Carter, Jimmy, 1924 – .   6. Chattooga River –
History.   7. Colorado River – History.   I. Title.

GV782.42.W66 W66 2006
797.1224092 — dc22
Library of Congress Control Number: 2006924812

First Edition — 2006

Printed and bound in the United States of America
by The Maple-Vail Book Manufacturing Group, York, Pennsylvania.

The paper in this book meets the guidelines for permanence and
durability of the Committee on Production Guidelines for Book
Longevity of the Council on Library Resources.

Cover design by Lynn Woodward — www.lynnwoodwarddesign.com

Credits listed on page 258

Life is a daring adventure — or nothing.

— Helen Keller

Wherever Waters Flow is dedicated to my children,
Cricket, David, Autumn, Forest, Rivers and Canyon,
expert paddlers in their own right, who would not let me rest
until I had put my whitewater memories on these pages.

Contents

Moment of Truth

Your life hangs by a thread. Your kayak is gone. But you have no time to notice. The icy water is quickly sapping your strength as you struggle to free yourself from the current surging through the strainer. The tree that your arms are wrapped around is slippery, worn smooth by time and the river. The odds of escape are small. Not thirty minutes ago Trish said she felt as if we might die today. Cricket and Dave were uncharacteristically silent. Out of sight upriver, these three, trusting your judgment, are now about to follow you into whitewater hell. Rain continues to fall as the river explodes and complains against the canyon walls. Hundreds of miles from another person, deep in the Yukon Territory, whatever fix you come up with must be totally your own. You stupid, egotistical whitewater nut, how could you put the lives of these three, who are closest to your heart, in such peril?

Does your life flash before your eyes? Not exactly. But for just a moment, think back. What was it that drew you here — whitewater challenge, wilderness beauty, or just the thrill of adventure? Did you spring into this scene with your whitewater psyche fully formed, knowing that this was where you someday had to be? Or did this passion develop gradually until it filled your entire being with the unquenchable desire to know what lay around each bend of every river?

For me it was the latter, that struggle for survival on Canada's wild Tatshenshini coming nearly twenty years and thousands of river miles after my paddle first thrilled to the excitement of entering a river rapid.

~

Trish, my close companion for the past year, had seen my slides of the 1978 Noatak river trip that I took with my kids, Cricket and Dave. She had been in the North Country herself a couple of years earlier, so the thought of enjoying that wilderness again had been intriguing. We researched rivers, checked logistics, set dates, and made plans in earnest. Cricket and Dave, now 17 and 15, would be included as we began to narrow our choices down to a handful of rivers in southeastern Alaska and western Canada. Finally, it was agreed that we would paddle the Tatshenshini River, starting in the Yukon Territory, eventually joining the ice-choked Alsek River near the Alaska border.

So, on July 15, 1980, we boarded the *Matanuska*, one of the large coastal ferries, and slid quietly out onto Puget Sound, watching the Seattle skyline recede behind us. Being low-budget travelers, we "camped" under the solarium with perhaps fifty others on the top deck. Music and conversation were in abundance. Privacy was not.

We came to know many of the travelers and something of the hopes, dreams and adventures that they looked forward to. A few we would be in touch with later. There was Richard, whose fiancée waited for him in California; he would canoe the Yukon River alone before returning for the wedding. It was not until the next year that we heard from him. He had stopped multiple times along the river, once to help a native family re-roof their cabin and on another occasion to fly with a bush pilot for several weeks on a surveying job. In the end, he was three months late, hitchhiking from Alaska to California as the snow began to pile up, often spending three days at the roadside before someone who could carry his canoe and gear would stop. When he finally returned to California, his fiancée promptly told him to get lost!

Four days after our Seattle departure, Trish, Cricket, Dave and I gathered our gear and tramped down the gangway to look for a ride into the town of Haines, Alaska, shrouded in mist and drizzle. We could not then have imagined the story of our own that we would be telling two weeks later.

Our plan was to paddle our kayaks for twelve days through the wilderness of the Yukon and British Columbia, join the Alsek River and cross back into the panhandle of Alaska. At the river's mouth, on the Gulf of Alaska, we gambled that we would arrive on schedule and that our bush pilot could find us among the glaciers, mountains and fickle Alaskan weather.

The remote Tatshenshini is far from any permanent human habitation. Until Bart Henderson pioneered the 140-mile run in 1975, only a handful of explorers and the native Tlingit Indians knew the river as a travel route. Now the Tlingits are elsewhere and Jack Dalton's post on the gold route (actually a tollgate for prospectors) near the river's headwaters has stood abandoned for more than a hundred years.

So, this was our kind of adventure — planned and carried out by the four of us. The boats and equipment were our own, much of the gear accumulated over years of such activity. Maps of the river were obtained from Denver and Ottawa. Food and clothing were carefully planned and packed in Atlanta. The logistics of getting in and out of this remote territory were made through long distance calls to Haines, Alaska. Likewise, specific details of the river were searched out through conversations with Sobek Expeditions. We also learned that Sobek had an expedition leaving a day after ours. But we expected to see no one on the river, nor did we want to. By nightfall of our first day, those feelings would change.

At this point in time, we could claim to be experienced whitewater paddlers, but on the remote Tatshenshini our abilities would be handicapped by a necessary equipment choice. The boats must be large enough to carry substantial supplies, but must fold or deflate to fit into a bush plane. This meant using either rafts or folding kayaks. A raft large enough and reliable enough to handle this river, with rowing frame and

At the Tatshenshini River put-in, Yukon Territory, July, 1980. Left to right: Lynn "Cricket" Woodward, David Woodward, Trish Severin, and the author. Boats are in the light colored bags at left; food, clothing and camping gear in remaining bags.

oars, would have cost $3500 at the time. Renting a professional rig like this is nearly impossible and even if we could afford to buy one, we would be limited to just one, a dangerous way to tackle a wilderness expedition. We opted for four folding kayaks at about half the total cost. Designed for two persons each, we figured that four of these would give us a margin of safety in case of mishap. But with a weight three times that of our slalom kayaks at home, plus the load of food, clothing and other gear, maneuverability would be limited. The low profile and long open cockpit makes the boats suitable for only moderate rapids. But that is all the Tatshenshini is supposed to have — under normal conditions.

~

Two hours ago, we knelt on the coarse stones of the riverbank, carefully lashing supplies and equipment inside our kayaks. We launched in the relative calm of a tributary creek, joining the Tatshenshini two hundred yards later as it churned impressively through the valley, carrying its load of glacial silt, the color of liquid cement.

The river is full, reaching beyond its banks in places. It's difficult to judge now exactly what this level will mean to us a few miles later as the river tumbles through a boulder-choked gorge.

My pulse is pounding with the river as I feel the powerful current grip the boat. Trish and Cricket follow at discreet intervals. David runs sweep to pick up the pieces. Dark clouds roll in before a stiff wind and sheets of rain make it tricky to pick the best channel.

Half a dozen miles on a writhing serpent — fallen trees in narrow channels — scattered rocks funneling water into jolting souse holes — dangerous, but avoidable hazards. The speed and power of the river continue to impress us. And the rain falls even harder.

In a fast-moving channel to the left of a narrow island, Trish catches a squirrely wave and goes over. Not a good omen. Swimming is not her style. We bump her in to the tail of the island, regroup and push on.

The Tatshenshini begins to narrow; dark canyon walls loom up through the weather. For the next seven miles, the river will be squeezed into a twisting canyon, where the most demanding rapids of the trip await our coming.

Early on, we realize that the run will be touch and go. Leisurely turns around sheer rock faces have now become driving currents, exploding against the walls, turning under and rising again as treacherous boils. Draw stroke, draw stroke! There are too many close calls as the heavy boats do not respond like our slalom kayaks. Some waves can't be avoided and are breaking into the open part of the cockpits. Two miles into the canyon, we are barely able to catch a narrow eddy on the right wall with all four boats. Stopping places — even this small — are almost nonexistent.

Unloading the kayaks to dump water will be too cumbersome, so we each remove a rubber boot for bailing. Trish wants to wait for Sobek or lower water, but there's hardly a place to stand, let alone camp. Cricket is unnerved from fighting her heavy boat, while Dave is somber, his thoughts turned inward.

I climb with some difficulty to a point perhaps two hundred feet above the river. The route is visible for a quarter mile ahead, then takes a sharp bend to the left and drops out of sight. My eyes are drawn to the chaotic maze of waves, boulders and holes before me. For a long time I stand and concentrate on what's fixed, what's moving, memorizing the route as I would a whitewater slalom course.

Joining the others, I describe what I think is the best route and voice the opinion that if the last five miles of the canyon are no worse than the first two, we just might make it. But the looks and the silence contradict me. I take the throw rope from David's kayak and put it in mine, saying that it's more logical to have it in the lead boat.

Even the re-entry of the main current is tricky and I stroke hard upstream to cross to the point where I want to enter the rapid I've just scouted. Sliding quickly into the rapid between two rocks, still moving left, I'm looking for a small eddy I had seen from above. Now some quick hard moves to avoid a monument-like rock protruding from the river that, within the next thirty minutes, will become known as "Trish's Boulder." I spot the eddy, set the boat angle and drive. Thump! A rock hidden underwater blocks my turn and the rushing water carries the kayak on past. Instinctively, I complete the move and grab a tiny stopping spot below the next rock.

The rest of the route that I had seen from the cliff still looks runable from river level and I motion for Trish to start. Peeling into the current again, I head for the turn. I'm thinking that if I can find another eddy below the bend, I'll stop and get set with the throw line in case anyone has trouble.

Now I'm into the curve and the waves and holes are much bigger than I had guessed. Unavoidable. Too many of them. One look at the part of the river I couldn't see before and I know it's all over. Our normal kayaks (light weight and fully decked) could make it, but not what we're in now.

A wave breaks over my head and water floods into the boat around my waist. Shake water out of my eyes — draw to the right — another wave hits — another, another and another. I feel the boat go under. I'm still in the cockpit, but the river is swirling around my ribs. If only I can somehow jam the swamped boat into the shore before it broaches on a rock.

This is not to be. I'm in river center, too far from either side. A van-sized hole suddenly stands the kayak on end and I'm swimming in the 46-degree water. I know the others can't see me now and will follow. That's the worst thought — I'm about to put three other people into the same mess and I'm powerless to help them.

Then I see the tree protruding thirty feet into the river from the right bank, the trunk just on the surface, angry currents swirling through the submerged branches. Boaters know it as a "strainer." A death trap. The faces of friends — competent boaters that have drowned that way — flash through my mind. Bob Goeke. Julie Wilson. Walt Blackadar. Lisa Sebacher.

Stay where I am and I'll go safely by the end of the log — but into even worse rapids. There's an eddy just upstream of the log. A slim chance. If I miss, I'll be in the strainer. Kick. Pull. Stroke. Repeat. But the current is far too strong to allow a swimming escape. I can see that I'm going to be swept right into the tree.

Can't let myself go underneath. Shove the boat away. Reverse the usual rule — get my head and arms downstream. I'm there. Grab the trunk and pull up. Crunch! The log hits me in the lower ribs like a blocking lineman. Suction on my legs is terrific. There will only be strength for one try. Have got to find a way to raise my body a few inches. My left toe finds a branch. Push with the foot. Press up slowly. Don't slip. As my hands desperately cling to the slippery trunk, my body weight moves over my arms with agonizing slowness.

Suddenly I'm up. Hardly thirty seconds, but an exhausting effort. No time to think of that. Trish should have been here by now. Was she swept past while I struggled in the tree? And what of Cricket and Dave? Now a kayak appears. Upside down. A wave tosses it and I catch a glimpse of the red deck. Cricket's boat! A yellow life jacket and small face appear in the wave ten feet to the side. She's clear of the kayak. But heading straight for the log!

Cricket would later sit down and pour out her feelings on paper. These are her words:

"I do not want to go on — I know I can't handle the water. Dad first peels into the current — stay left — he'll catch an eddy. I see him try to make the eddy, then disappear not around a bend left or right, but down.

Trish now, and my stomach churns — good thing I didn't have any bean stew. I would throw up. As I paddle to the current of no return, Dave shouts at me, 'Trish is out!' Oh shit — I should try to stop and help her — no, keep yourself going — Dave'll handle it.

Well, the rapid's not too bad. I'm out in the middle when I spot Trish — boat wedged between rocks, hanging onto the back of the boat — I can't move any closer to shore. There's no way I can get over to her.

The holes are getting to be monsters — I'm taking in too much water. Damn! The boat starts to sink — I see little wood braces floating off. No! I can't wreck a boat.

I see Dad kneeling on a sweeper. Now I'm holding onto the paddle and a boat end. The water is so fast and strong and murky — I can't see what's coming as far as rocks go.

I'm heading right towards Dad — good — no, not good — I'm going under that tree! It's serious — let go of the boat — throw Dad the paddle — grab the top of the tree — stay up. Dad's grabbed my left wrist — I have his wrist. My legs are under the log — I'm facing upstream — short of breath — keep calm. Pull, Dad! No progress. He moves and my head slips under — I can't get a breath — twist, struggle — don't breathe, you'll cough and choke.

Dad, I let go, let me go. Suddenly I'm floating, gasping for breath. How long was I under? Seems like an eternity of struggling — maybe a minute. It'll be a nightmare for a good while to come."

With great anxiety, I drop Cricket's wrist — I know that I can't keep her underwater any longer and yet I'm unable to pull her clear. If she doesn't come through under the tree, I'll drop off the downstream side and hopefully work her past the branches. She bobs to the surface and my heart falls back into place. Moments later, we stand at the river's edge and just hug each other.

Quickly our thoughts turn to Trish and Dave. Where are they? Do they need help? If still upstream, they must not run the bend. Downriver, perhaps a quarter mile, my eye catches a kayak hull grotesquely twisted around a rock in the center of the rapid, frame members protruding through the skin. A shape that could be a person appears to lean against the rock. My God! Trish? Pinned in her boat?

"Cricket, get upstream to a point where you can see someone and signal them to stay put. I've got to help Trish if she's caught downstream." No time for relief — it's not over yet. Cricket and I scramble off in opposite directions.

Halfway to the wreckage, I realize that it's my boat, not Trish's. What appeared to be a person in a rain parka is actually a combination of my black rubber camera pack and another blue waterproof bag, pushed up out of the boat and against the boulder.

I'll look later. Quickly, I get back to Cricket and we exchange information. Both David and Trish are still upstream on the opposite side,
apparently OK, but with only David's kayak visible. Cricket is sure they
know not to take to the river again. We chuckle over the double-take I
had made on my boat.

Just being alive is cause for celebration. But soon, we've got to take
stock. What's left? What can we salvage? What can we do with what
we've got? We're all wearing our rain gear and warm clothing — that's a
plus. My buck knife is on my belt. My pocket yields matches in a zip-lock
bag — soaking wet! But there are also matches in almost every waterproof bag — if we can get to them.

We look first at Cricket's boat. No more than twenty feet from the
end of our infamous tree, it has wrapped around a submerged rock,
pinned firmly in place by the strongest flow of the river. Within the hull
are all of Cricket's clothing and personal equipment. There also, is the
bag of group equipment — pots, stoves, fuel, utensils, rope, rain fly, tool
kit, repair materials, candle lanterns, spare batteries and a hundred similar items — all of the camping gear except tents (my boat) and sleeping
bags (Trish's boat).

We need to get to the wreck, but cannot find a way without putting
our lives at great risk again. Jumping from the end of the log would only
result in being swept downstream through more dangerous rapids. A
sheer canyon wall blocks our path fifty yards upstream. To swim out at
this point would wash the swimmer right into the log again. Since both
the kayak and rock are almost completely underwater in a swirling torrent, no eddy or foothold exists where a rescuer could work. We shake
our heads sadly and make our way down the narrow shore toward
my boat.

The salvage prospects don't look much better. With the river perhaps
150 feet in width, the kayak is broached squarely in the center of the
rapid. A glimmer of hope — a little more boat and little more rock are
exposed to view than at Cricket's wreck. Maybe we can nudge the boat
off of the boulder — but then what?

We wade into the icy water, floating a medium log about 35 feet long
— point upstream, let the current swing it — now shove! Too short. The
log spins by the rock and quickly disappears downriver.

A new plan — and Cricket's words again:

*"So we hike upstream to a logjam and select a larger log — perhaps
sixty feet long and a foot or more in diameter. It takes more than
an hour to roll it into the water and control its floating down to the
boat.*

We swing it out to the rock — too short — we almost lose it to the current. Pull! All right, we've got it. Reposition! Leaning against the rushing water, we wade out chest deep and swing it again. The end catches on the boat — barely.

I grab the bracing pole for Dad and he wedges it against the log and the river bottom. 'Can you hold onto this and brace the log?'

'I'll try.'

'If the log slips or you can't hold it anymore, shout, but jump clear of the log — it could knock you down and out.'

Dad holds onto the downstream side of the log, wading and swimming toward the rock. Just as he's to the end, the brace slips off the bottom — I re-ground it and try to brace with all my strength.

'Dad, hurry!' He has to cross the log and get up on the rock. The log overpowers me and I have to let it go — not a moment to spare. Dad looks over at me. Relief. I'm shaking.

He digs into the wreckage, pulls out the throw line, ties an end to the boat frame and tosses the rest to me. I tie it to a downstream tree, at an angle with the current.

First package to be ferried — camera, etc. — with plane tickets, travelers checks, cameras, lenses — safe! Open — dry! Photo-op!

After losing three of four boats in unexpectedly high water, the author, with daughter Cricket's help, engages in a difficult mid-river salvage operation.

More ferrying — use the 150-foot climbing line as a circular ferry — Dad's clothes bag, a canteen, the 30-.06 rifle, the medical bag, the tents, Dad's snack bag."

Now the water is jamming into the ends of the boat with tremendous pressure. The twisted skin and frame of the kayak, with the load removed, start to slide up onto the rock. My lower legs are numb from standing in the frigid flow — probably two hours — and I almost fall as part of the boat wraps around an ankle.

Time to leave. We don't need a hypothermia problem on top of everything else. I untie the climbing line and motion for Cricket to coil it in. Grasping the throw rope as far out as possible, I jump clear of the boat, which slides off of the rock as my weight in the rapid whips the rope taut. Hand over hand. Shore again. The wreckage of my kayak slides underwater and disappears downriver, leaving only a wooden cross-brace dangling on the end of the throw rope.

We're now significantly better off than we were several hours earlier. However, we're also wet and cold. It's getting dark and Cricket and I are still on one side of the river, Dave and Trish on the other. During our salvage efforts, Dave and Trish had hiked down the far side of the canyon to a position across from ours and — over the deafening roar of the water — motioned with hand signals that they had all of their gear, but only one boat.

Picking the most vital bags, Cricket and I work our way up the now familiar shoreline. I edge along thirty feet of rock wall with inch-wide toe and finger holds, swirling water below, realizing that this is where I sent Cricket to signal after our episode with the log. Meanwhile, Cricket is setting up the tents on a small patch of gravel dangerously near river level. No other choice — the canyon is too steep.

I see that Dave and Trish have managed to line David's kayak down to a point opposite the eddy where I now stand. David is preparing to ferry across to me, a tricky maneuver, to say the least. It's almost dark, and he'll have to cross a terrific jet of water, directly above the dangerous log and the rock where Cricket's boat is wrapped.

Trish beams a flashlight at the standing waves and holds the end of the kayak as Dave gets into position in the cockpit. Smooth, strong strokes away from the bank — keep a small angle with the current — lean downstream. Good. Now the main current to cross. Don't get spun out — tighten up the ferry angle — hard lean. Perfect execution and the boat whips into my eddy.

"Is everybody OK?" Dave and I ask each other as we hug. We each start to relate our own tales, then stop as we realize what remains to be done as the canyon darkens.

"Trish and I have found a pretty good spot to camp on a high bank," Dave says. Cricket is still working with the tents, out of sight and too far away to hear a shout, thirty minutes round trip by foot. She'll understand. I grab the paddle that Cricket tossed onto the sweeper and climb into the kayak with Dave. We can no longer see Trish, but her light blinks out at intervals from the dark of the far shore.

Crossing from this side is a more difficult task. The swirling eddy current is so strong that it catches our stern on the first two attempts. This completely destroys our ferry angle and forces a quick recovery to avoid being swept upstream against the sheer wall. Take a different approach. Work to the downstream tip of the eddy, spin the boat on the eddy line, and give it everything we've got up river. There's no margin for error — we're only two boat lengths above the log — but it works. In the dark we feel the grip of the river and respond with a hard lean. The angle is perfect and, moments later, Trish reaches past the flashlight and pulls the bow up onto the rocks.

More hugs. The three of us scramble up river over boulders, then up a thirty-foot bank, using roots for hand and toe holds. A quick inspection by flashlight confirms that we can squeeze two tents among the trees and bushes on a narrow but somewhat level shoulder of the canyon. Dave stays to try coaxing a blaze from the rain-drenched driftwood. If anyone can, he will.

I head back to the kayak. Cricket will be wondering about the delay by now. Another tricky crossing to make. It must be well after midnight for it's quite dark, even with the long Yukon daylight of July. Trish's flashlight sweeps over the black rushing torrent as the boat engages the river once more. Butterflies. Success again.

Cricket has one tent up and is working on the other. I tell her of the new plan and we quickly dismantle and repack the tents. Taking only the rifle, tents and my clothing bag, we climb into the kayak once more. The rest of the gear can wait until morning. Cricket will not paddle this time, keeping her weight low for stability. I'll repeat the procedure that worked for Dave and me last trip, entering the rapid at the tail of the eddy. Careful. No time for another mishap.

Drive hard again. Lean. Stroke quickly to maintain position. All by feel and sound. Finished. For the first time in probably eight hours, we're all on the same side of the river. We pull the boat high onto the rocks, then tie it to a bush another ten feet above water level. Trish opens a bag of gorp to share and we suddenly realize how hungry we've been.

We work our way upstream, boulder hugging and hopping again. Ten minutes later we're passing gear bags in a relay up and over a small cliff, David reaching down from the top. Tongues of flame blaze out from a nest of rock. Welcome warmth.

We change into dry clothes. Trish shares with Cricket, who has none. Their sizes are a good match, but at this point any dry clothing is welcome. Tents are soon up, barely squeezing between bushes. A little more food is shared as we warm by the fire, taking time at last to consider what we've all been through.

When Cricket had last seen Trish, she was hanging onto her boat at the top of the rapid, the swamped kayak wedged between "Trish's Boulder" and another rock. David had been swept by the same eddy that I had missed earlier, but had turned to face upriver, managing to pull in beside Trish's boat in position to help. Together, they were able to salvage all of the gear that Trish was carrying. Then, just as it appeared they might retrieve the submerged kayak, the river wrested it out of their grasp. They could only watch as the Tatshenshini swallowed it completely.

By the comfort of the small fire, we discuss our situation. Half of our food is lost, as are the pots, pans and stove. The bag must have been ripped out of my boat before Cricket and I could get to it. Much of the remaining food can be eaten as is, and the freeze-dried dinners can probably be reconstituted with cold water or heated in stages in their own foil packets. The countryside is full of berries. We won't starve.

Cricket's lost clothing is critical, but if she and Trish are careful to stay dry, they both can manage. I've lost two of my three warm tops — a heavy wool shirt-jacket in the general camp bag and a fiberpile pullover that didn't quite make it ashore in the salvage effort. At one point, my kayak was hung on the rock by the 30-.06 alone. The rifle looks intact, but I can't help wondering if it shoots around corners now.

None of us are hunters and our feeling toward bears — as with all wild beings — is friendly, but respectful. We don't wish an aggressive encounter, but if such a situation is forced on us, we intend to survive. Half of the ammunition is lost, but the other half (20 rounds) is safe in the rifle case.

The majority of maps are underwater in the general camp bag. However, the topographic maps of the immediate area, together with my engineer's compass, are safe in the camera bag. Many non-critical items are lost, too — newly purchased books and several hundred dollars worth of film mailers.

With only one boat remaining, there is no way we can continue down the river on our own. One person could paddle ahead for help, but that would take at least a week, even if the water dropped enough to make the canyon runable. The dangers to the lone paddler are too great — we quickly move on to other options.

Hiking cross-country back to the gravel road at Dalton Post is a possibility that offers some hope of success. If we made it, we might stumble onto a fisherman or get help from one of the half dozen or so vehicles that travel the road each day. The big task would be getting out of the canyon itself — we'll check the map in the morning when we retrieve my camera bag.

Our third alternative rests with Sobek Expeditions. We know that they will run large rafts with rowing rigs, but will they have capacity to take on four castaways with gear? It would be unfair to crowd their paying customers.

We're fairly sure that Sobek will start their expedition tomorrow. But what time? It would be disastrous if they passed by while we slept. Snuggled together for warmth, we sink into a fitful sleep. The physical and mental exhaustion of the day wage a tug-of-war with the necessity for being up and alert early in the morning.

~

First light in the canyon. What time is it? Six? Eight? Canyons are deceptive in shutting out light, even with the long northern day. The only watch is in my camera bag on the far shore. Surely Sobek could not have passed by yet.

A quick handful of food and we scamper down to the rocks above the bend. This spot commands a view upriver for nearly half a mile. Equipped with a whistle to alert us as well as Sobek, David will take the first watch. Lifejackets are draped on limbs and rocks to attract attention. I keep mine.

Trish and I follow the shore around to the kayak, while Cricket hangs clothing and camping gear to dry on the rocky shelf, which is now catching morning sun. Ferrying to the other shore is more reasonable in daylight, but still risky. As I lock paddles with the river once more, sunlight floods against the far canyon wall. For the moment, the rain is gone.

Bringing gear up the shore from the spot opposite my wreck is just as tedious as the night before. Two long and cautious trips along the narrow toeholds of the shear wall clear the area and all is loaded in the kayak.

One more task before I paddle back. This spot is highly visible to a boatman running the bend (if he can remove his eyes from the rapids) — a good place for a sign.

Still in my jacket is a waterproof marker that I had been using to mark bags in the airport. Taking the four-foot piece of inside floor out of the kayak, I carefully dry the white vinyl surface. "HELP" is printed in foot-high letters, followed by a brief explanation, our initials and the date. Rope from the boat is used to fasten the sign between two branches facing upstream.

Back together, the four of us look at the topographic maps and discuss the hiking possibilities. The map shows an old trail paralleling the river a half-mile back from the canyon rim, but on the opposite shore. This is probably the old Dalton route — or what's left of it — and passes near our put-in.

The real kicker will be the climb out of the 2,000-ft. deep canyon, carrying food, clothing, rifle, sleeping bags and other necessities. We study the walls and slopes on the far side — the prospects are not encouraging. I have the 150-ft. climbing line, but almost no hardware. Our hopes for help turn to Sobek again.

David wants to stay on lookout. I bring him some food and the rifle, which I have dried as best I can. We fire two rounds to test for accuracy and to clear the barrel of moisture. Except for water in the scope, which we can't reach without tools, the rifle works perfectly. My watch reads two o'clock.

Trish and Cricket work to put our salvaged gear in order. I look for a better route from our campsite to the kayak and almost step in some bear scat. Less than a day old.

Suddenly David's whistle shrills above the roar of the water. Half a dozen times the signal is repeated. Sobek! Rafts! Help! I know they can't stop where David is, so I scramble over the edge and down the bank above our kayak, almost tumbling into the river in my haste.

A raft appears fifty feet from shore. I motion frantically toward our spot. Three seconds more and it will enter the next part of the rapid, unable to land. "Catch you at Silver Creek!" shouts the oarsman.

"No! No! We need help!" I yell back. Silver Creek is eight miles down-river, their camping spot for tonight.

"Stiff neck! Can't pull the raft that way!"

Shivers run down my back as I see help disappearing, the raft sliding by the wreck of Cricket's boat and on into the rapid, our brief communication cut off by the noise of rushing water.

But even as I feel the frustration of the passing raft, head guide Bart Henderson has picked up on the signals and is driving the second raft toward the spot where I stand. "Grab my bow line!" Bart yells. I turn in surprise and the coil of rope hits me in the chest. In my excitement, I nearly pull the ton of raft, people and gear completely out of the water.

Behind Bart comes yet a third raft, whipped smartly into shore by a grinning red-bearded boatman. I tie off the two rafts to a stout tree and explain our predicament to Bart and Jack Morison (of the red-beard). Dave, Cricket and Trish soon join the group.

"No problem," Bart says. "With three guides and only five customers, we're actually running an extra raft. We've got plenty of food, particularly considering what you have left. Welcome aboard."

"You're life savers — literally! We'll be glad to pay whatever you decide is fair."

"We'll talk about that when the trip is over. Right now, relax. From now on, you're part of us."

Stan Boor, the elusive first boatman, joins us from downriver, where he's managed to find enough of a toehold to stop his raft on the canyon wall. He apologizes for passing us by, explaining that he realized too late that we needed help. With his river position and a badly aching neck and shoulder, he was unable to get the raft into our spot.

Now a flurry of action. I dismantle the kayak and pack it into bags while the others do the same with our camp. Passengers and guides help haul our gear and lash it inside the rafts. Within thirty minutes we're back on the Tatshenshini — as passengers.

Cricket's submerged boat and the treasures it contains are left to the elements and the salvage efforts of later river runners. Our perspective has changed. We strain inwardly with the boatmen as they bend oars to angle away from a hole or rock, but we no longer control our destiny.

The remaining five-mile stretch of canyon water is impressive — way too much for the folding kayaks. The guides tell us the river is the highest that they've seen in their five years of Tatshenshini experience and that normally it can be run in an open canoe.

We emerge from the canyon and set up camp at Silver Creek. The tension of the past two days is slowly replaced by a feeling of camaraderie with our rescuers and their group. Dutch ovens produce mouthwatering delights and we pitch in with chores whenever possible. But the rain continues and the power of the river grows each day.

Stan Boor pulls on the oars (foreground) as the Sobek rafts emerge from the upper canyon on the Tatshenshini River after having picked up the pieces of the Woodward family expedition.

A hundred miles away at the Alaska border, after the Tatshenshini has joined forces with the Alsek, Bart estimates the river's flow at 250,000 cubic feet per second. Even as we watch, we see the river cutting new channels, shaving tons of earth, dropping fifty-year-old spruces every few minutes and tossing massive blocks of ice as if they were Ping-Pong balls. Floating hazards are everywhere.

Then, as we approach Alsek Bay in Jack's raft, warning shouts from Bart and Stan suddenly alert us to the danger of our position. Jack has not guided on the Tat previously, and has chosen a line too far to the left. A rocky island rises out of the water, splitting the raging river into two huge, high velocity channels. The right hand channel is clear, but the left — to which we are now committed — is completely blocked by an ice dam over a mile in width. To follow our present course will be almost certain suicide for, on hitting the giant ice wall, we'll be quickly sucked far below the surface to become part of the frigid barrier.

We're still a quarter mile from the ice dam, but that distance is shrinking rapidly. The comparative safety of the rocky island is quickly slipping by too, 200 yards on our starboard side. Jack is putting everything he has into the oars while I visually give him slight corrections to his ferry angle. For the last ten minutes, I curl my hands over his on the oars and we both put all our strength into bringing the raft to shore before it's too late. We barely make it. The wall of ice is an awesome sight close up as we pause to regain a bit of energy for the long pull to the head of the island. An hour later, we engage the right hand channel and within minutes are spinning into the Alsek Bay eddy where we'll make camp.

Rafts drawn up at Alsek Bay camp after narrowly escaping disaster at the ice dam. The author with daughter, Cricket, and son, David.

~

The rest of the trip will blend together in retrospect. Exploring tumbling side creeks that have no name. Camping by glaciers that groan and crash all through the night. The superb culinary abilities of our adopted guides. Their tales — of the raft bitten in two by an angry hippo on Ethiopia's Omo — the raging cataracts of Chile's Bio-Bio — of Bart's being chased by a grizzly for more than a mile, the grizzly finally veering away to leave Bart spitting blood and gasping for breath. Bald eagles eyeing our progress. Each turn of the river outdoing its predecessor in a panorama of majestic glacier-covered mountain peaks.

Exploring a glacier at Alsek Bay with the Sobek crew.

We arrive at Dry Bay on the Gulf of Alaska to set up camp in hurricane-force winds. Nothing flying. Well, not quite. A sudden roar close by has us staring in amazement as a twin-engine apparition thunders into the teeth of the storm. Sixteen-year-old Catsy Williams is piloting an old DC-3 three times a day from the fish camp next to us to Yakutat and back with loads of salmon that won't wait for the weather. Hugging the coast and bucking the gusts, she flies at minimum altitude for the hundred-mile round trip.

Waiting out the weather for two days, we hit a brief lull and word comes over the fish camp radio to get it together — a bush plane is on the way from Yakutat. They're still not flying out of Haines, so we head north instead of south, needing two trips to get the four of us out. There is little time, tickets are changed to the new flights even as we fly, and the connections are unbelievably close. The other passengers probably wish we weren't so close, since we're still traveling in our river clothes, our bodies unwashed for two weeks. All too soon the sadness of really being home sets in as we think of the Tatshenshini and what we have just experienced.

But the memory — and the reality — which stands out the most, is the tough spirit of our small group on the day when our trip came apart. No one thinking of self. The strength of Trish in the center of crisis, stressing the positive and cheering us all. Cricket, fighting for her life, then turning in the next moment to signal the others and salvage gear. The coolness of Dave, in control all the way, able to share his strength when most needed. We may or may not face such a crisis again. But each time we've returned to the wilderness, our trust and confidence in each other has been even stronger and deeper. And for that, we can thank the Tatshenshini.

~

After *Alaska Magazine* had published my account of our Tatshenshini/Alsek experience, I received a note from Richard Tero, a priest in Soldotna on the Kenai Peninsula. A kayak paddler and river explorer himself, he was familiar with both the Alsek and Tatshenshini Rivers, adding greatly to my knowledge of the history of both. He had also been a good friend of Walt Blackadar, whose death I had mentioned in my article, and who had gained early whitewater fame with his 1971 solo run of Turnback Canyon on the Alsek.

Tero himself had run the Alsek in 1970 with Dee Crouch, Bill Evans, Vivian Mendenhall, Clem Rawert and June Weinstock. Rawert, running with John Dawson in a two-person Klepper in 1961, made what is likely the first paddling descent of the Alsek. Both groups portaged across Tweedsmuir Glacier in order to avoid Turnback Canyon.

Four years later, hoping to repeat his previous Alsek trip, Tero returned with Dee Crouch and Klaus Streckmann to again run the river in kayaks. This time however, upon arriving at the head of the canyon, they found the Tweedsmuir Glacier badly broken up and impassable. After a grueling five days of bushwhacking, the trio finally emerged at Dalton Post. They later flew in to recover their abandoned kayaks.

In 1997, seventeen years after our own Tatshenshini-Alsek adventure, I returned to Alaska for a two-week solo camping trip on my mountain bike. My ferry-connected loop included Anchorage, Seward, Kodiak Island, Homer, and of course Soldotna before culminating in Denali National Park.

Richard Tero was ready for my foggy two-wheeled arrival at his Soldotna home, including a dinner that would satisfy the appetite of the hungriest of bikers. Late into the evening we swapped river tales and shared memories of the many rivers we both had experienced. Tero and another friend had prearranged a canoe trip on the Swanson River, including food and shuttle. The three of us spent three days canoeing the Swanson and watching the silver salmon running upriver as they created their own waves. Before leaving, Tero gave me a video of Blackadar's Susitna runs and other Alaska whitewater history. It was a fitting way to tie together the tattered threads of our Tatshenshini trip.

Before I Knew

When I was four, my Dad, an excellent swimmer and athlete, told me to hold tight to his neck as he dove into the large spring on my great-grandfather's south Georgia farm. The water in those southern springs comes from deep underground, the temperature rivaling that of the glacier-fed rivers of the West. As soon as the waters closed over my pleasantly warm little body, I lost my grip, my breath, and any desire to try the stunt again. Of course my Dad's strong arms had me out in seconds, but there was no convincing me of a second try. Years later, as I wrestled my kayak down Alabama's Little River Canyon at fifteen degrees — paddle, boat and beard all iced over — I would remember that first introduction to frigid water.

A few months after the incident at the spring, as the United States rushed into World War II, my Dad was gone. He lay crushed beneath his half-track as it rolled down an embankment during blackout maneuvers of the First Armored Division. At 29, he had been a West Point graduate and commander of the First Armored's Headquarters Company. A diver of waterfalls, I had many times seen him plunge into Hawaii's deep pools from rocky cliffs beside the falling water during the two years he was stationed there. Dealing with our grief as best we could, Mother and I moved back to Pennsylvania, where she taught English and eventually bought an old farmhouse in Chester County, five miles from her childhood home in Oxford

Timberbrook, as we came to call it, was nestled against a steep wooded hill, and overlooked a large meadow through which flowed Muddy Run. An old mill, converted years before to neighbor Bob Hogg's cabinet-making shop, stood on the far side of the creek. The waterwheel and millrace, both long idle, beckoned me to explore. Explore I did, not only figuring out the engineering that went into making the mill do its thing, but getting to know every twist and turn in our creek from the old iron bridge to its junction with Octoraro Creek.

I would occasionally fish in the pool beneath the bridge and bring home bass or sunfish for Mother to clean and fry. But it was the water itself that I became intimate with — the feel of it on my skin in flood or drought, its power, its voice. The frog pools that it left when a flood receded, the little grassy islands, the path that a twig or leaf might take when running a mini-rapid, the futile attempts at rock dams — these were all my domain. The gift that Mother gave me in this country living experience was probably far more than she ever imagined.

But in those same years — the lean war years of rationed gasoline and scarce auto repair parts — Mother drove us to Mary Gwynn's Camp in the mountains of North Carolina so that I could have a two-week camp experience, made possible by trading her skills as a counselor during the same period. Long before the days of Interstates, such journeys were major challenges as we made our way through unmarked highway intersections with inadequate roadmaps.

Mary Gwynn's Camp had a small lake that always felt as if ice cubes had been added to it. But it was here, much to my delight at age seven, that I learned the watermelon float, crawl and elementary backstroke. "Stanny" was an unusually caring and competent instructor, probably in her mid-twenties. And I also remember how well she could handle a canoe on the lake.

Toward the end of those two weeks, I woke to a high fever one morning. After reading the thermometer, the camp nurse told me, "Get your bedding — you're going to spend the night in the infirmary!" Several hours later, a very concerned nurse tracked me down at morning swim and told me they had been looking all over camp for me and what was I doing in the lake. Shucks, I just thought they meant that I should show up that night, and besides, the lake seemed a great place to treat a fever.

Those early camp experiences brought me into contact with water time and again — not just at the lake, but hiking to the falls a mile or so up the creek that fed the lake, belly-sliding with my cabin-mates through a large road culvert after a heavy rain, visiting Conastee and Toxaway Falls, and sitting on the pebbly bottom of an infant French Broad River while ripples and sunlight danced around me. Little did I know at the time how deeply entwined with the rivers of this region my life would become.

Mother decided it would be an adventure to return to Pennsylvania by way of the Great Smokies. It was. The road through Newfound Gap was single-track mud, enveloped in swirling mist, and Mother later would say that I was looking for bears in the bushes — I found one — while she was looking for angels in the clouds. She didn't find any in the clouds, although one appeared in mechanic's garb later that day when our right front tire blew out. Against all wartime odds, he found one that fit our wheel, and the widow and her young son were able to continue their journey.

The next summer in Pennsylvania, my cousin Franklin, who was sixteen and had been a Boy Scout for several years, invited me to visit him at Camp Horseshoe for a day. I was eight. At one point we walked to the edge of the water where a canoe waited. Franklin held it steady while I climbed in.

"Sit there! Yes, right on the bottom! Don't stand up, don't move, don't even wiggle or we might turn over!" he admonished.

For perhaps fifteen minutes we paddled on the placid water, but it's the only memory of that day that remained. I sat obediently on the varnished, glistening ribs, surrounded by brass screw heads and a dark green skin. The Old Town — for that's undoubtedly what it was — had somehow captured a part of my spirit. Though as yet undefined, there was a subtle promise in those moments. A promise of a dimension of freedom that I had never before even dreamed of.

~

It would be four more years before I would again set foot in a canoe. Years filled with turmoil and changes in family life.

After six years as a widow, Mother married again and I was sent to live with her sister Sara, also widowed, at Sara's home in Drexel Hill outside of Philadelphia. A year later, in the fall of 1948, Mother and Pete (my stepdad) bought a house in Towson, Maryland and I was reunited with the family.

I turned twelve that September and immediately joined the local Boy Scout Troop. I had just missed the first season of the new Broadcreek Scout Camp, but nothing could hold me back from being there the following summer. Broadcreek, set deep in what was then farm country north of Baltimore, was actually many camps in one. Troop 312 of Towson, to which I belonged, made the Daniel Boone site their home for a week. In the middle of the huge acreage lay a sixty-acre lake, the centerpiece of water activity for all of the many campsites.

It was on this lake at Broadcreek that I was first able to paddle my own canoe, so to speak. Each succeeding season, I would devour all of the water skills that time would permit, until I had earned Scout Lifeguard and was teaching Canoeing Merit Badge to other Scouts.

Later, I became a student at Georgia Tech in Atlanta, and as soon as I turned eighteen, I signed up for the Red Cross Water Safety Instructor class taught by swimming coach Fred Lanoue. Lanoue was known for having developed the drown-proofing course required of all students at Georgia Tech and Emory University, the same training having been credited for saving the lives of many U.S. Navy personnel during World War II. His most dramatic tale was of a sailor who, with both arms and a leg fractured after his ship was blown out from under him in the Pacific, stayed afloat for nine hours, using only the survival float until help arrived.

Lanoue was tough as an "old salt," had a sideways crab walk and gave no quarter when it came to students meeting the requirements of his drown-proofing course. The same held true in spades for his Red Cross WSI (Water Safety Instructor) class. All candidates had their ankles bound together, hands tied behind their backs and were then pushed into a single lane of the pool to do the survival float for as long as he deemed necessary.

Then came the diabolical part. With a pole he began to herd us into a smaller and smaller area at the deep end of the lane until there was not room for everyone to remain on the surface at the same time. We were watched carefully by a number of helpers. Any candidate who was failing to surface and showing signs of distress, signaling for help, or could not remain within the designated area was immediately helped from the pool and dismissed from the WSI class. After this test, about three-quarters of the candidates remained, and nothing that followed was quite as difficult as that first hour. This, of course, was not standard Red Cross procedure, but those of us that finished knew that it was just a bit more special to have earned our WSI with Coach Lanoue.

The following summer I added Canoeing Instructor certification to the WSI and kept both current for many years as I taught within the Red Cross and Scouting programs. That same summer, 1955, saw me teaching full time for the Red Cross at Kramer's Pool, within walking distance of our Maryland farm. Pat Barnes, my fellow WSI instructor, boarded at Nell and Fred Kramer's house on the hill above the pool and together we taught the whole range of courses from Beginning Swimmer to Senior Life Saving. Having a terrific sense of humor, she was loved by the kids she taught. We spent the summer trying to one-up each other with practical jokes.

Every summer, no matter what other job I might have, there was always a week during which I would take the Scout Troop back to Broadcreek. But year after year, the lake seemed to shrink and become more familiar. The rules — for Scouts and leaders alike — remained familiar, too. ' Stay visible on the lake." "No horseplay." "Don't go near the dam." "Stay in your boat at all times." "Don't go up the creek."

Wait a minute. Don't go up the creek? Why not? That's exactly where I want to go. In fact, I begin to realize, this has been the missing link in my canoeing experience for a long time.

I ease my canoe into the mouth of the creek that feeds the lake. No one seems to notice. Some ripe blackberries overhang the bank. I stuff a few in my mouth and paddle around the bend, no longer "visible on the lake." At the next bend I notice that the water is moving, too. This is fun. How far can I go? Not much farther it turns out, as a large deadfall blocks the creek from bank to bank. I ease myself back into the lake proper, all my world looking just as it did fifteen minutes ago. But something has happened inside of my head. A new route to the wilderness has opened. The siren voices are calling and will not be denied. I must go to the river.

My first whitewater canoe trip — on West Virginia's Cacapon River in June of 1959 — marked a turning point in my life that had its effect on all that was to follow. The waves were soon to engulf family, friends and unsuspecting acquaintances.

First Love

Well, I could graduate from Georgia Tech this August if I just kept on taking classes…but I'll be damned if I'm going to give up my summer — particularly this summer. The dream that has been pulling at my heart for so long, is now within my grasp.

"Fred, please come back to Maryland with me. You know you'd like to see the farm and eat some good country cooking. Beth will get you a date with her sister Peggy for sure. And I know I can find a canoe somewhere. Two canoes? No, the girls aren't too keen on moving water, though they'll ride any horse you might come up with. Yeah, I do have a river in mind. It runs north out of West Virginia and there's nothing but green all around it on the map. There's a new Explorer Scout Base near Hancock, Maryland on the Potomac that has canoes and I bet they'll let me borrow one, my being a Scoutmaster and all. The river? It's called the Cacapon. No, I'm not stuttering."

The year was 1959 and Fred Scharar, my roommate at Tech, did come north. He was an excellent athlete and into healthy nutrition long before it became a fad. I never saw him eat a candy bar. He persuaded me to practice and compete in Judo at a gym in downtown Atlanta. After graduation, Fred became a pilot, first for the Navy and then with American Airlines. And we did double date with Beth and Peggy before heading for the river. But Fred wasn't the only one in shape. After enjoying an evening of Quaker beauty and wit with the Grey sisters, his comment to me was, "I don't think I'd want to have to arm-wrestle either of those girls!"

At Camp Strauss, Ranger Jim Collie not only had a 17-ft. Grumman canoe waiting for us, but had agreed to drop us off at our Capon Bridge put-in.

"Can't tell you guys much about what's down there, I mainly fish it, but there're no big waterfalls. The water's good — not too high, not too low — you'll have a lot of fun. Try to take note of any tough spots so we can tell the Scouts that come later."

I would make copious notes of each rapid and where to best run it all the way down the river. Obviously, neither of us knew of the existence of Randy Carter's guidebook for paddling rivers of this region, published a few years earlier.[1]

"Hang on a minute. I'll get you something that will help." Jim fished a hand ax out of his truck and stepped to the edge of the woods. In a few minutes he had cut two saplings about ten feet long and two to three inches in diameter. "Lay these on the bottom of your canoe — they'll help keep your gear dry."

In those days we had never heard of dry bags and few existed in 1959. At last we had stowed our gear and supplies and were ready to challenge the wilderness of West Virginia.

"Remember, portage the dam to the left, and then when you come to the Potomac, turn left and paddle upriver for three to four miles. Turn right when you come to the mouth of Sideling Hill Creek. You'll know you're there when you see the C&O Canal aqueduct crossing the creek. Good luck!" And with these words of advice, Jim climbed into his truck and was gone.

Well, it wasn't quite Lewis and Clark, but it sure felt like it. What lay ahead? Have we allowed enough time to paddle fifty-five river miles? How do we get through a rapid when we come to one? Will we recognize the dam before we get too close to the edge? Can we actually paddle up the Potomac for three miles? Do we have enough food?

Fred took bow and I the stern. Within minutes, we were around the first bend, immersed in a world that seemed every bit as wild and remote as we had expected. Although I had more experience in a canoe than

[1] Randy Carter and his wife Miriam dedicated much of their lives to paddling and documenting the characteristics of the rivers of Virginia, West Virginia and the Great Smokies. Their work was extensive, and an inspiration to other pioneer paddler/writers such as Roger Corbett, Lou Matacia and Ramone Eaton, to name but a few of the many touched by their lives. Long before automatic river level monitoring came into extensive use, Randy personally calibrated and marked scores of bridge pilings with his own "paddler-friendly" system of judging river levels. Randy's guidebook was packed with wisdom and humor. And there was a wealth of black & white photos — all paddlers sans PFD's, of course.

Fred, neither of us knew exactly how to apply our knowledge to moving water. Through trial and error, we gradually learned that draws were useful, sweeps much less so, and that back-paddling was a necessity. If we happened to perform a ferry or eddy-turn, we had no knowledge of what we were doing, only relief at somehow remaining upright. Our toughest lesson came on the second day as we caught a mid-rapid rock, swung broadside to the current, and of course leaned upstream. As water poured in, we leaped out, snatching what gear remained above the surface. We lost our bread and a few other perishables, but still managed to sleep dry that night.

In retrospect, I realize that our water level was ideal, probably a foot and a half over canoeing minimum at the start, and dropping no more than six inches during the trip. The weather could not have cooperated more, with sunny, warm days and mild nights. The month was June. We would spend three nights camping on the Cacapon.

First whitewater river trip on West Virginia's Cacapon River in June of 1959. Left, the author (right) with Georgia Tech roommate Fred Scharar (left), camped near the Beeler cabin. Right, Fred sliding the canoe down the covered spillway at the Cacapon dam.

In those days, canoeing the Cacapon really was a wild and remote experience. The main signs of human habitation occurred at Largent and Great Cacapon, where a scattering of cabins and houses could be seen from the river, perhaps a quarter-mile or less up and downstream from where the highway crossed.

I can't now recall the particular day of the trip, but we had begun to look for a campsite much too late. We had been seeing only forested riverbanks for miles, and darkness was beginning to close in. Then, as if it had been placed there just for us, a small cabin in a grassy clearing seemed magically to appear in the dusk as we rounded a bend in the river.

There was no question in either of our minds. We came ashore, put our tent up in the yard and started dinner in record time. The cabin was unoccupied and behind it a spring gushed out of the mountain. It was our longest day on the water and we slept well and late the next morning.

"Do you hear a bell?" I asked Fred as we woke to sunshine dancing on the tent. We zipped open the door to find ourselves surrounded by a dozen curious cows, all looking at this strange object that was standing in the middle of their breakfast. They backed off as we emerged, but were soon followed by two men in a pickup truck.

"What do you two think you're doing here?" accused the older of the two. "Get your tent and yourselves out of here. Can't you read? This road is posted as private property all the way out to the highway."

"But we didn't see any signs," I replied. "We were in our canoe and it was getting dark and we hadn't found any place we could pull off until we saw..."

"You came down the river?" The tone of his voice had changed completely. "In that case, you're more than welcome. I want to hear all about it. I'm Harvey Beeler and this is my place."

"He owns the whole mountain," added the younger man, "and most of the apple orchards in this part of the state."

We visited for the next hour as we packed our gear and loaded the canoe. "Be sure to stop again," Harvey admonished. "And camp here anytime you're on the river." We waved goodbye to the two men and the cows as we headed into another day of adventure.

~

My concern over not seeing the dam in time was ill founded. Long before we were anywhere close, we could feel the current drowning in the backwater and pick out the razor-sharp horizon line on the river. A diversion tunnel carried most of the river through the mountain to the powerhouse on the opposite side, leaving a mile and a half gooseneck of riverbed largely un-watered.

On this day, unlike many others, there was actually a flow over the top of the dam, though greatly diminished by the absence of the water diverted through the mountain. We scouted from the left shore and decided to aim for the covered spillway in the center of the structure, where it might be possible to wrestle our loaded canoe onto the ramp and slide it down to the riverbed below the dam. The strategy worked, and we spent the next two hours alternately paddling in spurts or dragging the canoe over rocks and low-water bridges.

Soon we were passing the little town of Great Cacapon, heading for our rendezvous with the mighty Potomac. At least she seemed mighty to us after the days of paddling the intimate twists and turns of a much smaller river. But these days had engraved their own images into our memories — the tinkling curtain of water falling from a mossy ledge into the river, the rock spire known as Caudy's Castle towering above the surrounding forest, the breathtaking cliffs along Cacapon Mountain.

Now it was time to turn our loaded canoe upriver on the last leg of the journey. In those days, railroads still held the low ground on each side of the Potomac and trains clattered by much more frequently than in these present years. So, to the serenade of whistles and wheels, we began a demanding lesson in ferrying and eddy hopping. We had learned more than we realized at the time and as evening began to brush shadows across our path we slid quietly into the mouth of the creek beneath the Sideling Hill aqueduct. The teacher had been kind.

I knew, of course, that we had passed through wilderness only in a very limited sense, and that others had traveled this river before us. Nevertheless, the experience had given me a taste of what I had imagined running rivers was all about. My heart embraced the feeling of freedom and challenge in those Cacapon days and created an unquenchable thirst for more. For all the years to come, my life would be entwined with rivers, sometimes in ways that I could never have imagined.

~

That same summer, Broadcreek Scout Camp decided to replace all their canvas-covered wooden canoes with aluminum canoes. Aesthetically it wasn't that pleasing, but from the practical standpoint of having the boats used by thousands of Scouts in a season, it made sense. The well-worn canoes were up for sale and I rushed to be in included in the bidder list. My bids were accepted, and I became the proud owner of two sixteen foot Old Towns, one for $24, the other for $27, complete with fist-sized holes and broken ribs, planking and gunwales. By retrieving the serial number from the inside stem of each canoe and sending them to Old Town, I was able to get exact replacement parts. After stripping both boats and restoring structural integrity, I replaced the skins with canvas and filler, the construction of choice in those pre-fiberglass years. I now had two canoes of my very own!

After the idyllic conditions of my first river trip, I would be drawn back to the Cacapon with quite different results. Late that same summer, I convinced three of my older Scouts of the joys of river travel and we were off for the West Virginia mountains once more. Buddy Musgrove, Mike Grimes Glen Johnson and I decided to put in on the North River tributary of the Cacapon, planning to paddle *down* the Potomac this time, to the vicinity of Point of Rocks, where our shuttle would meet us.

We dragged our loaded canoes the quarter mile or so to where the North River met the Cacapon, which proved to be only marginally better. Where had the river gone? Ignorant of the very basics of reasonable river running — the fact that you needed a river with water in it — we forged ahead. Days and miles later, tennis shoes falling apart from the forced march down the nearly dry riverbed, we struggled into the backwaters of the Cacapon dam. One look at the waterless trough below the dam and we decided to end the trip here.

Looking no further for an exit route — and there was an easier one — we began the arduous task of pulling our canoes by rope up the side of the mountain. We came close to giving up, but several hours later we had gained the dirt road that lay above. From there it was an easy matter to stumble exhausted down to the powerhouse cottage where we made an emergency call for pick-up.

While wolfing down ham and tomato sandwiches generously offered by the powerhouse operator's wife, we heard an astounding tale. Even though it came from the source, I still have trouble swallowing it. A small canoeing group similar to ours had reached the dam a couple of years before, under similar drought conditions, and was considering the best course of action. They encountered a man just packing up his fishing gear and asked for his opinion of the best way to continue downriver. Apparently thinking his reply would be taken for the wisecrack that it was, he remarked, "Why right through the mountain," and departed the scene.

On that day the bottom of the intake gate was a couple of feet above the surface of the small lake so that the group was able to get low in their canoes and force their way into the tunnel along with most of the diverted river. What their feelings must have been and how much life was left in their flashlights at this point I can only imagine. A half-mile later they reached the powerhouse end of the tunnel only to find that the gate at that end had been lowered to control flow to the turbines and that the water level in the tunnel was beginning to rise.

It was at this moment that the powerhouse operator, checking on some part of the generating process, came close enough to hear the frantic pounding and yelling from within the tunnel. Incredible as it all seemed, he realized that there must be people on the other side of the water gate. Springing into action, he had the gate raised in minutes, the desperate group bursting out of the mountain. All were able to extricate themselves from the open channel to the powerhouse before being swept against the trash screen protecting the turbines. Anyhow, that's the story from those who were there at the time. Our own trip was totally exhausting, but not nearly as hair-raising.

〜

I should point out here, if it's not already obvious, that I was essentially operating in a vacuum with my whitewater paddling. No one I knew had any experience with rivers and the Water Safety Department of the Maryland Red Cross had actually begun to refer swift water paddling inquiries to me! It would still be several years down the river before I would become a friend with Ramone Eaton, vice president of the National Red Cross in DC and an experienced river runner of long standing. I had no idea that there were actually a few paddlers who would go out for a day of whitewater without making it into an expedition. Each time I would convince someone to accompany me on a river, that person would invariably have less experience than I, and often none at all.

One small piece at a time, I was learning. No water — no fun. How much water would be good? Well, I really didn't think of that — I just knew that I needed more and a whole lot must be just dandy. So it was that when the rains came in the week preceding Memorial Day, 1960, I grabbed my good friend Jack Cotton and headed for the Cacapon once again. We would only spend one night on the river, and thus avoid dealing with any problems that might arise at the dam.

It was still raining as we arrived at our North River put-in. "Hey, this is great," I said to Jack, "We won't have to drag the canoe like we usually do on this first bit of river." Somewhere far away there seemed to be a little voice saying, "You really don't know very much about what you're doing. In fact you hardly know anything at all."

I bent down and pulled a coil of rope from one of the packs. "I think it might be a good idea to tie our gear to the boat, Jack." A few minutes later we climbed in with our supplies, noticing that about four inches of freeboard remained.

At the junction with the Cacapon, all hell broke loose and we almost lost it right there. Now we were in it — big, rolling, noisy brown water, with haystacks rising and exploding in our path like mortar rounds. We tried to maneuver the loaded canoe to avoid holes, but with the speeding current and sluggish response, it was only a matter of time before we foundered. A very short time. Less than a quarter mile from the junction, the bow buried and did not rise again. For perhaps thirty seconds we continued upright in our submarine, nothing visible but our torsos and paddles.

Just before we did an involuntary slow roll to port, Jack swiveled around to fix me in his gaze, his words still calm and controlled. In a steady voice without detectable anxiety, probably in the same manner that carried him to the presidency of the Great Western Banks years later, he asked, "Woody, what in the hell do we do now?"

What the hell *do* we do now, I thought to myself. This is deep doo-doo.

"Hang onto your paddle and stay with the boat," I replied, trying to sound as if this sort of thing happened on every trip. "We'll look for a place to come ashore."

Now we were each clinging to an end of the canoe, only our heads visible above the seething surface. It was in this posture that we amazingly realized we were not alone. There on our left, his Foldboat drawn up above the river's reach, squatted a lone paddler in the rain. He seemed as surprised to see us as we were to see him. Any exchange of words was impossible over the roar of the river. We simply managed a friendly wave before disappearing around the next bend.

We clung to that canoe for at least a mile, without PFD's, competing for swimming space with logs and other debris, until I saw an area where the river was rushing through the woods. "If we can swim the canoe far enough to the right, I think those trees will help us stop." Side-stroking as hard as we could, we just made it.

But with megatons of water pushing from behind, landing a swamped canoe was not simply a matter of park and walk. Jack's glasses, hanging from a string around his neck, snagged a bush and separated him from his grip on the boat, creating a few tense moments until he was able to free himself. Fortunately, neither of us was on the downstream side of the canoe as it crunched, scraped and rolled into the woods and I was finally able to stop its progress by snubbing the bow line around a tree.

Having shortly worked the canoe to land, we began to take stock of our situation. Our gear and supplies were soaked, despite being wrapped in tarps, but it appeared that we had lost only a canteen and Jack's boots to the river. Our bodies soaked and shivering in the rain, we attempted to squeeze excess water from our gear. "I don't think we can risk repeating that experience," I said through chattering teeth. "Let's stop at the first possible camping spot."

The river gods smiled and apparently thought our lesson sufficient for that day. Bursts of sunshine appeared, the rain stopped and we made camp before encountering more river hazards. We soon had a good fire blazing, thanks to a stash of matches in a waterproof container. Our dinner was heated from canned goods. The biggest problem was our wet cotton sleeping bags. We spent half the night trying to dry them and the other half with the two of us squeezed as far into the driest bag as we would fit. Morning was never so welcome.

Having placed a stick at the river's edge the night before, we noticed that the water level had dropped significantly overnight and while we were packing, the man we had seen the day before eased his Foldboat into our spot.

"I saw you go by yesterday, but knew I couldn't help. You both looked very philosophical about the whole thing. The river was running eight feet at the bridge — almost touching it. Too much for my kayak without a sprayskirt." Our new friend was a professor at the University of Maryland, also addicted to river expeditions.

My Cacapon had shown her many faces — from that of the eager, perfect lover promising so much more; to that of the bored, indifferent companion; and now the wild reckless coquette on a spree, leaving suitors strewn along her path. I would seek her out again, but would also come to know many of her sisters.

Still Blundering On

Overnight canoe trips on the Potomac would follow, but they seemed to offer less wilderness and whitewater challenge. Obviously, I hadn't discovered the Great Falls to Little Falls section as yet. At night I would pore over topographic maps, making comparisons within my limited experience. The Potomac that I know churns along with a drop of three feet per mile while the Cacapon does a little better at five feet per mile, I said to myself. But hey, here's one that looks a lot better! The Youghiogheny. This section in Maryland drops 150 feet per mile.

Now, if you are a whitewater buff, you may think that this is one of the sections of the river known as the "Upper Yough," or perhaps the "Top Yough" by the cutting edge paddlers of today. Actually, it's neither. It's upriver of both. Nor is it the "Ultimate Yough," a narrow, torturous descent near the headwaters, first paddled by the CCA's[2] Ed Gertler[3] in C-1[4]. It's the stretch of river connecting the "Ultimate" with the "Top," a run just waiting to spring its surprises on us, not the least of which was

[2] Canoe Cruisers Association of Washington, DC.

[3] Ed Gertler has been actively exploring rivers for the CCA for the past four decades. Author of several area guidebooks, he is, at the time of this writing, program chairman for the CCA, often contributing accounts of his own whitewater adventures for the enjoyment and education of the group.

[4] A C-1 is a decked canoe paddled by one person, often confused with a kayak by the casual observer. In the C-1, however, the paddler kneels and uses a single blade, while the kayaker sits and uses a double-bladed paddle. A C-2 has two paddlers kneeling, each using single blades.

the load of raw sewage arriving from the town of Oakland as it flowed untreated down the Little Youghiogheny[5]. I would later christen it the "Stinky Yough."

But looking at the map, I thought, that's familiar territory. I've camped at Deep Creek Lake with my folks and visited Swallow Falls. I know there's a road to the falls. We can take out there. So who's arm can I twist for this adventure?

Even though I had been working for Western Electric in Baltimore for only two years, another young engineer had been assigned to learn some basics from me.

"Hey Jim, how would you like to do some unusual field studies next weekend?" Not only had Jim Rew not been in a canoe before, he had never even been camping.

"No problem. I've got the boat and all the gear we'll need. It'll be a trip to remember." Actually, my river trips were all turning out to be memorable. This one was to be no exception.

Saturday was warm and sunny as we pushed our canoe into the current a few miles northwest of Oakland. The year was 1961. Leaves were brilliant splashes of color reflected in the mellow waters of October. It was already mid-afternoon and we would paddle less than seven miles before making camp.

As we finished dinner, it became evident that the temperature was tumbling toward the twenties. Our tarp-draped shelter was rigged to catch heat from the campfire, but an all-night fire must be periodically stoked. So we slept rather fitfully and awoke tired, not relishing any early contact with chilly water. The river would shortly have its own say in the matter.

For a few hundred yards we cruised idyllically as we had the day before, rounding the first bend below our camp. The elusive sound that had been growing for the past twenty minutes had now become a roar.

"Where did the river go?" It was Jim echoing my own thoughts.

Looking down from the brink, I now realized what a drop of a hundred and fifty feet per mile really meant to a paddler. Here I was once more, in a situation I had only vaguely anticipated, with a boatload of gear and a novice partner. As if the water quality wasn't bad enough, we were now about to be flushed.

"Maybe we should portage," I suggested, and so we began to toil down the right bank, heaving and sliding the loaded canoe from boulder to boulder. An hour later, we were still within sight of the ledge where we had started our efforts.

---

[5] Even for decades following our 1961 "Stinky Yough" canoeing adventure, Oakland would remain the largest town in Maryland without a sewage treatment system, straight-piping it all into the Little Youghiogheny and ultimately into the Yough itself.

"Jim, I think we might make it back to work by Wednesday at this rate — that is, if a search party doesn't find us first," I joked, the seriousness of it still gnawing at the back of my mind. "Let's try the river again."

We were dealing, of course, with the low flow of a normal Appalachian autumn. For a decked-boat paddler day-tripping the river, this water level would have been completely unacceptable. She would never have gone near the Yough under these conditions. But for us, it meant survival. We found short stretches that we could navigate, pinchy pour-overs that we could slide over if we exited the canoe, and some parts of the labyrinth where we both just remained in the river, guiding the boat along. We learned a lot about avoiding undercuts and foot entrapments.

Just as daylight was beginning to fade, we reached the approach to Swallow Falls. I breathed a sigh of relief. We unloaded the canoe and carried boat and gear around the falls in two separate trips. But I noticed in my mind that I now regarded the falls with different eyes. Although I had no desire to do so at this point, something inside me suggested that maybe — just maybe — this falls could be run without dying, perhaps in a different boat at a higher water level.

~

During the course of my first several whitewater years, I would return to the Potomac and Cacapon, usually with some of my older Scouts. At least I had learned enough not to take my open Old Town back to the "Stinky Yough." Gradually, after again poring over topo maps, I began to add other rivers to my list — Monocacy, Patuxent, Shenandoah. Then one day, Jack Cotton, my old canoeing partner from flooded Cacapon times, and now the veteran of several subsequent trips with me, said that he had the word on a good river in West Virginia — the Cheat.

The pair that he knew were more fishermen than river runners, but they had names for several of the rapids and were inviting us to join them, rather than just pointing us toward the river. We would paddle from Albright to Lake Lynn, spending a night camping in the Cheat gorge. You may laugh at our continuing ignorance of what lay ahead, but I would point out that we had not as yet crossed paths with any of the handful of paddlers in the region who ran rivers for sport in those days. To us, and most folks who lived in the vicinity, the Cheat was forbidding wilderness. And even to that handful of experienced paddlers, the neighboring Gauley was still unknown territory.

As the fortunes of summer would dictate that weekend, the Cheat was running three inches over zero at Albright, probably an optimum level for four intermediate canoeists and their loaded boats. The river still demanded some tight moves, even at minimal flow, but Jack and I managed to complete the whole two-day run without swamping. There was, however, a moment of maneuvering when we both pitched bodily out of the boat, the canoe remaining upright beside us. All in all, we enjoyed the challenge of the trip and felt rather pleased with our performance.

That winter, my life would change in another direction. Western Electric always sent their new engineering personnel to New York City for education and company orientation. I would spend nine weeks in the Big Apple, watching Broadway shows, enjoying time in Central Park, and occasionally even studying. While visiting the Scout Troop of a friend on the East Side, and describing the magic of whitewater to his Scouts, my friend gave me an unlisted phone number for Roberta Kendall. Roberta and I had met on a snowy evening in Gainesville, Georgia several years before while she was visiting friends at Brenau College — she had been a student there before transferring to Southern Cal — and I had driven up from Georgia Tech. When I briefly saw her in New York the winter before, she had been engaged to a medical doctor.

After a whirlwind courtship of two weeks that left Bonnie, the girl I was dating back home, feeling as if I had slapped her in the face, Roberta agreed to marry me. The wedding was large and formal, and took place in her hometown of Louisville, Kentucky in March of 1962. Two of my early canoeing partners, Fred Scharar and Jack Cotton, were in the wedding, but we were greatly outnumbered by several hundred friends and business associates of the Kendall family. More than a few of them probably shook their heads as Roberta and I left our elegant surroundings for our wedding trip in my VW bus, complete with boat rack. And Roberta herself probably wondered about the longing eyes that I cast toward the Greenbrier River as we spent our first night in White Sulphur Springs, West Virginia.

We came back to live in the Maryland hill country, where I had by now spent nearly half my life. The old Riley farmhouse in Glenwood caught my eye, largely because of its location on a hill overlooking Cattail Creek, and I spent several weeks before our wedding sanding and refinishing the floors, and painting the interior, room by room. To me, the scene was soothing and pastoral, as we were just downstream of the old Roxbury Mill, a mill still grinding grain under the capable hands of neighbor Raymond Smallwood. A huge white oak, having been given the space to spread, dominated the yard.

But to Roberta, who had just spent the past two years of her life in Eastside Manhattan, the shock of rural life was almost too much. A blacksnake dropped out of the oak tree beside her. The flue pipe on the oil furnace fell apart, nearly setting the cold and drafty house on fire. The last straw was added when she tripped on her nightgown and took a frightening headfirst fall down the steep stairway, ramming her head into the wall where the stairs turned. She was already pregnant with Lynn, our daughter to be. I kept her in the same position, with pillows and blankets, and woke up Howard Hall, our doctor in Sykesville, who made the ten-mile house call in record time to determine that Roberta's neck was not broken. We moved within the month to "downtown" Glenelg, next to the post office, gas station & general store combined. Lurlyn Hobbs, Jack Cottor's father-in-law, owned the well-insulated little rental house.

But there was little marriage could do to slow down the passion of whitewater paddling. Canoeing had become entwined with Scouting, and at least two weekends a month, sometimes more, would be spent on rivers. Roberta tried. She went canoe camping with me, and even entered a flatwater slalom as my C-2 partner — we finished first. But paddling and the out-of-doors did not grip her soul as it did mine. As a therapist, her own passion was the medical world. She was attractive and competent, and specialized in hand rehabilitation. As soon as the ages of our two children, Lynn "Cricket" and David permitted, she returned to work in her field.

Kindred Spirits

In February of 1964, a newspaper item caught my attention. There was to be a first-ever whitewater race on the North Fork of the South Branch of the Potomac near Petersburg, West Virginia in April. Anyone interested should contact Dan Sullivan in DC. I called Dan immediately.

"Several of us are going out this weekend to the North Fork to check it out from a racing standpoint," Dan informed me. "Would you like to join us? Oh, do you have a decked canoe?"

What in the world is a decked canoe? My mind raced, trying to come up with an answer that wouldn't sound too stupid and thus eliminate me from their weekend. "No," I finally replied, for lack of a more intelligent answer. "I paddle a sixteen foot Old Town."

"You could make yourself a deck, at least for the bow area," Dan suggested.

"Sure," I replied, "I'll do it."

It was enough — I was in. We rendezvoused on a Friday night and pinpointed the area to which we were heading in West Virginia. Through pouring rain and falling temperatures, I kept Dan's taillights in sight. The rain was so hard that twice we had to dodge showers of rocks loosened from the steep slopes of the winding West Virginia backroads. With my VW camper bus, I always had my accommodations with me, but Dan had told me that we would all be spending the two nights under roof.

"Bob Harrigan and John Berry have rented an old farmhouse on the North Fork for $200, and they've offered it to their paddling friends when they aren't using it."

"That sounds great, but two hundred a month? Isn't that a little steep for a West Virginia farmhouse?"

"Did I say 'month'? That's $200 a year!"

"Wow! That's unbelievable. Who are these guys?"

"Well, they paddle C-2 — that's a two-person canoe, completely decked — and they're two of the founders of our small club, the Canoe Cruisers Association. We paddle area rivers and meet once a month at the Red Cross building in downtown DC. You're welcome to join us. Berry and Harrigan just represented the United States in the World Whitewater Championships."

A club of whitewater paddlers! I mentally filed that piece of awesome information and other tidbits away for future reference as I drifted off to sleep in the warmth of the woodstove. I could already see my paddling horizons expanding.

The morning dawned cold and crisp, the rain having passed. Snow dusted the ridges, but spared the valleys. The North Fork was still running clear, but very full, and as yet, I had had no experience with winter paddling. Our run today, I was told, would not cover the entire fourteen mile length[6] of the proposed race course, but mainly Hopeville Canyon, where the river parted company with the road, and the rapids were not easily accessible to scouting on foot.

Five of us would paddle that day — Dan in his kayak, Lee Lewis and Swede Turner in C-2, Bill (a young doctor whose last name has disappeared into the river mists of my mind) in C-1, and myself in the only open. Outwardly, they treated me as a fellow paddler with some measure of skill and knowledge, but inwardly I knew that they would be watching and evaluating my every move.

It started on land, as Dan inquired if I had either wetsuit or part of one. Dry suits, of course, were unheard of in those years. I had none, although I noticed that each of them was well protected by neoprene, including gloves and booties. I did have a wool sweater, but Dan offered a spare wetsuit vest that I was happy to wear beneath the sweater. The rest of me, in cut-offs and tennis shoes, was woefully unprotected.

Then there was the deck I had improvised for the Old Town, a magnificent piece of "under-engineering." I rigged it up at the put-in,

6 That first year (1964) of the Petersburg Races, the wildwater racecourse was 14 (or 15, depending on who was doing the estimating) miles in length and the race brochure contained 12 pages. By 1966, the brochure was a single tri-fold sheet. To encourage top level competitors to attend, a travel allowance of $25 was offered that year (and that year only) to any contestant who had to travel over 250 miles to reach the race. Two years later (1968), Race Chairman John Berry announced that the wildwater event would be shortened to a length of five miles to better match the length of similar races being held in Europe.

wedging in place four brass strips that curved upward from the gunwales. Over these I stretched black plastic to shed the waves, taping it to the canoe at the gunwales. Flotation? Never heard of it. The group was kind enough not to comment on possible deficiencies in my equipment. At least I had a spare paddle.

Well, I was certainly not fool enough to be the first on the water, nor did any of my companions expect it. I stayed silent, watched intently, and waited my turn. Why in the world is he pointing upstream, I wondered? After each of them had entered his boat in that direction, taken a few strokes upriver, and then turned into the current, I realized that the technique must be intentional. I was gradually learning, but I was not yet astute enough to have picked up on the downstream lean. It would be the river that would teach me that one.

I tried to imitate my predecessors, made a shaky turn downriver, and we were on our way. Within a mile I was swimming in ice water. My deck had shed waves for a while, but the big ones began to collapse it in short order. I had a bailer, but in the brief moments when I could spare a hand to bail, I realized there was no way I could keep up with the water coming into the canoe. My swim was relatively short, and my new friends commended me for hanging onto boat and paddle. But I was shivering uncontrollably.

We all stopped on the rocky beach where I had come ashore, and some foresighted member of the group produced a small bottle of gasoline and matches while others collected firewood. After a half-hour of warming, I told the group that I was ready to go on. As we headed for our boats, Dan offered some advice.

"Whenever you can, take the waves and holes off to their shoulders where they're not as heavy, rather than hitting them in the center. With your deck not working, you'll have to minimize the water trying to get in."

I took Dan's advice to heart. My extremities were numb, but I was quickly learning a little technique and what it took to survive cold weather paddling. Already, I was planning what I would do differently next time. We were catching eddies regularly and each stop would give me a chance to bail. Then it happened.

We had paused in a substantial eddy on river right. There was perhaps half a mile of continuous rapids ahead, the kind where you're so occupied with the move at hand that you never have a chance to look back upriver. A strong differential between the upstream eddy current and the downstream flow of the river made for a tricky exit of the eddy, but each of boats peeled smoothly into the main channel. I was the last, and not so smooth.

It was probably a combination of my inexperience and the lack of any feeling in my hands, but whatever the cause, I crossed the eddy line and wobbled to port, where the river immediately seized my upstream gunwale and rolled me under. It was a rocky swim, and I came ashore bruised and gasping, still gripping my canoe. My paddle was gone, but the spare was still in place. No one was in sight.

I was so unbearably cold that I didn't move for perhaps fifteen minutes. Still no one in sight. Where were they? Cold, yes, but not so cold yet as to lose rational thought. I knew there was no way I was getting back on that river and risking another swim. I would never survive it. The only option now was to walk out of the canyon — but not without my canoe.

Lining would be difficult, I knew. The boulders were large, so I removed the bow line and tied it to the stern line for greater length, slowly working my way down the canyon. Control with one line is poor, and the canoe tended to wallow and roll, taking on water and showing a mind of its own. As I was stepping from one high rock to another, the beast went over a small drop and, determined not to let go, I went over a large one, holding tight to the line. As I sprawled in pain on the rocks eight feet below, I watched my canoe disappear downriver.

"Damn," I said to myself, "Damn, damn, DAMN! Now you've really done it, Woodward."

I had hit hardest on my right shin and it felt as if the leg were broken. It wasn't, but within seconds my lower leg, sock and tennis shoe were bright red. I had severed a large vein in my leg and the blood flow showed no sign of slowing down. My cut-offs were too thick to cut into strips without a knife, so I ripped my boxer shorts off and bound the wound with them. The boxers turned red as well, but the direct pressure was enough to get the bleeding under control.

A good bit of time had passed when I finally found a walking stick and felt that I could bear a little weight on my leg. I began to hobble down the canyon, crawling over obstacles, and occasionally having to wade into the edge of the river at sheer places. My canoe was nowhere in sight.

I had traveled like this for perhaps another hour, shadows creeping into my path, when I spied a figure approaching in the distance. It was Carole Lee Lewis, Lee's wife, searching for me, or what might be left of me. The others had waited far downriver, seen the wreck of my canoe float by, and then paddled to the takeout to decide what should be done.

Carole Lee, an expert paddler in her own right, was running shuttle that day. She was as delighted to see me as I was to see her, although I probably looked more like a war refugee than a canoeist at that moment. With her assistance, I was soon out of the canyon and back to the farmhouse, where Bill stitched up the gash on my leg. My canoe was not so lucky. Broken in two, and held together only by the skin, it was beyond any practical repair.

I was tactfully kept clear of the newspaper reporter who was being told by Dan at the takeout what a safe sport whitewater paddling was and how there would be no significant danger to contestants in the upcoming competition. Only whitewater paddlers whose abilities were known to the organizers would be competing in this first race, thus it was advertised "by invitation only." However, a classic misprint in the ad material read "by initiation only." After my frigid and bloody day on the North Fork, Rosemary Bridge, who would help organize this race for decades to come, jokingly pointed out that if anyone had passed his "initiation," it was Doug Woodward. The only problem now was that I didn't have a boat since I had sold my other canoe and this one was demolished.

~

Despite the apparent outcome, I had gleaned a lot more than cuts and bruises from that February day on the North Fork, not the least of which was an appreciation of paddling with those whose skills were more advanced than my own. I was present at the CCA (Canoe Cruisers Association) meeting in DC the next week. Marian Hardy had a kayak for sale and I wanted it.

"Can you tell me a little bit about it?" I asked, trying to sound as if I might know something about the differences between various makes of kayak.

"It's a Coffin," she replied, as if that might explain everything.

"I hope not," I gulped, no more enlightened than I had been a moment before.

"No, no. It's an all glass boat, made by Stew Coffin in Massachusetts. Come by one evening and you can try it out. We'll go over to Angler's Inn," she suggested.

Marian, as I soon learned, was one of the premier kayak paddlers of that era. She and Barb Wright were usually at the top of the women's division in both slalom and wildwater races. Marian was also an astronomer by profession, and was engaged in mapping the moon in preparation for the Apollo Project. I bought the kayak. But I would

Marian Hardy (left) and Terry Franz (right) load boats following a slalom race on the Potomac River.

not quit pestering her until she sewed me a custom sprayskirt (I traded her a telephone installation at her house) and taught me to roll. She was good. We accomplished it in one session at Difficult Run on the Potomac and the following week I did my first combat roll just below Great Falls.

As I rolled up to the applause of my fellow paddlers, I felt as if I were ready to run Great Falls itself. It was not until many river trips later that I realized that only about half of the applause was for my personal accomplishment. The other half was expressing the feeling, "Thank God. Now we don't have to chase that dude and his boat down the river for the next twenty minutes!"

I would take the kayak to the Potomac when I could, or by myself to the Patuxent or Patapsco, which were closer at hand. Back then, almost all boats were given names by their owners, particularly boats that the paddler had personally built. The name that I inherited with my kayak was the *Half-Fast*, which always got a laugh wherever we appeared. But one fellow paddler was so embarrassed by the boat name that he would always address me in a whisper, "Hey, *Half-fast*," until he learned my own name.

So I had a boat for the North Fork, after all. I didn't enter the race that year, but later had a good run of the canyon, and the *Half-Fast* and I even ended up on a *Wild West Virginia* poster, my tongue pinched between my lips in concentration. The Petersburg Races, as they became known, went on for many years, to the mutual benefit of the paddling community and the good folk of Petersburg, West Virginia.

～

A door had opened for me. Suddenly I was among kindred spirits. Rather than blundering onto unknown rivers under extreme conditions — due to my own ignorance or inadequate equipment — I now had friends with the whitewater skill and knowledge to accompany me on the rivers I longed to paddle. There were movies and slide shows at the CCA meetings, trip reports in the newsletter, a slalom division being formed for those concentrating on competition, and a schedule of trips yet to come. CCA members were becoming active in river conservation issues, as well as analyzing accidents and near misses in order to make whitewater paddling a safer sport for all.

This new world had so many dimensions. I listened with fascination to John Lentz describe the first of his many North Country river expeditions. Bob Harrigan made us all laugh as he described his time with the Robert Kennedy family during their introduction to whitewater paddling on the Upper Hudson under his guidance. And, as kayakers, we were awed by the smooth skills of Czech paddler Milo Duffek — for whom the paddle stroke was named — as he shared his expertise with us at Little

Falls. I began to hear of more races, both slalom and wildwater, on nearby rivers. There were CCA members who provided connections to other paddling clubs — Roger Corbett to the Blue Ridge Voyagers and O.K. Goodwin to the Coastal Canoeists, to name but a couple.

I found myself paying attention to water levels. When torrential rains flooded the Maryland countryside, Jim Stuart and I kayaked a low-lying portion of Old Annapolis Road. As Jim later said with a chuckle, "It was the only time I was almost hit by a car while surfing!" That incident made the *Howard County Times*, our local newspaper.

Later that summer, a front page spread in the recreation section of the Baltimore Sun caught my eye. Complete with photos, the article included interviews with several members of the Baltimore Kayak Club (BKC) following one of their outings. Here was a club closer to home whose existence I wasn't even aware of until now. If interested in BKC activities, call Astrid Nielan, the article suggested. I did.

My first encounter with the BKC was to join them on a Sunday afternoon for a Class II Potomac trip, starting at Dam Number Six. I was amazed at what I saw. Nearly all of their boats were identical. As it turned out, the Baltimore Kayak Club was almost totally oriented toward the classic folding kayak, the German-made Klepper Foldboat. The Cadillac of touring boats[7] surely, but not one that lent itself to tight moves on a technical river. No small coincidence then, that the president of the club was Hans Lewenz, the area Klepper dealer. It was a hot lazy afternoon on the Potomac and I rolled often to cool off, darting into eddies at will in my smaller and lighter slalom kayak. The comparative boat performance was not lost on the group that day. Some of the BKC paddlers had already been thinking in this direction, but seeing a glass boat in action inspired many.

---

[7] So much equipment that we take for granted today did not exist at that time. When I say that the Foldboat was the Cadillac of touring boats, it was not for quality alone, but also because it claimed a unique place in its category. Jack Kissner's Folbot, the lower priced U.S. competitor to the German Foldboat, was just beginning to take its place on the whitewater scene. Sea kayaks were virtually unknown, except to the indigenous people of the North Country and the dedicated individuals who spent months at wood strip construction.

C-2's were beginning to appear in glass form, usually pirated from Europe, whose paddlers were then a decade ahead of us, both in boat design and paddling technique. It was much more common then to see a Grumman morphed into a C-2 by screwing aluminum decking fore, aft, and midship, leaving two spray-skirted openings for the paddlers.

The molding of fiberglass whitewater boats was limited mostly to private individuals such as Stu Coffin, Bart Hauthaway, Jim & Fran Raleigh, John Berry, Bob Harrigan and Dave Kurtz (not a complete list!) I was shortly to join their ranks, along with Jim Stuart, Charlie Walbridge, Tom Wilson, Les Bechdel and many others.

PFD's (the word had not yet replaced "life jackets") were beginning to be used with decked boats, but were still considered by many to be unnecessary for open canoes. Neoprene appeared in wetsuits, but not yet in sprayskirts, which were still made from vinyl-impregnated nylon or rubberized cloth.

Creating Our Own

There was another group inspired by the versatility of slalom kayaks — my Explorer Scouts. Post 757 had evolved from my old Boy Scout Troop that same year and we had designated it a whitewater paddling Post at birth. Other boys (in the 15 to 18 age range) who had never been in Scouting were attracted, and a few years later Explorer Posts were allowed to become co-ed. Enthusiasm was high, but funds were low.

I knew that certain members of the Baltimore Kayak Club had an interest in boat building, but as yet had not constructed anything resembling a kayak. Upon closer investigation, I found that after a year, and untold cases of beer, they had produced exactly one level worktable. The appealing part of all this was that BKC member Fred Nelson had a workshop on Pennsylvania Avenue in downtown Baltimore, where serious boat building could take place. It even came complete with — a level worktable.

I was still short on knowledge, though — very short. As an engineer, I had a general feel for what the process of molding a fiberglass boat might be, but I had questions about so many details. At each meeting of the Canoe Cruisers in DC, I would ask Jim and Fran Raleigh to call me collect whenever they planned to start building the next boat. They never did. But I did convince them to rent me their K-1 mold and to sell enough glass and resin to lay up a kayak. They were also kind enough to share ordering information for their sources of material with me. Hey, it might get that guy off our backs!

Working in Fred's shop was a test of patience in itself. An austere brick building from the previous century, connected on each side to its neighbors in typical Baltimore row-house style, the structure lacked insulation, ventilation, and most importantly, a heating system. We would aim a large portable gas heater in the general direction of the work area for whatever comfort it could provide. That meager comfort was balanced on the other side by a noise akin to a jet airliner on takeoff, noxious fumes and frequent headaches. Sirens from emergency vehicles on nearby streets would cut through the jet noise, and when the heater was resting we could often hear angry voices and running feet on the street outside the door.

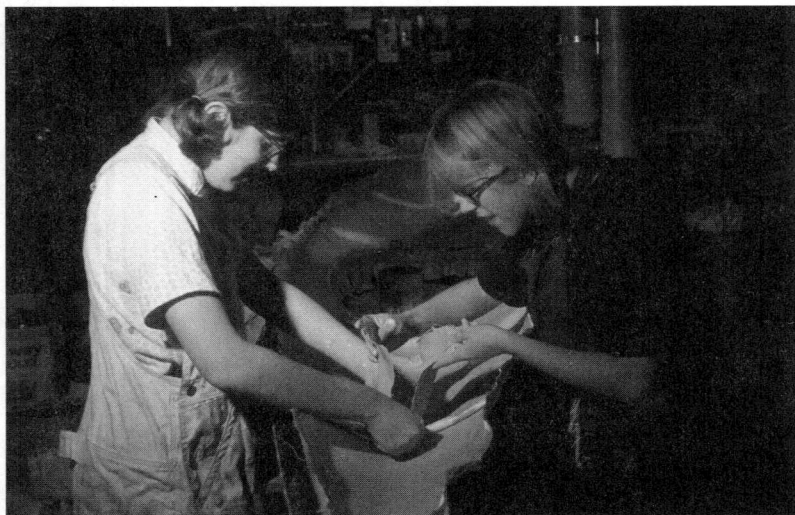

Nancy Rayburn, left, and Mimi Hayman, Explorer Scouts of Maryland Post 757, put the finishing touches on the deck of a new epoxy and fiberglass slalom kayak.

Despite the challenging conditions, our first attempt at producing a kayak was reasonably successful. There were imperfections in the outer layer, but it looked and performed as it should and, to our great relief, had not stuck to Jim and Fran's mold. Occasionally one of my Scouts would come to work with me, and Fred was sometimes there, but the continuity of the process was left to me. A step at a time, I discovered ways to make a boat better. I found that a "round weave" of glass could produce a defect-free outer surface, "flat-weave" for the inner layers would use less resin and make for a lighter boat, and that a layer of polypropylene (kevlar had not yet appeared on the scene) sandwiched between the glass layers of both deck and hull would provide good fracture resistance.

We once made an all-poly kayak. It was great for bouncing over river rocks and you couldn't damage it with a loaded dump truck, but if you left it in the sun at the river, when you went to re-enter it would be so soft and flat that you couldn't get your legs into the boat. We experimented with nylon, Dynel, satin-weave (a densely woven glass fabric) and microspheres, but rejected each for different reasons. Dynel, which would fracture easily with the normal flexing of the hull, worked well in our paddle lay-ups because of its resistance to abrasion.

As more of us paddled these kayaks, we began to make other improvements. Strategic reinforcement of critical wear points at the bow, stern, and beneath the seat. Ribs to strengthen the deck. Adjustable foot braces from aluminum shelf brackets. A D-ring inside the rear deck to secure gear. We tried and discarded the idea of bulkheads. Although later they would become an integral part of sea kayak design, they invariably leaked for us after a demanding whitewater run. We stuck — no pun intended — with the epoxy used by the Raleighs because of its strength, long pot life and ease of cleanup.

Shortly after the second kayak was built, and before it saw a river, I used it to make our own mold, split at the parting line between deck and hull. This was an interesting process in itself, involving the construction of locking flanges, heavier shells, and a supportive framework for keeping the mold stable while laying up kayaks in it. A variety of molds for different boat designs would be built over the next dozen years.

To make a plug — the starting point for a mold — we would sometimes glue blocks of rigid foam together and shape the larger block into a boat of our own design, then coat it with epoxy, but more often we would work from an existing boat design, changing certain aspects of the hull and deck to make it unique. Occasionally, I would buy a mold from another boat builder and by the time I moved to Atlanta four years later, I had molds available for laying up a whole range of K-1's and C-2's, both slalom and wildwater.

The long blue line of Baltimore Kayak Club Foldboats began to be infiltrated by insolent little slalom kayaks. Astrid Nielan named hers *TNT*, swearing that it was for her explosive personality, and *not* "two nice... uh, parts of her anatomy." A few boats began to appear among my Explorer Scouts, the appeal being that they could acquire a boat of their own just for the cost of materials. But Fred's downtown Baltimore shop was an inconvenience to Scouts living thirty-five miles away, and I finally made the decision to shift operations after my VW bus was vandalized as I was inside the shop, working on a boat.

Astrid Nielan paddling the "TNT," in a time when almost all homemade boats were given names by their owners.

So the boat factory moved into my own basement at our Centennial Lane home in Howard County. There were some differences. Now the noxious odor of epoxy would waft its way upstairs to mix with the more pleasant smells of dinner unless the basement door was tightly sealed. A nominal charge was added to the boat cost for fledgling builders to cover tools stuck to the workbench, epoxy on doorknobs and telephones, and other lapses in judgment. Roberta would complain that my breath smelled like epoxy when I came to bed. It did. I could even smell it myself. And the delivery man would wonder where my fork truck was when he came to deliver the 500-lb. drums of hardener and resin.

The vitality of the Explorer Post, and especially boat-building, was a magnet for many. We had already started doing joint camping and river trips with a Senior Girl Scout Troop in Baltimore. The Post took mold and materials to a Scouting exposition in Towson and built most of a C-2, named *Blood, Sweat & Epoxy*, over the weekend. That performance attracted Carl Flynn of Bel Air, and his whole family. The glass boats intrigued Carl — he was already an open canoeist — and we arranged a trial run for him on the Lower Yough the next weekend. He became an assistant advisor for the Post, and a lifelong paddler, retiring to live at the Yough with his wife Beth in later years.

Fred Nelson's daughter, Lisa, knew two nurses at Johns Hopkins Hospital in Baltimore who were interested in kayaking and building boats. Both Eunice Lokiec and Mary Lund built their own kayaks and Eunice stayed to work with the Explorer Scouts for a number of years.

The author carefully examines a new kayak as the mold is broken loose, the critical moment at which the boat-builder gets a quality check on his work up to that point in the process.

While we were working on Eunice's boat, a reporter from the *Baltimore News American* called and asked for an interview about my boat building. I said, "Sure, but I'd like to read it before you print it, and please don't mention anything about cost, since this is basically a non-profit venture for my Scouts." She agreed.

A couple of days later, Deborah Lavery appeared, camera and note-book in hand, and was there for the popping of Eunice's kayak from the mold, always the most anticipated part of the process. I had forgotten about the story a couple of weeks later when I came in to work at Western Electric on a Monday morning. "Hey, there's our celebrity!" quipped a fellow engineer. He had brought a copy of *Maryland Living*, Sunday's magazine section of the *News American*. Deborah obviously hadn't let me preview the article. But what about mentioning dollars? The headline read, "For $80, It Floats."

It was boat-building that precipitated another memorable incident. The same Monday evening after the *News American* article had appeared, the phone rang and Roberta handed it to me.

"Is this the Doug Woodward who was in the Sunday paper?"

"Yes."

"This is Blaze Starr." I paused to swallow. "...The dancer," she added.

"Yes, I know who you are."

"I liked your looks in the story. Do you give kayak lessons?"

"Of course!" ("And do you give lessons in your specialty, too?" I would have loved to add, but didn't have the courage.)

We talked for a half-hour that day and I assured her that I could supply kayak and all related gear and that she would be in good hands, so to speak. I did wonder, though, about the size of the life jacket I should bring. I suspect Roberta wondered about a lot more than that.

Blaze gave me her unlisted phone number and her address on Park Avenue in Baltimore. We spoke several more times and finally a Sunday afternoon was set for the kayaking. Boats and camera were loaded. I called a couple of hours ahead to make sure everything was still on. It wasn't.

"I'm so sorry Doug. I was all ready to go and took my poodle across the hall for my neighbor to keep. Until she reminded me, it had completely slipped my mind that I'm supposed to be at the Annapolis Clam Festival today. We'll have to make it another time."

Sure enough, her picture was in the *Baltimore Sun* the next evening, clad in a bikini, while eager artists at the Clam Festival painted her body for charity fund raising. "Another time" never came.

Eunice christened her kayak, which had a green deck and white hull, *Green Side Up*, not only reflecting her paddling desire, but recognizing a popular joke of that era (the crew laying sod that had to be regularly reminded of which side went up) connected to her own ethnic heritage.

About the same time, I built a wildwater racing kayak using a bright plaid in the outer layer of the deck, naming it *Scotch on the Rocks*. The craze caught on for several years. I'm sure there were salesladies who scratched their heads in puzzlement at the teenage boys who pored over different dress fabrics in their sewing shops, wondering about their sudden interest in what appeared to be domestic sewing.

We were not alone. Dave Kurtz, of State College, Pennsylvania had preceded us in creating a whitewater Explorer Post, although we didn't realize this until running into him on the Yough on one of our own trips. His Explorer Scouts of Post 32 were also very much into boat building, using polyester rather than epoxy as their binding resin. At that time the C-1, which was their boat of choice, was dominant in western Pennsylvania with such whitewater heavyweights as Les Bechdel, Bill Bickham, Steve Draper, Gay Gruss, Dave Guss, Tom Southworth, John Sweet and Dave himself. All of these paddlers were National Champions in many of the years between 1961 and 1972.

But our own Explorer Post was not without its share of success in whitewater competition. Brad Hager would go to the World Championships in 1969. He would paddle C-2 Wildwater with Norm Holcombe that year in France, then become national C-2 champion the next year with Bill Endicott, who would later coach the U.S. Team for many years. Liz (Boo) Hayman was one of our Maryland Explorers — after I had departed to the South — who, paddling with C-2M Slalom partner Fritz Haller (NOC), would not only make the U.S. Team, but win a gold medal in the 1981 Worlds in Bala, Wales.

Even though Scouting provided a framework for outdoor activity in those times — and I had been an enthusiastic Eagle Scout and Scoutmaster — I gradually became disenchanted with certain aspects of the program for the younger Scouts. I tended to rebel at the regimentation, the wearing of uniforms, the similarities to the military, and the push to have Scouting "show off" in front of the public with camporees and even indoor exhibitions. Explorer Scouting presented an opportunity to escape from these constraints and concentrate on the experience itself — in our case the thrill of spending days on a wild river, the fulfillment of building your own boat, or the satisfaction of improving your paddling skills, whether for competition or running more difficult rivers. And being coed certainly didn't hurt matters, either.

Early Rivers

Paddling with the Canoe Cruisers Association (CCA) of Washington, DC, opened my eyes to many more whitewater possibilities. Spontaneous trips were now possible. I can recall dashing out with fellow kayaker Jim Stuart in a pouring rain to western Maryland and Pennsylvania on old US 40 (there were no Interstates in that direction then.) As we ran shuttle, the rain was still falling, but by the time we returned to the put-in, the sun burst out of the clouds over Wills Creek and the waters were surging nearly over the banks. It was a run of pure joy as we pounded through hole after hole for an exhilarating hour on a creek that is so hard to catch with water.

We hooked up with the Bridge family for the rest of the weekend and ran everything we could cram into the daylight hours, putting our boats into drainage ditches and small creeks that may never before have seen a paddle. Three of us burst out of the woods on Jennings Run and passed within ten feet of a man mowing his yard. He nearly dropped his pipe as we flew over small drops and quickly disappeared into the dusk. We had devoured everything we could in that rare window of time.

Jim was always ready to seize the moment for new paddling territory when conditions cooperated. My phone rang early one Saturday after an all-night deluge of rain.

"I just drove by Rock Creek and it's full! How fast can you get into DC? It won't last long."

"I'll meet you at nine." With a VW camper mini-van, I was always ready, my gear stowed inside and my kayak usually on the roof rack.

We rode the high water through the park, twisting around boulders and slamming over drops. The creek was so narrow that at times it seemed we could reach out and touch both banks at the same time.

Jim Stuart, hot-dogging in Swimmer's Rapid on the Yough in western Pennsylvania.

Five years later, CCA paddlers were slipping onto Rock Creek sporadically as water level permitted, although the wisdom of such a hazardous descent was being questioned by a few other CCA members. At least one group was ordered off the creek by the District of Columbia Park Police. Park regulations said that the waters were closed to swimming, wading and water skiing, but not boating or fishing. Could one of the boaters possibly have become a swimmer or wader?

The Potomac, of course, more than any other river, belongs to the CCA. The paddling club was literally born on the river on October 15, 1956 when a small group of paddlers met on Sycamore Island to officially launch the organization. Most of these founders, which included John Berry, Grant Conway, Chris Christy, Bob Farr, Bill Gilbert, Aubrey Graves, Bob Harrigan, Jack Hazzard, Sid Hess, Jim Johnston, Hal Leich, Henri deMarne, Todd Miles, Bill Richardson, William Rhodes, Andy Thomas and Spike Zywicki, had canoed the Potomac and other rivers for many years, often discussing the possibility of a formal association. Bill Richardson had pioneered canoe camping trips on the Potomac in the twenties and thirties, becoming known for his camp cookery. Henri deMarne and Hal Leich later took on the responsibility of leading the CCA in the mid-sixties and early seventies. Although I came to the CCA when the club was nearly eight years old, I enjoyed the company and competence of many of these individuals as we paddled together on area rivers.

It was natural then, for CCA paddlers to experience the Potomac intimately in all seasons, to know the changes caused by each variation in water level, and to be a force for river safety and conservation concerns in the broader community. Possessiveness surfaced when it came to environmental threats and unnecessary regulation. After all, it was our river!

The Potomac was enjoyed by many of us in the CCA on a daily basis. On a summer evening with long daylight hours, we — even those of us who didn't live in DC — could savor an evening run from Great Falls to Carderock, or simply park at Old Angler's Inn and spend a couple of hours playing the chutes at Difficult Run, where I had learned to roll. The Potomac became familiar territory — we loved her and became alert for any changes that might detract from the paddling experience and natural beauty of those waters. There were many.

Throughout the sixties and into the seventies, CCA paddlers provided first-hand "wet education" for our elected and appointed officials. Henri deMarne, Bob Harrigan and Jimmy Holcombe led many of these trips, which sometimes had as many as thirty canoes, each carrying a guest or a member of a guest's staff. Included in this group at one time or another were U.S. Representative Morris Udall and most of the Maryland and Virginia congressional delegation. Seeing and feeling the Potomac from a canoe was a new experience for the majority of these folks. Pollution sources and insensitive development were pointed out and discussed.

Unbelievably, eighteen new dams had been proposed for the upper Potomac basin and its tributaries. In June of 1969, CCA founder Henri deMarne remarked, "Unfortunately, the Potomac and Shenandoah are getting dirtier every year — no more blue-green and silvery water — all dark brown and smelly." Four years earlier, President Lyndon Johnson, calling the Potomac River a "national disgrace," had signed the Water Quality Act of 1965 into public law, but more legislation was desperately needed.

Justice William O. Douglas weighed in against the dam building in the upper Potomac basin, stating, "What is really needed, is to clean up the Potomac, not dam it up." Over a decade before, Douglas had almost single-handedly turned public opinion away from a proposed C&O Canal Scenic Highway and toward a C&O Canal National Park[8].

8 In 1954, a scenic highway, proposed by the National Park Service in a moment of short-sightedness, and approved by Congress, would have been built over the C&O Canal, essentially obliterating that part of our nation's history. This proposal appeared at the time of Eisenhower's push for an Interstate Highway System, was supported by the Washington Post, and seemed to many to be a done deal.

His reasoning against the proposed dams, together with the work of many others, including CCA members, had a similar effect. Only two of the dams were built.

Representative Henry S. Reuss of Wisconsin also took a shot at turning the direction of the Army Corp of Engineers when he introduced legislation (HR 10316) to redefine the mission of the Corps:

"The Corps' passion for construction threatens to destroy the ecological balance of some of our most beautiful rivers and estuaries. Instead of putting all its resources and skilled manpower into increasingly marginal navigation, flood control and power projects, let us turn the Corps loose on building the sewage systems and waste disposal plants which the Nation so desperately needs if we are ever to enjoy clean water again."

In the days when Republican congressmen were not embarrassed to stand up for an environmental cause, it was Maryland Representative Gilbert Gude who brought before the U.S. House of Representatives, National River legislation for the Potomac. Congressman Gude had been Jimmy Holcombe's canoeing partner on a "Get to Know Your Potomac" trip in November of 1969, and would introduce his legislation with these words:

"The choice is between a river comprised of wilderness, open space, developed recreational areas, and farmland, interspersed with towns and areas of commerce, or a mammoth open storm drain running through a nightmarish strip of oversized cities, suburbs and Coney Islands."

By the mid-sixties, the pollution problems of the Potomac had become infamous. Although the National River legislation was not successful (many folks in Virginia and West Virginia regarded it as a federal land grab), enactment of other river-related laws began to have a positive effect. As the decade of the sixties came to a close, river conservationists were on a roll.

Not the least of these successes was the passage of the National Wild and Scenic Rivers Act of 1968, which initially brought segments of nine

Justice Douglas was not so sure. He challenged the Washington Post editors to hike the entire 185 mile length of the Canal towpath with him to see if they would stand by their original position. They accepted his challenge and by the time the trek started, there were 58 participants, including North Country author Sigurd Olson, and Dr. Olaus Murie, president of the Wilderness Society. Douglas, then 55, set a brisk pace of 23 miles a day, and not everyone who set foot on the towpath at Cumberland, MD, was able to finish the trip.

Publicity generated along the way began to snowball, the Washington Post editors reversed their position, and two years later the scenic highway proposal was withdrawn. Justice Douglas continued to lead "reunion hikes" each year and in 1961 Eisenhower proclaimed the C&O Canal a National Monument. Finally, in 1971, after much lobbying and many more hikes, the C&O Canal became a National Historical Park, offering superlative recreational opportunities as well as exceptional educational experiences.

rivers under its protection. Over the next thirty-seven years, 145 more would become part of the Wild and Scenic Rivers System. Jim Johnston, Jr., CCA's super-active conservation chairman and a driving force for environmental protection throughout the mid-Atlantic region, conveyed the Club's support[9] when the original legislation was introduced in May of 1965 with words from his heart:

"It is with keen pleasure that I submit an opinion on behalf of the Canoe Cruisers Association of Greater Washington, DC in respect to S 1446. The Wild Rivers Act...We support the principle of the Wild Rivers Act wholeheartedly and deem it one of the crucial legislative proposals in the history of the Nation's conservation movement. The preservation of wilderness is fast becoming a lost opportunity, and as the population continues to burgeon, the as yet unborn citizens will know of wilderness and clear streams only as an echo out of the past. It behooves the leaders of this Nation to take quick steps, such as this bill, in order to set a precedent. We hope that the bill will become an Act in this session of the Congress..."

As early as the thirties, concerned leaders in the Potomac watershed had seen the need for a cooperative approach to managing the problems of the river and in 1940 Congress gave its consent for the states of Maryland, Pennsylvania, Virginia, and West Virginia, as well as the District of Columbia, to enter into a compact providing for the creation of the Interstate Commission on the Potomac River Basin (ICPRB) and the Potomac Valley Conservancy District.

Such an approach was a step in the right direction, but through the forties and fifties, action was largely limited to measurement and evaluation of water quality. Both rural and urban populations increased. Industrial and municipal waste flowed untreated into the Potomac. A huge fish kill occurred in the summer of 1951, the result of low dissolved oxygen levels in the water. Some reaches of the river had no biological population whatsoever. In 1957, the U.S. Public Health Service declared the Potomac unsafe for swimming. A sign fastened to the pier at Mount Vernon in the sixties advised visitors to "Avoid Contact With Polluted River Water."

Against this dismal historical backdrop, CCA paddlers labored to instigate and support legislative measures that could help the river. Bob Burrell, Ross Hales, Jim Johnston and Bob & Lucille Harrigan met time and again as part of the Potomac River Basin Compact, voicing their opinions on water quality improvement, aesthetics and recreational needs. Jim Stuart testified with strong words before the Senate Public

[9] In a letter to Henry "Scoop" Jackson, Chair of the Senate Committee on Interior and Insular Affairs.

Works Committee, trying to crack the Army Corp of Engineers rationale for building the dams in the upper Potomac basin. Others, including Jean Dunn, Dick Bridge, Randy Carter, Grant Conway, Anna Marie Herfindahl, Mary Ollry, Betty Reidel and McKelden Smith kept the pressure on for restoring the river as they met or corresponded with key legislators.

The next two decades would see continued cooperation among the basin states and DC, with sediment limitation laws, phosphate bans, and acid mine drainage controls put in place. Maryland and Virginia both instituted moratoriums on new sewer hook-ups until adequate treatment facilities could be constructed. De-chlorination was achieved at treatment facilities throughout the basin. On a national level, the Environmental Protection Agency (EPA) was established and the Federal Surface Mining Control and Reclamation Act was passed, as were more stringent amendments to the Clean Water Restoration Act. By 1998, with broad-based support in the basin area, including many individuals from the paddling community, the Potomac was designated an American Heritage River.

~

Along with their love for the Potomac and its health, it was natural for CCA paddlers to recognize her hazards, both to the boater and the spectator. Many near tragedies would find a CCA canoeist or kayaker in the right place at the right time.

On May 4, 1969 Ben Tracy was ferrying back and forth below the fish ladder on the Maryland side of Great Falls, warming up for the start of the Potomac Whitewater Race when he was startled by an unusual sound from the cliffs above. He looked up to see a small figure crashing down the rock face, finally splashing into the river a hundred feet away.

"Save the boy! Jump in the water!" Ben shouted to a fisherman who was closer to the victim. The fisherman, who, unbeknownst to Ben, was a non-swimmer, leaped in with terrified demeanor, but heroic intent. In the end, it was Ben who brought them both to shore. The boy, unconscious and bleeding, was laid on a large flat rock. He had fallen seventy vertical feet.

At this moment, Ben thought his mind had gone into replay as the scenario began to repeat itself. Another young boy — brother to the first one, as it turned out — came hurtling down the cliff face. His fall arrested, he lay precariously on the edge of a small ledge thirty-five feet above the river. Knowing how critical each moment was, Ben immediately abandoned his kayak, scaled the rocky face and brought the second boy down.

By this time a ranger had reached the accident scene, and after radioing for additional help, worked with Ben to assess and apply first aid to the boys' injuries as best he could. Thirty minutes later an ambulance arrived on the C&O Canal towpath and the pair was evacuated from the river by stretcher. And with all that energy expended, was it time for Ben to relax? No way. He climbed back in his kayak and paddled on to a first place finish in the wildwater race!

According to fellow paddler Lamarr Knapp, it was not the first time that a river had demanded life-saving action from Ben. Four years earlier, Lamar had seen Ben, without hesitation, leap into a swift rapid on the Yough to hold Jim Reber's head above water until he and Rick Green could extricate Jim from his submerged kayak.

Two months later, CCA paddlers would again be on the scene of a near tragedy. Frank Daspit, John Dirst and Cay Hathaway were preparing to run Little Falls after a welcome rain. John and Cay were scouting the run from shore when they saw a figure on the opposite shore plunge from a steep path to the rocks at river level. They shouted to Frank in his C-1, who immediately ferried across the river above Rock Island, reaching the fallen man within minutes. John and Cay ferried to a different point and were able to get to the scene by land a short time later.

As it turned out, the fallen man, who was eighty years old, was still conscious and able to direct first aid efforts for what was later diagnosed as a broken shoulder, broken ribs and a punctured lung. John Dirst used the ski belt the man was wearing to immobilize his arm. Cay Hathaway climbed to the man's house to call for a rescue boat. The powerboat was unable to reach the accident location, so the victim was laid in an open canoe that was then carefully lined down the shore to a point where the transfer could be made.

It was inevitable that CCA paddlers would continue to be instrumental in Potomac River rescues. In February of 1972, Frank Daspit (again!), Jean Goertner and Sam Huntington put their own lives in considerable danger for more than an hour during the icy high water rescue of fellow paddler Nick Cullander, who suffered two broken legs when his kayak was pinned in Difficult Run. Jean Goertners's husband John played a vital part in getting two stranded novice canoeists ashore later that year when Hurricane Agnes drove the Potomac into flood.

But it was an incident on October 7, 1972, as the Potomac was surging and rising toward ten feet, that suddenly catapulted the CCA into prominence as a vital force for river safety. A small group of advanced CCA boaters had enjoyed the high water at Difficult Run (where else?) that morning and were taking out at Old Angler's Inn. Four paddlers in two open canoes had just climbed into their boats at the same spot. It was obvious to the CCA group that the four were novices — the way paddles are held and used, and the paddler's position in the canoe are usually dead giveaways — and they stopped to warn them of the danger of the river at its current level.

"Thank you very much, but we'll be fine," was the gist of their reply. They departed downriver.

The CCA'ers loaded their boats and started to head for home. It was at this point that Tom Yanosky, mulling the scenario over in his mind, decided that the probability of the four canoeists getting into trouble was so great that he should unload his boat and gear and try to catch up with them. Enough time had passed that he was unsure that he could be of help at this point, even if he did overtake them.

Indeed, both canoes had capsized — in the vicinity of Stubblefield Falls — two of the paddlers making it to shore, while the other pair clung to a rocky islet in mid-river that was rapidly disappearing in the rising waters. Help had been summoned, but the would-be rescuers were becoming increasingly frustrated with their failed attempts to get a rope to the stranded pair. The police had radioed for a helicopter.

As Tom hove into sight and quickly evaluated the scene before him, both the predicament and its solution were evident. With the National Capital Park Police, and the Glen Echo and Cabin John Volunteer Fire Departments looking on — and the Channel Nine TV news cameras grinding away — he proceeded to eddy out at the tail of the islet, take one of the stranded pair aboard, ferry him to safety, and then return to rescue the other in the same manner. The police and fire department personnel were impressed. How is it that four paddlers could be at the mercy of the river while another was in such complete control?

To help answer that question, CCA'er Bill Carr and Chairman John Seabury Thompson met at lunch with C&O Canal Superintendent David Ritchie. Ritchie was already a canoeist himself and, after the favorable publicity of Yanosky's recent rescue performance, was quite open to a working relationship with the Canoe Cruisers Association. The trio discussed river safety programs (in which the CCA was already quite involved), improved put-ins and take-outs for paddlers, the resolution of post-hurricane (Agnes) problems on both the river and the canal, and the possibility of river rescue squads similar to the ski patrol. The paddling club had already been working for several years to establish a close relationship with park personnel through the CCA's "Know Your River" trips, but now there was new respect for the skill and maturity of this local paddling association.

That relationship did not extend to the running of Great Falls, however, which was generally considered certain suicide by Park personnel as well as most of the paddling community. John Berry had once listed, in the CCA Cruiser, a tongue-in-cheek Great Falls trip on April Fool's

Day, 1965. Little did he know then that only ten years later, fellow CCA'ers Tom McEwan, Dan Schnurrenberger, and Wick Walker would make the first intentional descent of Great Falls. At dawn on a Sunday morning in August, 1975, at a time when the Park was quiet and deserted, they would do what couldn't be done. Many would follow.

~

Close behind the Potomac in popularity with CCA paddlers was the Youghi-ogheny in western Pennsylvania. When I first saw a scheduled trip listed in the CCA newsletter, I immediately thought of the hair-raising October canoe camping trip a few years earlier when Jim Rew and I had been fortunate enough to survive the stretch of Class V water above Swallow Falls.

Here, on the lower Yough, the potential for disaster was less, but the thrill and beauty of the ideal whitewater run would draw us back time and again. We would take turns leading monthly trips, where often fewer than a dozen paddlers would make up the group enjoying the rapids and the solitude of the day between the sleepy town of Ohiopyle and Stewarton, where a single occupied home marked the site of an old logging settlement. In those early years, there were as yet no outfitters on the Yough and you might make the whole run without seeing anyone on the river outside of your own group. Open canoes would often outnumber decked boats.

The Stewarton take-out was an alpine challenge — nearly as tough as the river itself. There was no path. The paddler exiting the river at this point would scramble sixty or so vertical feet, grabbing bushes and trees with one hand while dragging the boat with the other. Then it was a matter of pushing your boat up onto the railroad track after listening for an oncoming train, which were plentiful in those days. The occupants of the house by the tracks let their golden opportunity slip away by not opening a refreshment stand in their front yard. In 1978, Chesapeake & Ohio Railroad officials, afraid that it was only a matter of time before a train hit a boater, closed the Stewarton take-out, forcing the outfitters and Park to find another option.

My own first run of the lower Yough, in the early summer of 1964, was one to remember. It was my third or fourth time in a kayak, having only kayaked on the Potomac up to that point. I was paddling the *Half-Fast*, a bit smug with my newly acquired roll, but hesitantly trying to surf the outflow of Cucumber and other rapids that my companions were enjoying. Learning the river and getting familiar with my boat were all that mattered as I experienced that exhilaration which would draw me back to whitewater time and again.

Then came Dimples Rapid. I stopped and scouted with my companions, then decided that I knew the moves I wanted to make. Avoiding the boulder that the main current was piling into, I drew right, leaned too far into a crosscurrent and flipped. Coming out at the top of Dimples can make for a long swim. I rolled. And broached. And wrapped. Within seconds, my kayak was U-shaped, my legs firmly pinned by a crushed deck, my torso being pushed underwater by the force of the current.

My reaction was basic and unsophisticated. I jammed the tip of my paddle into the river bottom and worked my hands up to the other blade. River depth and paddle length just permitted my head to remain above the surface. My position was stable, but the minutes were definitely numbered by muscle endurance and water temperature. Personal survival progress had reached its limit.

At such a point it pays to paddle with quick-acting, safety-conscious friends. The line-up that day was in my favor, for it included Ramone Eaton, Dick Bridge, John Bridge and Charlie Bridge. Dick's throw rope whistled overhead and came to rest across my shoulder and the kayak. But in my precarious position, I could do no more than curl the rope against the paddle blade with the fingers of one hand.

Realizing the urgency of the situation with their first look, John and Charlie had worked their way into an upstream channel and now arrived bodily at my rock. While Charlie helped support my head and shoulders, John tied the throw rope to my bow loop. With Dick and Ramone — and several others — applying a considerable pull at an upstream angle, the kayak straightened enough for my legs to be extracted. While I worked my way ashore via the rope, John and Charlie slid the boat around and off of

Left to right; Dave Kurtz, Dick Bridge and Dan Sullivan at the first Youghiogheny River slalom, held at Entrance Rapid.

the rock. Most of a roll of duct tape was required to make temporary repairs to the badly fractured kayak, but I was able to finish the run.

I had received a very large measure of expert help in the rescue, but another lesson had been etched into my mind. Self-help. Self-help can give you the necessary seconds for a companion to effect your rescue. Self-help can put you in the only position from which rescue is possible. Sometimes self-help is all you've got. It can keep you alive. The lesson would serve me well in the years and on the rivers that would follow.

I often brought my Explorer Scouts to the Yough for a week in the summer. We would check in with Ohiopyle Mayor Bill Holt and his wife Adalene (they even joined the CCA in 1967), who always gave us permission to camp on the grassy strip between the empty homes[10] on Front Street and the Falls. The camp was idyllic, serenaded by the Falls on one side and shielded from the road by the abandoned houses on the other. The Holt's general store was close enough to keep our camp supplied with necessities and we could hang slalom gates from the road bridge, a short walk upstream, to practice our whitewater moves.

By this time, we were building our own kayaks and canoes, both C-1's & C-2's, and had a twelve-foot military surplus raft along for those who were new to whitewater. Scouting was still four or five years from becoming coed, and our group of guys tended to attract the local teenage girls. They would raft with us, eat with us and often hang out in our camp, much to the consternation of the local teenage males. I don't remember any nasty incidents, but the Ohiopyle guys several times challenged us to a touch football game in Ferncliff Park, where they would invariably whip our fannies.

One evening we were in the midst of dinner preparations when we overheard hysterical voices nearby. "Help! There's a boy in the river!" a man dashing toward our camp called out. Removing our food from the fire, we grabbed a throw line and sprinted to the riverbank. A young boy of eleven or twelve had lost his footing under the upstream bridge and been swept down to within fifty yards of the Falls. He stood chest deep in an eddy below a mid-river boulder, but was separated from us by a powerful chute. Quickly tying a large loop in the rope with a bowline, we made a perfect first toss and the boy slipped it over his head and under his arms. Within seconds we had him ashore, where he spotted a swimming buddy and disappeared into the dusk without a word.

---

10 The empty homes, acquired by the Western Pennsylvania Conservancy, were part of Ohiopyle's disappearing past. The process had started in 1951 when Ferncliff Park, the peninsula enclosed by the Loop, became the first acquisition of the Conservancy. By 1970, these and twenty other buildings had been torn down and the Conservancy began to step out of the picture, with Pennsylvania's Department of Environmental Resources stepping in. The river and much of the surrounding land would become Ohiopyle State Park, Pennsylvania's largest at more than 18,000 acres.

As my own children, Lynn and David, grew into toddlers and beyond, I would bring them to the Yough to camp and canoe selected portions of the river, particularly the family stretch between Confluence and Ohiopyle. Our favorite, however was Railroad Rapid, the last of the Loop's distinct drops. Here I could give them a small taste of kayaking by loosening my spray skirt and placing one of them just forward of me in the cockpit. I would eddy-hop almost to the top of Railroad, then peel out and give them the thrill of punching through whitewater as we descended to our starting point.

The sixteen of us who paddled the Yough on Labor Day weekend, 1964, would be considered a large group, but made up of names that the seasoned paddler will well recall — Bob Belton, Bill Bickham, Peter Brown, Randy Carter, John Delabar, Ramone Eaton, Terry Franz, Panalee Ikari, Jack Knapp, Tom McEwan, Ralph Netterstrom, Betty & Bob Reidel, Barb Snyder, Karl-Heinz Weinberg, and myself. We made multiple runs of the Loop, a two mile river segment which bends back to nearly touch its starting point, and some of us ran all the way to Connellsville on Sunday, just to see what that part of the river was like.

By way of contrast, consider a late summer Yough trip I led two years later in August of 1966. The number of participants had nearly doubled, including many Yough first-timers from Maryland — a Foldboat contingent from the Baltimore Kayak Club — and a group of open boaters from the coast of Virginia. As part of the latter group, six-year-old Jonnie Frye sat close behind her dad, Les, directing him to a perfect Saturday run in their Grumman. I was not alone in introducing my own small family members to the joys of Youghiogheny whitewater.

The first day was rainy, and two Foldboaters from the BKC took a battering in Entrance rapid, deciding to exit the river at that point. The rest of the large group continued on, mist on the water so thick that the lead and sweep boats were invisible to most of the procession. Three boats would stay below each rapid for safety, waiting for the next to appear before one would move on. It was always a relief to see the *Rock-n-Roll*, with Lamarr Knapp running sweep, emerge from the mist. On the second day, we judiciously split the group into two trips, one making the milder run of the Middle Yough while the other repeated the Stewarton run.

Commercial raft trips were becoming a factor in river traffic as new outfitters rushed to compete with Lance Martin's Wilderness Voyageurs. Paddling groups from Ohio, West Virginia and Penn State, like us, could not get enough of the Youghiogheny and were also contending for river space. The feeling of solitude was fast disappearing from the Yough experience, regulation of boaters was on the way, and during 1978 nearly two million visitors came to the river and the newly created Ohiopyle State Park.

~

There were other rivers that we often ran, though not with the regularity of the lower Potomac or Yough — some for beauty and solitude, some for challenge. Back in my isolated paddling days — when my Old Town canoe was still intact — I enjoyed a leisurely solo canoe/camping trip down the mild waters of the Potomac's Trough, a seven mile straight stretch of the river in West Virginia. It wasn't entirely soloing as Scout, my German Shepherd, accompanied me as bow-dog. I later learned that this trip was a CCA favorite for enjoying the brilliant foliage of October.

The Shenandoah, particularly the Staircase section beside Harpers Ferry, was a run with moderate rapids through an area steeped in history. High water could dramatically increase the danger and challenge, however. Paddling there in the sixties, we would often see raw sewerage floating in the water below Millville, a condition that would not be remedied for several decades.

For runs that would leave us few chances to catch our breath, the North Branch of the Potomac, and the Savage (a Potomac tributary that could be run with a dam release) provided complete fulfillment. On a run of late-winter water — clear and frigid — John Sweet introduced me to the pounding drops of the North Branch. The following year, Jim Stuart, Bill Funk and I, with a dozen or so other paddlers from the CCA, West Virginia and Penn State ran, in March of 1969, the first scheduled release for whitewater boaters on the Savage. This was actually a wildwater race, sponsored by the Appalachian River Runners Federation — the weather was bitter, with snow covering much of the ground along the river. Jean Goertner, an experienced CCA paddler, took a nasty swim near Monument Rock that, even though she was wearing a full wetsuit, left her drained of energy, barely able to crawl out of the water.

The *very* first Savage River water release for paddlers — unscheduled — took place several months earlier and is recalled here by Jim Stuart[11]:

"In October of 1968, Bill Funk, Kent Taylor, Henri deMarne and I went up to Harry Bittinger's (the dam keeper) house and knocked on the door. I sheepishly asked if it was even possible to release water from the dam. 'We're kayakers, and are interested in running the river between here and Bloomington.'

Harry replied, 'Why sure — how much would you like?' We restrained our astonishment and gladly accepted his offer to tour the inner working of the Savage River Dam. We descended a spiral

---

11 From personal correspondence of 11/8/05, Jim Stuart to Doug Woodward.

staircase disappearing downward into the belly of the structure. Before long, we emerged deep below onto a gantry above the outflow — sort of an unimpressive ten-foot wide mossy culvert.

Harry said he would go turn the spigot on, and we could say if it was enough. A few minutes later, we felt a rumble, then 5,000 cfs exploded out of the discharge tube and soared eight feet high into an explosion wave. We ran back in and shouted up the stairs, 'Too much, too much — cut 'er back — cut it in half!'

Harry, who was coming back down the stairs, said, 'OK, OK, I'll turn it down and you let me know when it's about right.' So, after a few adjustments, we agreed that 2,000 cfs seemed about right.

We hopped in our boats right at the base of the dam and headed downstream. Harry followed along in his truck to watch. Five exhilarating miles later we all knew, then and there, that this river had the right stuff for a major international race. Twenty-one years later it did just that — hosting the 1989 World Championships."

Rarely was a CCA trip canceled, except in times of extreme drought. When water was at the other end of the scale, flooding out an expected run, it presented an opportunity to paddle small rivers and creeks normally unavailable to us, such as the Lost River or the Castleman, a tributary of the Yough.

Even though the use of dry suits would be many years in the future, cold weather was rarely a deterrent to our enthusiasm for paddling. I can remember icy trips on Virginia's Cedar Creek, clad in wetsuits or multiple layers of wool clothing. Carter Hearn, Panalee Ikari, John Seabury Thompson and others would gather around a lunchtime fire on the riverbank, absorbing warmth for the remainder of the trip. Paddlers with foresight — any of us who had previously experienced such conditions — would bring a thermos of hot drink, and sometimes, hot food. A canoe was the craft to be in on such trips — those of us getting washed by waves in the lower profile kayaks definitely had an additional chill factor.

I once paddled the Patapsco River — near Ellicott City, Maryland — in high water during a breakup of river ice. However, the cold weather adventure that most stands out in my memory occurred on the Cacapon, the river that had been my introduction to whitewater in 1959. The Baltimore Kayak Club had a trip scheduled there one March in the late sixties, hoping for a spring break in what had been a very cold winter.

The day dawned bright and blue, but winter still reigned. Nobody showed. Nobody with any common sense, that is. Astrid Nielan, the sparkplug of BKC activities, was there in the *TNT* — the glass boat she had recently built — and so was I. Sure, it was colder than a witch's mammary, but there was sunshine and it would be an adventure. We would do it!

We had selected the shortest section of river, the twelve miles from Capon Bridge to the Forks, where North River joined the Cacapon after its journey around Ice Mountain. Several ledges to run. The fairy waterfall. Castle Rock. Plenty of time to enjoy a winter wonderland. Or so we thought.

The ice formations along the riverbanks at the put-in were intriguing. We breathed the crisp air, and the dark flowing water felt good beneath our kayaks. We'd have such a day that the rest of the BKC would be sorry that they hadn't shown up!

Well, not too sorry. A mile or two later, and too far down the river to abort, we ran into the first of the ice. River-wide ice, white and glistening from bank to bank, and extending to our limit of sight.

"Do you think we could slide over it?" Astrid asked.

"You might," I replied, "but I don't think it will hold my weight. I know one thing, though — I sure as hell don't want to go under it!"

About fifty feet from the edge, Astrid began to accelerate, and was moving at full speed when she hit the ice. The kayak lifted and she slid onto the surface of the sheet. Control then became the obstacle to forward progress, first with the slipping of the paddle as she dug for a grip and then with the boat spinning crazily with each stroke.

My own attempt to go topside was not so successful. Cracks ran out through the sheet at my point of impact and, close to the kayak, chunks of ice began breaking loose. My own progress would depend on my efficiency as an icebreaker.

Half an hour later we reached black water again, with a welcome current to carry us along. But as the river slowed once more, a similar obstacle loomed before us. With forest close to the river's edge and ice-covered rocks along the shore, portage was not an option. We slid and crunched on as the scene repeated itself time after time.

Lunch was brief — we could see the day slipping away relative to our minuscule downriver progress. The daylight hours flew by, dusk was at hand, and we were still miles from the take-out. There had been no sign of escape possibilities — roads, houses or even a clearing — on either side of the river. Darkness closed in. We were hungry again, and cold to the bone, right through our wetsuits.

The CCA antidote to hypothermia on the river — after a warming fire and hot drinks — suggested that the victim be stripped and wrapped in a blanket with a warm body (also stripped) for gradual and total warming. The procedure sounded delightful, but we were lacking the basics — we had neither blanket nor warm body!

I did have a small bottle of gasoline and matches along, but that would be saved for the unthinkable — spending that winter night on the river. Our thoughts were just reaching the desperate stage when a small light flickered in a window far back from the shore on river right. Stumbling through a long meadow on frozen stumps that were legs only that morning, we dragged our kayaks past barking hounds and up to the door of the most welcome farmhouse we had ever seen. The door opened cautiously, but warmth poured out. After explaining our predicament, we were invited in for a cup of tea, then driven to our take-out vehicle.

It had definitely been a day — and part of a night — to make for a memorable river tale. We told the Baltimore Kayak Club folks about it at the next meeting, but I doubt that any of those paddlers were sorry to have missed it!

Astrid, with her speedy and accurate typing skills — to this day, I'm still a two-finger typist — would collaborate with me on an endeavor of a different nature. In the fall of 1968, I was transforming the CCA *Roster/Schedule* into a new publication, a small booklet that would include not only the basic information on our trips and members, but much more. There would be sections on safety, equipment, instruction, competition, recommended guidebooks, and contact information for other clubs as well as our national paddling organizations. Advertising would be included for the first time. It was a daunting task and without Astrid's help I would have foundered. In the end, the 1969 *Schedule/Roster* appeared on time and was a piece of work of which we both were proud. CCA Chairperson Jean Dunn wisely suggested that the job be given to a committee for the 1970 edition.

~

In the late sixties, despite the fact that the CCA had a membership of more than 500 active paddlers, there were still Appalachian rivers waiting to be explored. One of these, the scene of a hair-raising river tale and still shrouded in mystery, was West Virginia's Gauley.

Sayre & Jean Rodman of Oakmont, Pennsylvania, CCA members throughout the sixties, had been exploring challenging whitewater well back into the previous decade. They felt limited by the open canoe and had developed their own technique for handling heavy water and technical moves within a demanding rapid. Each of them used a twelve-foot military surplus raft, rowed with reinforced oars. Although their oars were positioned in the large grommet ears on the side tubes rather than mounted on a rowing frame, they sat facing downstream, realizing the same advantages of today's rowing rigs — quick lateral movement in a rapid and the ability to slow down the raft's descent to allow more time for course changes.

On Easter weekend in 1958, the Rodmans were part of a small group led by Ray Moore, hoping to explore the Gauley, for which no river running information existed. The paddlers put in near the town of Summersville and ran to a point below the site of the present dam where they were turned back by "white water of unprecedented violence."[12] (The section we know now as the Upper Gauley.)

Jean and Sayre would return to the Gauley three years later (May 26 – 28, 1961), leading a group of six rafters that, in addition to themselves, included Kay and Ralph Krischbaum, Dave Barbour and Ken Hawker. With the river running an estimated 600 to 700 cfs, they put in under the Summersville Bridge, amid "a deep snow cover [that] was melting fast...trying to stay out of a downpour."

They ran about seven miles the first day, camping near Initiation Rapid — not then named, of course — to patch rafts, dry clothes and warm up around a large campfire. Not having seen any of the Gauley below this point, Sayre "wondered if the dam was going to take out all the best white water."

"It won't," he remarked in his description of the next day's run. He goes on to describe the drop we know today as Pillow Rock and then arrives at the Iron Ring Rapid experience that would define the Gauley for years to come. His words tell it best:

> "About twenty feet above an attractive pair of five foot waterfalls, the river churns past a big rock face. Two of the first three to run it reported (later) a strange sideways tugging. Boat four went a trifle closer to the rock face. It was jerked sideways, flipped, and its passenger pulled under almost at once. Seconds later, the raft vanished too. About twenty fairly long seconds later, the passenger was spit out from under one falls, tossed over the second and washed into quiet water, damp and shaken, telling tales of trips around an underwater chamber with small air space. The boat popped out intact a bit later. Hidden suction that can engulf a 6x12 boat, displacing at least 1500# without even denting the six foot oars in the oarlocks, it, well, best [be] avoided. The other two people carried boats around this one."

Although Sayre does not state in his account the identity of the underwater explorer, through process of deduction (in other accounts of the same event) it would seem to be Kay Krischbaum.

---

12 This, and quotes in the following four paragraphs, from Sayre Rodman's personal account of the 1951 Gauley trp in the Cruiser, newsletter of the Canoe Cruisers Association of Washington, DC, August, 1965.

For the next seven years, tales from that Gauley descent would reach mythic proportion. Whitewater paddlers were intrigued by the prospect, but none actually ran it. Following the completion of Summersville Dam in 1966, John Berry hiked the de-watered riverbed to scout the run. He got a good look at the bare bones of Iron Ring and reported back to the CCA at one of our meetings. The run (of the entire Gauley) looked doable for decked boats, but extremely demanding. According to John, Iron Ring appeared absolutely lethal and should not be run under any circumstances.

On Labor Day weekend, 1968, Jim Stuart — one of CCA's more intrepid river explorers — got his chance to kayak the Gauley. In a trip report[13] for the club, he mentions how it came about.

> *"...the New River was run as always, but was disappointingly low (1,600 cfs). Our dampened enthusiasms were getting the better of us when John Sweet, decidedly enfrenzied about something, just bubbled out the horrifying news that the Gauley would be running 1,200 cfs out of the dam on the next day."*

John Sweet in his C-1 (decked canoe), proving that you don't need a paddle to enjoy the surfing spots.

Six paddlers — Jim Stuart and Jack Wright in K-1, Jimmy and Norm Holcombe, John Sweet and Miha Tomczech (from Yugoslavia) in C-1, headed for the Summersville Dam. The twenty-four mile run — the take-

13 Jim Stuart's personal account of the September 1, 1968 Gauley River trip in the October, 1968 *Cruiser*, newsletter of the Canoe Cruisers Association of Washington, DC.

out between the upper and lower portions of the river was unknown then — would have been daunting even without the mandatory scouting of Class V rapids. Evan and Anne Shuster, well-known paddlers from the Penn State Outing Club, with infant daughter Amy, hiked in to take photos at the rapids near the junction of the Gauley and Meadow Rivers.

At Pillow Rock, Jimmy Holcombe, whose strong C-1 side was on the left, was unable to draw right at the Room of Doom, smashing into the wall and ripping out his thigh braces. To his credit, he ran the rest of the river with a single strap over both knees. John Sweet smoothly negotiated two "exciting drops" (as Stuart described them), the rest of the group carrying around them. One of the two (with the highest single drop) subsequently became known as "Sweet's Falls."

Despite the demands of the river and the length of their run, the party made it to the take-out at Swiss by dark and combined their camping food into a mystery stew. Not a group to dwell overly long on their accomplishments, they headed over to the Yough and more familiar water on Monday.

The following fall (October 18 – 9, 1969), another group of CCA adventurers headed west to take on the Gauley[14]. The Gauley was equal to the challenge, however, chalking up boat damage, equipment wrested away, several swims, and even a broken rib. After Barb Snyder lost her paddle in the rapid below the mouth of the Meadow River, and following a dangerous and fruitless search for it, she and Peter Brown decided to hike out with their boats. This was not an easy task, as they had to bushwhack for half a mile until they intersected the trail that led to the Carnifex Ferry Battlefield State Park. They were accompanied by the rest of the paddlers, who had decided to return to their camp and continue the trip the next day, leaving their boats beside what would henceforth be known as Lost Paddle Rapid.

Al Jenkins, who had suffered the broken rib, apparently took a different escape route from the others and became lost. When the group realized that Al hadn't made it out, Jim Stuart and Bill Funk started their own search for him. Jim described it to me years later by email.

"Bill Funk and I walked all over the woods that night looking for him, even though it was dark. We climbed up into the tops of trees to shine flashlights so that he might see them. I had a piercing whistle and we kept hollering as we went. Despite all the commotion, he never called back until I was almost on top of him.

---

[14] According to Al Jenkins' firsthand account in the November, 1969 Cruiser, the newsletter of the Canoe Cruisers Association of DC, this second decked boat descent of the Gauley (running at 1,500 cfs the first day and 1,800 cfs the second), was led by Jim Stuart, the only paddler in the group to have run the river previously. Accompanying him were Peter Brown, Bill Funk, Al Jenkins, Ed Richmond, Barb Snyder, and Gorman Young.

I found him sitting in a hunter's camp under a rock overhang. He was still in his wetsuit, type II horse-collar life vest, and hockey helmet. Two local mountaineers with rifles were sitting on either side of him. A dim fire was glowing — it was a scene they could have used later in the movie Deliverance. *Fortunately, these hunters were nice West Virginia country boys, so we talked a while about why the deer liked the canyon and such, and successfully extracted Al without incident."*

It would be two more years before I ventured onto the Gauley in a kayak. Like Jimmy Holcombe, but with less excuse, I was quickly trashed in the Room of Doom. The rest of the day flowed well, even as I chose a very careful line through Iron Ring.

Today, the Gauley is commercially rafted and run by thousands of individual paddlers during the fall water releases. Many boaters, as well as other concerned individuals, worked tirelessly, particularly over the decades of the seventies and eighties, to stop a proposed Army Corps of Engineers dam from being built at Swiss, a dam that would have flooded the entire Gauley valley almost to the Summersville Dam. One of the early leaders of this opposition was Jim Stuart, arguing the case for free-flowing rivers, just as he had done in the upper Potomac basin.

~

During this period of my life, I was trying to balance my whitewater activity among three groups; the Canoe Cruisers of DC, the Baltimore Kayak Club and Explorer Post 757. The Post was, in many ways, closest to my heart. Explorer Scouting had recently become coed and the gang met in the basement of my Howard County, Maryland home — the boat-building shop. They were a super-active group of teens when it came to kayaking or canoeing the whitewater rivers of the East, always looking for the next adventure. One blustery and chilly November evening, we rented a 16mm projector and scheduled a movie for our program.

The Grand Canyon, with its panorama of geological history and color, fern-shaded glens and beaches, and turquoise waters cascading from intriguing side canyons had come alive in the Sierra Club's movie, *The Colorado River*. The clicking of the movie projector ceased and the room lights came on, but there was a pervasive silence that was out of character for this bunch of teens.

Then Mimi's words voiced the collective feeling, "I want to be there! I mean — really!"

Other voices sprang to life.

"Our rivers here are great, but ... the Colorado... it's like it's a whole different world."

"If those folks who made the movie could get down the river, so could we!"

"Can we go this summer?"

And so the comments and questions flew back and forth, each giving rise to the next. A fire had been kindled that I hadn't foreseen. The summer after next would be more practical from a planning standpoint, but I knew what that would mean. Momentum would be hard to maintain and by then we would have lost some of the kids that were now so enthusiastic. And it wasn't just teen Colorado fever. It didn't hurt matters that fellow Post advisor Carl Flynn and I had both had a similar dream tucked away in our hearts since our early years of whitewater paddling.

But my engineering mind reeled with the practical questions. What will it cost? How will we get there? How much time will we need? A hundred sub-questions to these. I didn't have the answers, and I wasn't sure I could get them all, but I knew I had to do everything possible to make this dream happen.

We needed information in a hurry, but there wasn't a whole lot of precedent for this sort of adventure in the winter of 1969. Some of us wanted to kayak the Colorado and that would add another dimension to the trip. As far as I knew then, only one expedition with kayaks and decked canoes had made the run before us. This was a group of nine cutting-edge paddlers from the DC area, Pennsylvania and California, including one from England, that had made the Lees Ferry to Diamond Creek descent in June of 1968[15]. Later, I would learn of others who had preceded them.

I called Dan Sullivan, who had been one of the organizers of the 1968 trip, having run the Colorado himself by kayak. He had, I knew, built a custom kayak, with greater length and volume, just for that river.

---

[15] In 1968, rafting business n the Grand Canyon was just beginning to emerge. Demand for trip space was relatively low, and if you wanted to run the Colorado you could do it without a wait of any kind. Aided by the stunning knowledge of all that had been lost in Glen Canyon, the Colorado River had survived a terrific push for another dam between Lake Powell and Lake Meade. Over the next decade, the publicity that had helped preserve the river would make it one of the most popular trip destinations for river runners.

The group of decked boaters that descended the river in 1968 were pioneers in their own right. This was the largest water by far that most of them had run and there were doubts as well as anticipation as they planned their trip. None of their raft guides had ever seen a decked boat on the Colorado and insisted that all of those craft be lashed to the rafts for the trip through Sockdolager — because of the difficulty of rescue below — even though they had already seen their excellent performance through eighty miles of Colorado water. Caution was the word at Crystal, as the right side sneak route was taken by some while others ran center, cutting right of the lower rock. Five paddlers ran Lava Falls, all down the rocky left side.

This intrepid group included: Mark Fawcett, Jim Raleigh and John Sweet in C-1; with Joe Lederle, Chris Hawkesworth. John Newdorp, Peter Reilly, Dan Sullivan and Art Vitterelli in K-1. Aboard the rafts were: Ruth Abronski, Gail & Ray Beach, Al Behall, Jean Dunn, Paula Ganser, Vickie Grant, Gay Gruss, Amy & Pete Hellier, Bill Jahn, Ken Laidlaw, Bernie & Diane McManus, Fran Raleigh, Dorrie Reilly, Harvey Shapiro, Barbara Snyder, Michael Sullivan, and Nancy Tighe. The Hatch boatmen were Warren Herlong, Jerry Hughes and Earl Staley.

"Dan," I asked, "What does it take to kayak the Colorado? I mean, not just equipment, but the kind of paddler who can handle it?"

"Good judgment and a bomb-proof roll," he replied. "By good judgment, I don't mean just the ability to pick out the best line which, of course, is important. You've got to know when you're up against more than you can handle, when you're too tired to be at your best — when it's time to carry or get aboard the raft."

The following Saturday I met with two of our Explorer Post leaders, John Morar and Mimi Hayman, and we began to outline the costs and other requirements of a Grand Canyon adventure. Within a month we had formed the necessary framework upon which the trip could be built and presented the results to the rest of the Scouts.

We knew then that we would go — whether three of us, or thirty — it didn't matter. The dates were set with our Colorado outfitter, Hatch River Expeditions, and a group rate for Scouts was agreed upon.

Work began in earnest. Red Cross Senior Life Saving certification was made a requirement for all participants. Three Post work projects earned nearly $1,700 and individual earnings began to accumulate. We sighed with relief as our transportation problem was suddenly solved. Beth Flynn, Carl's wife, drove a bus during the school year for John Titus of Bel Air, Maryland. After discussing our hoped-for Colorado adventure with him, he generously agreed to donate a retiring school bus for our use.

All during the winter and spring, we kept up with our regular activities; backpacking on Virginia's Old Rag Mountain; caving through the Sinks in West Virginia; competing in slalom and wildwater at Petersburg (WV), the Loyalsock and Brandywine (PA), the Potomac and Savage (MD); as well as paddling a dozen rivers for pure enjoyment. But through all these times together, we were aware that the Colorado River was just over the horizon, creeping ever closer.

I was in a period of frequent travel in my engineering job, ironically not far from the Colorado River, so the burden of transforming the sixty passenger, 1960 International school bus into the vehicle we would need for a cross-country expedition fell on the shoulders of the young men and women of Post 757. Post president John Morar guided his welding torch far into the night as counters, racks and tables took shape within the bus. Curtains were sewn for the side windows. Even the exterior of the bus took on a new look as the yellow body was gradually transformed to green. (Actually, because of rain, the complete transformation never quite happened and the bus was still distinctively two-toned when it left Maryland.) Menus, equipment lists and park reservation letters were generated. We were going to turn this impossible dream into reality!

Canyon Dreams

Kenton and Noel are gone. Blasted away. With an empty steering platform, the huge raft now angles helplessly toward the sharp rocks in the center of the channel. I look at Carl and Frank, shaking their heads as if trying to clear their sight. Where are the guides? In the water? Swept into the abrasive volcanic rock that constricts the channel? From where we crouch and watch on a narrow ledge of the inner gorge, distance and surging waves prevent the three of us from an accurate assessment of what has occurred. We do know, however, that we had not until now seen the power of the Colorado River unfold with such sudden fury.

Horn Creek Rapid is short, but steep and treacherous. Moments before, the lead raft a 33-foot inflatable tail-dragger[16] with eleven Explorer Scouts and a week-and-a-half's provisions aboard, had slid left of center and entered the seething water under the careful eye and quick hand of head boatman Kenton Grua. Close beside Kenton on the stern platform had sat his working companion, Noel Cox.

[16] In the early days of running large (28 and 33-foot) inflatables down the Colorado River, Hatch Expeditions mounted their outboard motor on a wooden platform that overhung the stern of the raft. In order for the motor prop to reach the water, some of the air was released from the stern compartment, thus the name "tail dragger." Introducing this limpness into the raft profile meant that the raft — and particularly the guides positioned on the platform — were often subject to violent whiplash in the heavier rapids. Hatch and other outfitters using motor driven rafts later moved the guide station and motor inside the "doughnut" of the raft, providing better protection to both guides and motor.

From our vantage on the wall of the gorge, the raft looked tiny in the grip of the Colorado's turbulence. It was lost from view for a moment behind a boulder, appeared again, then dropped nearly out of sight into a deep trough. The bow rose skyward and the silver raft bent forward over the crest of the next wave as the Scouts clung tightly to lashing ropes.

Then the wave below — as Colorado waves are inclined to do — exploded upward at a critical point just behind the center of the raft. The stern hung low in the hole for a half second longer — Kenton and Noel still hidden from view — then catapulted upward twenty feet and down again as if on the end of a giant "crack-the-whip" game. The quickness of it left us blinking, searching the empty stern platform and rushing waters for some sign of the guides.

We hear a warning shout from boatman Jack Williams to his passengers, "Hang tight!" and turn to see the sweep raft, already committed to the same course, about to challenge the waiting violence. Meanwhile, someone has crawled to the stern of the lead raft and manages to get it under control in the nick of time. The sweep takes the run with plenty of thrills, but no mishaps, and moments later both rafts pull into the heaving eddy at the base of the north wall, a quarter-mile downriver.

Now, with Kenton and Noel's fate still unknown, it is our turn. Both of the rafts are already below the rapid, and given the steepness of the inner gorge, we're committed. Our three lightweight slalom kayaks are about to meet the same foaming, tossing challenge. We have already seen intimidating water upriver: Sockdolager and Grapevine Rapids had given us a ride through the tallest waves we had ever put a paddle into, and, at Hance Rapid, Carl Flynn and I had been torn from our cockpits while running a monstrous double hole for the benefit of the movie cameras. The three of us have ninety miles of Colorado rapids already under our kayaks, but each rapid is a new challenge to be approached with the proper caution, particularly after what we've just seen.

We ease into our boats, testing thigh and foot braces, checking spray skirts for tightness, and one by one peel off into the main current. Our chosen route follows closely that of the two rafts as we slice to the left of a submerged rock whose peculiar form and effect give the rapid its name. A sculpted, smooth, twisting waterspout stands six feet above the river's surface; in times of greater flow it can rise to even loftier heights.

We drop into the turbulence, angling again to the left to avoid center rocks, at times seeing nothing but brown water seething around and above us. A series of strong draw strokes brings us to the right, avoiding the granite wall that the current is sideswiping on the left. We cross a strong eddy and maneuver among the ever-present boils and whirlpools to where the rafts are now moored to several large boulders.

Both Kenton and Noel are still aboard the raft. They had been catapulted into the air when the wave exploded beneath them, Noel landing on the pile of gear amidships while Kenton crashed into the spare motor and aft supply box. Bloody and barely conscious, with an open gash at his right temple, it had been Kenton whom we had seen crawling aft to bring the raft under control and into the eddy at the last moment.

He now lies stretched across the stern of the raft, legs raised and face shaded from the sun as Jack, Noel, and Eunice, our Johns Hopkins nurse, work to dress his wounds and treat, as best they can, what has now been diagnosed as a concussion. We decide to camp at the first practical spot. Boatman Chuck Liley switches to the lead raft and three miles later we come ashore at a beautiful tamarisk-screened beach backed by gray cliffs, just above the formidable Granite Rapid.

Eunice Lokiec and Bonnie Buchwalter tend to injured head boatman Kenton Grua as Horn Creek Rapid thunders in the background. Rejecting evacuation efforts, Kenton recovered sufficiently from his concussion to finish leading the ten-day trip on the Colorado River.

That evening we are passed by the Sanderson expedition, supposedly a day behind us and surprised that they have overtaken our group. With Sanderson camping at the foot of Granite, a doctor in their party is summoned to our camp and confirms the "probable concussion" diagnoses, recommending that we have Kenton evacuated by helicopter. Their head boatman lends us a transceiver that may be used to make contact with a passing plane.

Noel keeps an all-night vigil beside Kenton, waking him periodically to see if his concussion has worsened. In the dim light of pre-dawn, boatman Jack Williams and I quietly check in with Noel, take the radio, a bit of food, considerable water, and make a 1200 foot climb up the steep draw behind our Granite Rapid camp. Hopes of obtaining help through contact with a passing plane vanish after three hours of fruitless efforts and we return to the river, finding a determined and healthy-looking Kenton ready to push on.

~

Two weeks earlier, on the morning of July 11, 1970, we had left our staging area at my family's Maryland farm only an hour late, almost a record for Post promptness. With seventeen tired but eager explorers and leaders aboard, and twelve kayaks and canoes racked overhead, the old green and yellow bus chugs onto U.S. Highway 40 heading west, leaving behind a crowd of nervous parents and envious fellow explorers. We are all in high spirits, but we also know that the heart of the dream still lies 2,600 road miles toward the setting sun. The bus is to be our home for the next month and will take us on an odyssey of some 6,700 miles through nineteen states before returning to Maryland in mid-August.

"You don't need tents on the Colorado," was the word from Hatch Expeditions. "Just stretch your bags on the sand and be sure to shake the scorpions out of your clothes in the morning." Actually, we weren't given the latter bit of advice until we were well underway on the river! No tents necessary in the Grand Canyon? Great! We're tight on bus space, so we won't bring any tents period.

We have an ace in the hole, however, since we are traveling under a National Scouting Tour Permit. This means that we can enjoy the hospitality of military bases en route, sleeping in barracks or on gymnasium floors. At campgrounds, we will just stretch out on the ground, hoping for clear skies. As it turns out, we're quite lucky that way. And the river? Actually, a rainstorm catches us each day in the Canyon, but always in early afternoon while we are on the water or having lunch. Only once, just before dawn, does a sneaky cloud that apparently didn't check the storm schedule let loose on our peacefully sleeping bodies.

School buses aren't really built for extended high-speed freeway travel, and some of the weaknesses begin to appear early in the trip. By the end of the second day, we limp into Granite City Army Depot in Missouri with a radiator leaking in several places. It appears unrepairable, as the core is prone to crumble at a touch, so we pull it out. We resign ourselves to an unscheduled day's layover while the radiator is re-cored by a mechanic who gives us top priority. The delay gives Eunice and others a chance to finish hanging the curtains and to reorganize the bus storage area.

The Grand Canyon bus gang , July, 1970. Left to right: John Morar, Al Jenkins, Damon Wilson, Tish (hitchhiker), Mark Beck, Barry Martin, Sue (hitchhiker), Nancy Rayburn, Anne Rayburn, Ron Eike, Carol Clark, Collins Downing, Eunice Lokiec, Charlie Morar, Ed Sheldon, Arthur Downing, Frank Birdsong, Bonnie Buchwalter, Doug Woodward and John Zirpel.

One recurring and unavoidable delay that we haven't taken into account occurs at each gas stop. The thirty-gallon bus tank is quickly filled, but emptying our own tanks is another matter. With only two restrooms — sometimes just one — it often takes forty-five minutes for us to get underway again.

As we roll out of Granite City, we know that we will have to drive through the night, despite the rules to the contrary in our National Tour Permit. The river launch date, on which the whole trip depends, is not negotiable. But with four adult drivers, and the bunks that have been built into the rear storage area to give drivers a rest, the marathon is not an impossible task.

A few hours later, steam again billows out from under the hood of the bus. The miles we travel between water fill-ups become shorter and shorter. Our four five-gallon jugs are almost empty as we greet the dawn in Hutchinson, Kansas. Spotting an International dealer on the outskirts of town, we pull into the parking lot, remove the faulty water pump and wait for the parts department to open.

Later in the day, the charge indicator drops into negative territory and once again we're forced to find the cause of a problem. The generator is the culprit, but fortunately we're carrying a spare and underway once more with no more time lost than a gas station stop.

But despite these delays, the bus seems to adapt to its new life as it trundles through the hot, barren deserts of the Southwest and over the high mountain passes of Colorado. After a grueling 32-hour, 965-mile non-stop push (except for gas and maintenance) from Granite City, we at last catch up with our schedule as we pull into the Air Force Academy outside of Colorado Springs. Dan and Pat Gold, paddlers from Baltimore who will join our rafting group on the Colorado, have spotted the bus and are the first to rendezvous with us.

The next morning we're curbed by a Colorado Springs police officer, blue lights flashing as he frantically tries to bring us to a stop before we enter the downtown.

"How tall is that thing you're driving? Our traffic signals only have a fourteen foot clearance here."

I'd already been concerned about clearances myself and measured the total height before we left Maryland. "Exactly twelve feet to the highest point on the 'T' rack, officer," I reply.

"Well, I hope you're right. I'd say it was more like fifteen feet. You're going to be in a heap of trouble if you take out any of our overhead." He follows us through the downtown.

Fifteen minutes later we're pulled over once more, but this time by familiar faces. Frank Birdsong and Bonnie Buchwalter hop out of their car to exchange hugs. Frank will be kayaking with us while Bonnie will be aboard one of the rafts.

"No trouble finding your bunch. Everyone in town has seen the green and yellow bus with boats on top, knows what time it was seen and what direction it was headed!" It's becoming obvious that we're not slipping across the country unnoticed. Like some uprooted drifting beacon, the strange-looking bus is gradually attracting the other nine members of our Colorado River party.

We are drawing inexorably closer to the Colorado, yet there remain other places to explore before we reach Lee's Ferry. That night we will stretch our sleeping bags out near Salida beside the Arkansas River, still running full from snow melt in the high country. At last the boats can come down from the roof of the bus and provide us a much-needed workout after five days of confinement.

The river run is fast — with very few eddies — and we cap the day with an hour of play in Cottonwood Rapid. It is here that the Arkansas exacts its dues. Paddling C-2 together, Carol Clark and Collins Downing ("CD") flip and do not roll. Coming out of a tight cockpit in a hurry can often be a challenge and Carol's leg becomes wedged, badly wrenching her knee and hobbling her for the rest of the trip. Within minutes, John Morar ("The Sundance Kid") gets slammed while surfing and as he rolls up, his right shoulder dislocates. He will float the Grand Canyon with his arm immobilized in a paisley sling.

The continental divide lies between the Arkansas and Gunnison Rivers, and will present a major test for our bus. We creep ever upward, keeping our oversized turtle as close to the edge of the road as we safely can so as not to back up traffic behind us. At one point, Barry Martin hops out, betting that he can run up the mountain highway faster than the bus can climb it. He's right.

On the west side of the Divide, the limitations of the bus become more critical. Sundance makes his way to the front of the bus where I'm trying to keep our descent at a reasonable pace.

"The rear brakes are smoking pretty badly! Can you smell them up here?"

"Yeah, but I'm already geared down to third."

"Well drop it down one more. It's a long way over the edge and there's not even a guard rail."

I hear similar comments from others, as a mutiny seems a distinct possibility. We're probably all envisioning the tragic bus accidents of Central America, where old retired, and often mechanically deficient, school buses ("chicken buses") from the U.S. are used routinely for public transportation. I "double-clutch" the beast, a tricky maneuver on a steep curvy downgrade, and pop into second gear. There is a tense, nervous silence throughout the bus, out of character for this group, until the grade finally begins to gentle out.

We arrive late — standard operating procedure for us by now — at the Black Canyon of the Gunnison. The campground is full, so we simply swing back into the main parking lot and deploy our sleeping bags on the gravel beside the bus. Dinner in the dark.

Dawn has barely begun to illuminate our sleeping forms when another vehicle appears, sporting a kayak with similar lineage to those on top of our bus. Carl and Beth Flynn, driving almost non-stop from Bel Air, Maryland, also have had no trouble getting a fix on our location. Carl, our assistant Explorer advisor, completes our Colorado kayaking party of three. His wife, Beth, drove the same bus we're in now for several years, when it was used to transport kids to school in Bel Air.

We're long gone before a ranger can question our sleeping arrangement of last night, heading south through the spectacular peaks that surround Ouray and Durango. Innovation is the word of the day as someone perusing the bus maintenance box discovers that a metal funnel and two-foot length of heater hose can be attached to each other. Thus is born the "alpine horn," a musical instrument of questionable tone and irritating volume.

As we pause at a Durango intersection, the bus suddenly empties as the occupants race around it in a Chinese fire drill. How such a maneuver got pinned on the Chinese, I have no idea. One of the Scouts, Arthur Downing, has gone wild with the alpine horn, bringing most of the town, motorists and pedestrians alike, to a standstill. I pull the bus to the curb in the next block and a Durango police officer approaches.

"You in charge of this bunch?" he inquires.

"Once in a while," I reply.

"Well, I suggest that all of you be out of town before sunset," as another blast on the horn nearly drowns him out. There is the hint of a smile at the corner of his mouth, yet I get the feeling he is dead serious.

"What did he say?" Arthur wants to know.

"He said he's going to lock you up for disturbing the peace. Or maybe put you in the town stocks for the afternoon." We re-board and head for Mesa Verde.

Camping on grass is more comfortable than gravel and the campground has plenty of space. We catch the first tour of Cliff Palace the next morning, climbing rustic ladders and contemplating what life might have been like for the Anasazi a thousand years ago in this region. So many questions that even the rangers and anthropologists can't fully answer.

Pulling out of Mesa Verde, we see two teenage girls hesitantly trying to thumb a ride so we invite them aboard. Sue and Tish have hitched from Massachusetts, where they told their parents they were taking the bus to the Grand Canyon. For the next two days, as they become part of our company, that will be true! The lure of having a bit of extra spending money as well as the ability to stop and see more places had prompted their change to hitch-hiking, though I suspect that may have been the plan all along. They eat and sleep with us at Navajo National Monument and at the end of the day at Grand Canyon we bid them goodbye and godspeed.

We take our first close-up look at the river and then, full of nervous energy, try to find sleep in the Lee's Ferry Campground. The last human pieces of this adventure are now falling into place without a hitch. Dave Demaree, Sara Richard, and son Matt Richard, arrive at dusk to complete the river company at twenty-three rafters, three kayakers and four guides[17]. We speak briefly with our head guide and the shuttle driver, and pack only the bare necessities into our river bags.

~

Morning comes, the river is real and the Dream has become reality. Two huge silver rafts are already afloat in the clear greenish water at

[17] Our Colorado River Expedition was made up of thirty individuals. Kayaking: Frank Birdsong, Carl Flynn and Doug Woodward. Rafting: Mark Beck, Bonnie Buchwalter, Carol Clark, Dave Demaree, Arthur Downing, Collins Downing, Ron Eike, Beth Flynn, Dan Gold, Pat Gold, Mimi Hayman, Al Jenkins, Eunice Lokiec, Barry Martin, Charlie Morar, John Morar, Nancy Rayburn, Anne Rayburn, Matt Richard, Sarah Richard, Ed Sheldon, Damon Wilson and John Zirpel. Guiding: Noel Cox, Kenton Grua, Chuck Lilley and Jack Williams.

Lee's Ferry and our three homemade kayaks lie dwarfed beside them. Kenton Grua, with brown curly hair and beard, and exuding confidence to our group, is only in his second year of river work — yet destined to become one of the most sought-after Colorado guides in the years to come. He will be our trip leader for the next ten days. Joining him are Jack Williams and Chuck Lilley, graduate students at the University of Missouri, Kansas City, and Noel Cox, a student at Prescott College.

An NPS ranger is methodically running down his checklist with Kenton to make sure the upcoming trip complies with all Park rules and safety requirements. Meanwhile, our shuttle driver is ready to take the bus to Peach Springs, which puts the explorers into a small frenzy, making sure that no river items have been left behind in the bus and, just as important, no gear that should stay in the bus is lying ignored on the pebbly beach.

Was it only eight months ago that we said, "Let's do this thing!" having little idea then of how it could all be pulled off? Yet here we are, introducing ourselves to the guides, lashing gear amidships to the rafts, climbing aboard, three of us easing into kayaks and testing our rolls in calm waters. We are ready — physically and mentally. The river now belongs to us and we to the river. It deserves, and receives, our respect. It is wide, deep and powerful — and very much alive.

We soon recognize our dependence on this moving thread of life. We sleep unsheltered on its soft sand beaches; we cook over fires built from driftwood left by its floodwaters; bathing or swimming we emerge refreshed from its coolness; twenty times a day — clear or muddy — we drink its waters. Ultimately, it will deposit us with sad farewells at Diamond Creek.

All is ready, but still we wait. Kenton will determine the appropriate moment. At last it comes — the flood tide from Glen Canyon Dam that he wants us to ride this first day. We take to the river as the surge of frigid blue-green water passes by and the excitement is electric.

Marble Gorge draws us in and lulls us with its lazy pace. We pass under Navajo Bridge. Then, almost eight miles into the Canyon, Badger Creek Rapid adds it voice to that of the alpine horn, which has been echoing back and forth between the walls for hours. The boatmen watch the kayaks carefully and seem pleased at what they see. Four miles later we've still got those first day jitters and Soap Creek decides to slam us. We roll up and the guides begin to breathe a little easier.

Rivalry between raft crews develops immediately and water battles with bailing buckets break out whenever the two rafts come close to each other. As kayakers, we learn to stay clear of a raft's stern as the boatmen have a trick of bringing the motor prop to a position near the surface of the river where they can inundate us in a blinding power spray.

House Rock, next to the rapid of the same name, provides the perfect first night's camping spot as we all stretch our bags under the overhang and a steak dinner is cooked on a driftwood fire at one end of the protective ceiling of rock. No rain, but we're soon scrambling to cover our food as a small sandstorm blows through our hideaway.

The next morning, we carry the kayaks up to the head of House Rock Rapid and enjoy it one more time. Nancy Rayburn, one of our Scouts who was later to become a western river guide, borrows Carl's kayak to make a fine run of her own. A few miles of relatively calm water bring out the pirate instincts of the group again as the rafts maneuver, trying to ram each other. Bailing buckets, the alpine horn and Mimi go overboard. Mimi is retrieved, but the alpine horn is lost forever. Not everyone misses its presence. At least no one will be able to entertain us with a horn concert when we stop at Redwall Cavern later in the day.

Four rapids in succession grab our attention, culminating in Cave Springs, where we're happy to avoid the huge center hole. Frank and I play the big waves below Cave Springs, both flipping and rolling at the same time on a wave face. Bonnie later commented, "It looked as if it were choreographed."

The next day our lunch stop is memorable as we climb to the Nankoweap ruins high above the river. Were the rock and daub structures just granaries or were there dwellings here? In any case, the immensity of the vista — both up and down river — from this promontory is awe-inspiring.

We pause again as the Little Colorado River joins its waters — today a milky gray-blue — with those of the larger river, now having taken on the look of tomato soup from the heavy afternoon rain storms. Across the river, high up on Chuar and Temple Buttes, gleam a few silver fragments left from the 1956 mid-air collision of two airliners. At the time, it was the worst civilian air accident in U.S. history, claiming 128 lives.

In the mid-sixties I was flying regularly for my engineering job and happened to make conversation with the man in the next seat on one cross-country flight. As we flew over Arizona, the 1956 collision came up.

"Strange that you should mention that," he replied. "In all my travels — and I fly a lot — I've never missed a flight — except one. I was in a Los Angeles motel and never heard my alarm. By the time I rushed to the airport it was too late to catch United 718. I had to wait several hours for another flight and it was not until I arrived in Chicago that I saw the newspaper and realized that the plane had gone down. My flight."

Camp is set at Tanner Wash, where we can see the Desert View Watchtower far up on the Canyon rim, intruding upon our wilderness experience. The guides are just setting up for dinner when the afternoon rain squall, running late and making up for lost time, comes barreling down the Canyon. The high winds send pots and pans flying and we all scramble to protect and hold down what we can. In twenty minutes the rain has passed, the sun breaks through and all is calm.

We're learning what it means to be a minimalist from Kenton. A floppy black hat, two pairs of cut-offs, a couple of faded denim shirts, no underwear and a pair of sandals (rarely worn) make up his entire wardrobe for the ten days on the river. Any piece wet from the day will be hung out to dry during the night.

As we head out the next day, the nervous jitters return. Hance Rapid is getting high water and the boatmen decide to walk folks around. Bonnie sets up her tripod and telephoto. Someone grabs my movie camera. Carl and I decide to tempt fate and run directly through the center maelstrom. We pay for it. Frank watches, then wisely moves his line left and clips the edge of the holes.

Around the bend, Sockdolager and Grapevine Rapids welcome us to the Inner Gorge. What an elevator ride those towering twenty-foot waves give us! As my speed slows toward the peak of one tall wave, I feel that I'm about to fall backward into the trough and become trapped in an endless river cycle, much like the inside of a treadmill. But we're quartering the waves, holding the kayak at a diagonal with the current, and as my momentum grinds to a halt, I lean into the wave face with my paddle deep and the river itself pulls me the last few critical feet to the top. Then it's a rush down the fast face to challenge the next uphill slope. The sweep raft takes such a flexing that one of the wooden frame pieces breaks. With evening approaching, we camp downriver of the Kaibab suspension bridge near the trail to Phantom Ranch, where the guides make repairs. A ranger joins us for dinner.

The next morning we're startled by a sudden yell from the part of the beach where Dan and Pat Gold have spent the night. We come on the run to find that Dan has been stung on the inside of his thigh by a scorpion that has crept unseen into his pants.

"Well, you should know in an hour or two if it's the deadly variety," says Kenton encouragingly.

"Can't you tell by looking at it? It's still here." Dan is pretty agitated.

"I'm not that intimate with scorpions," Kenton replies, "But chances are, it's more annoying than lethal." Dan survives.

Today we'll cover only three river miles before Kenton is injured at Horn Creek. Later that night, while Jack and Eunice and I discuss the possibility of evacuating Kenton, the Explorers build a roaring fire. Three self-appointed witch-doctors chant and dance around the flames far into the night. Whether their magic has any effect on Kenton or not, the next morning he tells us that he's ready to push on.

Yesterday's enforced rest gave me a chance to finish the waterproof housing for my movie camera that I had designed before I left home and had been constructing for the past week in the rare scraps of available time. Granite Rapid is a good first test, both to find out if the housing is waterproof and to see if the whole assembly stays on the boat. The big water descent lives up to its scouting report, but the eddy is even more fearsome. I'm grabbed by a sucking whirlpool that pulls the boat under and finally releases me when only my head and shoulders are still above the surface. The camera mount is still in place and the housing has allowed no water to enter. It's not often a new design works on the first try.

Since Jack and I have spent a good part of the morning trying to radio for help while Kenton rested, we cover only eight river miles before camping again. But there are a couple of thrills in that short distance — Hermit and Crystal Rapids. We're riding the crest of a release plus some pretty heavy rain run-off. At Hermit, Frank and I both flip and roll in the towering waves; Carl runs it clean. Five years later I'll hike the Hermit Trail to the bottom of the Canyon in January, camping beside what looks like a different rapid with its clear water and five-foot waves.

At Crystal, the raft passengers walk once more and the boatmen carefully scout the rapid. A 1966 flash flood in Crystal Creek turned this spot into a major rapid and it has changed several times since that event. There is a new boulder rearrangement in the center and Kenton decides that the best route to avoid damage and keep the rafts from hanging up is to run the "killer channel" to the left. He and Jack handle their runs with admirable skill and manage to cross back to river right for passenger pick-up. Carl, Frank and I all run cautiously to the right of center. An hour later, we camp beside Sapphire Rapid, knowing that we'll soon have to make up our lost river miles.

That day has arrived. With a near-dawn start, we cover thirty-eight miles, running sixteen named rapids in the process. Despite the marathon on the river, we pause twice, once for the climb to Elve's Chasm and again for the thundering spectacle of Deer Creek Falls. As I step into the falls, the force of 130 feet of free-falling water rips my shorts completely off. This brings applause from the explorers, who are delighted to see their leader caught with his pants down.

The long day is not without its misadventures. As the afternoon wears on, the river swings from north into west, making it almost impossible to read the current as we're blinded by the dancing glare from the sinking sun. Both rafts miss their lines and damage their motors, requiring the spares to be put into service. Frank gets trashed in Dubendorff, but manages a one-arm, no-spray skirt roll to recover. Running almost blind, Carl and I luck out on our own lines and come through unscathed.

Kenton is exhausted and we all try to take up the slack at our Fishtail Rapid camp.

We're still pushing the next day as we put twenty-eight more miles behind us, but the whitewater challenges are almost nonexistent. Frank, Carl and I climb aboard the rafts and let the Scouts take turns in the hard boats. Even boatmen Jack Williams and Chuck Lilley have a go at the kayaks and enjoy the change of venue.

The highlight of the day is a lunch stop at Havasu Creek, where we explore the tiny side canyon on foot. Before the decade is over, I will have backpacked in twice from the top, climbing past awesome Havasu and Mooney Falls and swimming in the turquoise pools behind the naturally formed travertine dams. Today, however, Havasu Creek is spouting forth the tomato soup waters with which we've become so familiar.

Our day ends at National Canyon, a spot where you could become mesmerized by the evening and morning light playing on the canyon walls, the scene changing by the minute. One of the raft pontoons has been leaking, so the guides take the opportunity after dinner to detach and pull it up on the beach, where they sew up and seal a fifteen-inch gash. Darkness falls at last, but suddenly there's a sharp cry, followed by what sounds like muttered curses. Mimi is caught in the act of sneaking cookies out of the food box when her weight shifts on the raft floor and the wooden lid falls on her fingers. We're all eating twice as much as we normally do, yet we feel trimmer and more fit.

At this point, the three of us in kayaks should be exuding confidence. The Colorado is the biggest water we've paddled up to this time and there have often been unexpected tests and surprises. Gradually, we've dispelled the fears that the boatmen held for our safety, as our mobility and Eskimo rolls have proved equal to the big water. None of them has ever seen a kayak on the Colorado before.

Yet those nervous jitters are building again. As we shove off from National Canyon, we know that this will be the day. Thirteen miles to the infamous Lava Falls. There is talk of little else from the boatmen. We can feel various parts of our anatomy tightening.

Hours of apprehension pass and suddenly we're there. We land next to the rafts and, with a very large measure of respect, examine this thirty-nine foot drop from every possible vantage on river left. Deciding we need more information, Frank and I ferry across to the opposite shore, and climb high on the sharp black boulders for a view right down the throat of the action channel. Satisfied as to the "where," but still dubious about the "how," I agree to take the first crack at the heavy side of Lava.

Sliding close by a dark boulder which juts into the channel from river right, I get my first cockpit level glimpse of this whitewater madness. Arm muscles seem to lack strength to even hold the paddle and I wish that somehow my stomach butterflies would fly me right over the seething caldron below.

The first drop galvanizes my whole body into action as I slam into a wall of water, replacing the queasy feeling with one of total exhilaration. The next drop wipes me out — utterly and totally. I can feel the neoprene spray skirt go, and my body slides out of the hip and thigh braces as I fight to get my paddle in position for a roll. Turbulence threatens to pull me completely out of the cockpit and all I can think of in my inverted posture is that heaving fifteen-foot pillow of water climbing the rough volcanic rock at the end of the channel. The rock I had planned to miss with a couple of well-timed draw strokes to the left had I been in a happier position.

Keenly aware of each phase in the thrashing I am being given by this granny-gobbler (as the boatmen call it), I feel boat, body and paddle rise skyward in a corkscrew motion. The glimpse of daylight gives me a much-needed gulp of air, and with renewed effort I grasp the cockpit rim and force my legs back into position.

The next roll attempt brings success and, finding myself clear of the dreaded black rock, I strain to keep the waterlogged kayak upright and making headway for shore. My headway is largely of the negative variety and only a last-ditch lunge gains me the haven of a small eddy-line rock where I'm able to scramble out and empty the boat before being swept against the canyon wall in Lower Lava.

Safely ashore, I find Frank and we discuss his strategy for surviving the same run, including the double vee-shaped hole which had inundated me a short time before. Frank adjusts his line accordingly and is more than equal to the task as I watch — through my movie camera lens — his helmeted form blast through one stopper after another on his way to a perfectly executed run. Carl prudently decides to carry his kayak around.

Both rafts have suffered motor damage upriver and are running on their spares, so the guides will take no chances. As the passengers walk, the boatmen decide to pull the motors out of the water and bring the rafts down the shallow left side of Lava under oar power, two boatmen rowing each raft. Their runs are rocky, and the rafts nearly hang up several times, but eventually make the big eddy on river left.

The rest of the day is void of excitement as we tack another twenty-five miles onto the thirteen above Lava. The long day brings us to the beach below Two Hundred-Five-Mile Creek. It's spacious and ideal for camping, but a melancholy mood has already begun to grip the group.

Everyone is keenly aware that it's our last night on the river. The songs are poignant — Mariah, Scarborough Fair, Bridge Over Troubled Waters. There is more than one wet cheek as each of us is deep in private thought — what bonds have formed among us during the days in the Canyon — why, why does it all have to end?

Kenton approaches me just outside the fire circle. "You know, Doug, when Ted [Hatch] told me a month ago that we were scheduled to take a bunch of Scouts down the river, I about choked. I said to Jack, 'What did we do to deserve this punishment — or is it just the luck of the draw?' But now — and I speak for all the boatmen — I can't remember a trip that I've enjoyed more than this one. I just want you to know that."

I nod and ponder his words. "Thanks. It was our Dream — and you brought it to life. You can't help but know what the trip has meant to all of us, too." We join the circle.

The last day disappears like gold running through our fingers. We have no power to hold it in place, to make time stand still. All too soon we're unloading gear at Diamond Creek, leaving the familiar routine of our Canyon days. Tears are streaming down Mimi's face as she hugs our guides in an embrace that says, "I love you all, I love the River, I love the Canyon, but will I ever see any of you again, you who have given me beauty, solitude and companionship?"

"One more picture before you deflate those rafts," Dave yells as he gets Jack and Chuck to pose with him on the stern tube. Several cameras point that way as Dave drapes his arms around the two guides. Suddenly the arms tighten and there's a terrific splash as he wrestles the pair into the river, something no one had been able to do in all our river miles. Kenton and Noel escape.

Left, Hatch River Expeditions guides Noel Cox and Kenton Grua. Right, Shenanigans at Deer Creek Falls.

Now comes one of the most hair-raising parts of the whole trip. Somehow we all pile into two pickup trucks, most of us crammed in atop our bags in the rear. There appears to be no road, and the drivers roar right up the bed of Diamond Creek, over boulders and washes at what feels like highway speeds. We desperately grasp for handholds or cling to the person next to us as the trucks lurch and bounce violently up the draw. We can't help but wonder what holds these vehicles together long enough to come back for another shuttle run.

An hour or more later, we throttle down for arrival at Peach Springs. There sits our green and yellow turtle, the remaining boats still racked overhead. And, as in Tolkien's epic Ring adventure, there will again be a "breaking of the company." The time has come to bid farewell to Carl and Beth, Frank and Bonnie, Dan and Pat, Sarah and Matt, and Dave as they head east and we board our bus once more.

It springs to life, though not with the pizzazz of the pickup trucks, and eventually crosses the Colorado once more at Hoover Dam, heading for Las Vegas. We arrive at Nellis Air Force Base just before dark, and are shown to our quarters, a suffocating storage room in the basement of the mess hall. Pulling mattresses from the stacks against the wall, we stake out our individual sleeping spots. I toss a mattress onto a table and collapse in exhaustion. A gigantic fan roars through the night, but does little but move the stifling heat around the room. In the blackness of the wee hours, I suddenly wake in alarm, thinking that I've crawled onto a rock in the middle of Lava Falls, surrounded by thundering whitewater.

We're out of Las Vegas by 7:25 AM, setting a new bus record. A four-hour stop in St. George, Utah for laundry, mail and relaxation helps our spirits a bit and we pause briefly for the requisite photos at Zion and Bryce National Parks. Nothing compares to our time in the Canyon and we're all still feeling the emptiness.

Now we're working our way north, stopping to enjoy places that most of the Scouts have never seen before: Great Salt Lake, where the increased buoyancy provides us with an unusual swimming experience; the Tetons, sudden giants rising from the surrounding, more subdued terrain; and Yellowstone, where we see bear, buffalo and elk. We fill the bus with 24-cent/gallon gasoline, a sight none of us are likely to see again.

Leaving Yellowstone through the northeastern Silver Gate, the bus labors over Beartooth Pass and into the high country of chilling winds, snow fields, deep tarns and a sea of wildflowers that covers the slopes to the limit of sight. The narrow mountain road from Lovell, Wyoming is spectacular, but another challenge for the bus. Night is falling as we enter the Bighorn Mountains, downshift to first gear, and suddenly find ourselves confronted by switchbacks so sharp that the bus must back up and reposition itself in order to make the turns. During each such maneuver, we send out a signal person with a flashlight to make sure we don't back over the edge of the road. Spontaneous singing breaks out — the melancholy songs reminiscent of our last night on the Colorado — and at midnight we at last pull up beside the Tongue River to make camp.

In the morning, six of us enjoy the Class III+ kayak run from our camp to the town of Dayton where we're met by the bus. Afternoon finds us hiking the Tongue River trail into the high meadows, again enjoying the vast expanse of wildflowers. That evening, at our campfire, we surprise our youngest Explorer, Anne Rayburn, on her fifteenth birthday with a candle-lit cake and a sweatshirt autographed by all of us.

Sheridan Lake, in the Black Hills, is our next camping spot, where we have "chicken fights" in the lake and then Mimi, Sundance and Butch (Damon Wilson) create the "bus song" after dinner. There is a verse for each person on the trip, as un-flattering as possible (within the rather loose bounds of common decency), each set to a well-known tune of the day, and uproariously funny.

We will continue to camp, but now we must try to make some serious mileage each day as our band heads east in earnest. Just beyond Rapid City, we pick up another hitchhiker. Linda has been living the hippie life-style for several years, traveling from commune to camp to gathering. She immediately begins describing her experiences to the Scouts, adding quite a bit to the education of our group with her "shock and awe" tactics. She has kept a journal of all her sexual encounters, with description of technique and a rating for each of her partners. It's not a small book. She claims to be the daughter of a prominent Presbyterian minister in DC and I heave a sigh of relief as she asks to be let off several hours before we make camp.

With our return to long driving days at highway speeds, mechanical problems begin to rear their heads once more. We're still an estimated three and a half days from home when our generator goes out again. The brushes have disintegrated and we borrow the ones from the bad generator to make a good unit.

As we creep slowly along in a thick nighttime fog, hoping for an open gas station, the engine sputters to a halt. There is spare gas in a can strapped to the back of the bus, but at seven miles per gallon it won't get us far. Looking for anything resembling a camping spot, we pull into a picnic area at Gavins Point on Lewis and Clark Lake — we're still in South Dakota — and sleep under the shelter roof.

We quickly find gas in the morning, point the bus east once more and by nightfall we're at Le Claire on the Mississippi River. Sleeping bags are stretched out between the river and the railroad. We talk to some of the trainmen and take turns scaring each other between the deserted buildings along the tracks. Trains rumble past all night.

The next day, we're making good time toward East Harbor, Ohio, when our generator goes out again. The shaft has twisted right in two, but not at the bearings. Using what parts we have left, we build a mechanically sound generator — so we can keep tension on the water pump pulley and fan — even though the unit itself is electrically dead.

After several stops to charge the battery, we finally pull into East Harbor where Ed Sheldon's sister Judy is still waiting for us at three in the morning! Three hours later, she and Ed head for North Carolina while we charge our battery once again.

With no rested drivers, we're out of East Harbor by 6:30 AM, heading for the Pennsylvania line on what we hope will be our last day on the road. We stop to recharge in Pittsburgh, knowing that if everything else goes well, we shouldn't have to pause for another charge since we're running in daylight. In Hancock, Maryland, we make several calls to Baltimore to alert the home folks of our schedule.

At 7:30 PM, after a month on the road (and river), we at last pull into the Normandy Shopping Center in Howard County, Maryland, to the cheers and tears of parents and friends, a "welcome home" banner stretched across our path. Again, there are sad farewells as our company of adventurers is split once more. I drive the last handful to my family's farm, where the parting is final. The bus is empty. The odyssey is finished. Tomorrow I'll be in Atlanta.

～

The Colorado River adventure has had a far-reaching impact on many of our lives. Some would be drawn back to the River or the Canyon again and again, and a majority of us have stayed active in whitewater paddling.

Two long-term relationships grew out of the time our small group spent together. Bonnie Buchwalter and Frank Birdsong were married shortly after the trip. And, although it took eleven years to finally tie the knot, in 1981 Mimi Hayman and Dave Demaree were married at Ohiopyle Falls on the Youghiogheny River. Since that time they have given birth to their own raft manufacturing company, Demaree Inflatable Boats. They both have run the Colorado many times since our 1970 trip, Dave usually guiding a raft or dory for one of the commercial outfitters. And Mimi, owner of that clear and insistent voice that pointed us toward the Grand Canyon in 1970, six years later would become the first woman to run every rapid of the Colorado in a C-1.

Beth and Carl Flynn, after spending years in Connecticut and on the coast of Maine, finally realized a lifelong dream and retired to live near the Yough in western Pennsylvania. They have spawned a host of whitewater paddlers, as most of their children and grandchildren have become skilled in the sport. And their home has become a magnet for many of the veterans of that first Colorado expedition.

Nancy Rayburn worked as a guide on the New River in West Virginia and later guided on several of the western rivers. Most of the other explorers stayed active in whitewater, even carrying the connection into adulthood to share with new families.

Our kayaks had generated interest among the boatmen and both Jack Williams and Chuck Lilley wanted their own. Design and colors were agreed on and that fall Carl built Chuck's while I built one for Jack, shipping them both to Kansas City.

Kenton Grua would become one of the most skilled and respected Colorado river guides over the next three decades, switching from rafts to oar-powered dories the year after we met him. I even ran into someone who knew him while I was camping with the family in Patagonia in 2001. Anticipating a meeting to reminisce and hear some of his river tales, I was shocked to learn that he had been killed the next year in a mountain biking accident.

~

Writing these words thirty-five years later, it is interesting to put our run of the Colorado into the perspective of those times. We had been drawn to the river by the magnificent beauty and vastness of the Canyon. It had been the Sierra Club film we had seen the year before, as well as two of their books published in the mid-sixties that had begun to awaken our consciousness; *Time and the River Flowing — Grand Canyon* and the heart-breaking *The Place No One Knew — Glen Canyon on the Colorado*.

Although we would never see them ourselves, we knew that the mysteries and intimate beauty of Glen Canyon now lay deep beneath the waters of Lake Powell. In one of the great tragedies of the century, the handful of people who were familiar with the treasure that was to be lost were too few to stand up to the political forces that would profit from putting a concrete plug in the Canyon. The gates had closed and the waters had begun to rise seven years before we came to the Canyon.

We were aware, too, of the more recent battle against the proposed dams at Marble Canyon and Bridge Canyon, having passed both sites in our descent of the river. How Martin Litton, with his "no dams" stand, shook the complacency out of the Sierra Club when they would have settled for "tasteful marinas" on the lakes and elevators in the dams to get tourists down to the river below. That David Brower had been responsible for the *New York Times* newspaper ads saying, "Should we also flood the Sistine Chapel, so the tourists can get nearer the ceiling?" in response to the BLM's claim that the new lakes would benefit tourists by bringing them closer to the upper walls of the side canyons. It was later said that as soon as that ad hit the streets, the dams were dead. The proposal was withdrawn in 1967.

All of this was fuel for our after-dinner discussions as we sat around the campfire with Kenton and the other guides, watching the ever-changing evening light paint the canyon walls. We were on the cusp, though we didn't realize it then. Few people had run the river through the Canyon at that point, and most of them on commercial trips. Martin Litton, who had labored so hard for the past eight years introducing friends and decision-makers to the Canyon through his intimate dory trips, had been forced at last to begin charging for his services. Within a few years, the publicity that had saved the river from the dams would bring throngs of eager folks to the Canyon, seeking the thrill of the rapids and an escape to wilderness. The reservation system suddenly became restrictive and new Park Service regulations were introduced to protect the river. The days that we experienced, when you could pick up the phone and reserve a launch date — either privately or with an outfitter — quickly passed into memory.

How unique was our kayaking descent of the Colorado, running all the rapids between Lee's Ferry and Diamond Creek, including the heavy side of Lava Falls? Let's look back over the forties, fifties and sixties. The trips that preceded ours were few and scattered, major rapids were often carried or snuck, but we should all doff our helmets to the courage of these intrepid individuals.

Kudos for the first complete[18] kayaking run of the Grand Canyon must go to an eastern paddler, Alexander "Zee" Grant of Bedford, New York. Grant was a multi-dimensional whitewater enthusiast, having organized the National Whitewater Championships on Maine's Rapid River in the summer of 1940 and later became involved in the formation of a national organization for whitewater paddlers, the AWA (American Whitewater Affiliation). He was also drawn to the solitude and challenge of wilderness rivers and got in touch with Norman Nevills, who at that point in time had twice run the Colorado from Lee's Ferry to Lake Meade. Nevills felt that a craft as "fragile as a kayak" could not survive the abuse it would undergo in the Canyon. He finally agreed after Grant assured him that the trip would be for their mutual convenience and neither would bear responsibility for the other's safety.

They met in July of 1941 and spent the night at the Nevills home at Mexican Hat, Utah. Nevills was looking for high water to protect his wooden cataract boats from rock damage. Grant was hoping for low

---

[18] Three skilled kayakers from France, Bernard de Colmont, Genevieve de Colmont and Antoine de Seynes made a self-contained run of the Green and Colorado Rivers in folding kayaks in the late summer and early fall of 1938, taking out at Phantom Ranch.

water to give himself more time to maneuver. As it turned out, pre-trip rains came in torrents and Nevills maintained that the river had never been so high in July. Grant would paddle a 16-1/2-foot folding kayak of his own design, the bow and stern carved from balsa wood, a skin of rubberized fabric, and the interior filled with an array of flotation which included eight inner tubes and five beach balls. Huge sponsons, made from the inner tubes of New York City bus tires, were attached to each side. He named it the Escalante, in honor of the explorer-priest who first crossed the Colorado.

After a missed line in Badger Rapid resulted in a wet exit, with another at House Rock, Grant's run became smoother and more precise. Hance and the rapids of the Inner Gorge were run without mishap. At Hermit and Lava, the huge explosion waves were intimidating and as Grant states in his account[19], "Two rapids forced us to line or drag the boats around them over the rocks, Hermit and Lava Falls." After eighteen days on the river, the party reached the backwaters of Lake Meade, and Zee Grant had accomplished a kayaking "first," disproving Norm Nevills' ominous prediction.

Nineteen years later, Walter Kirschbaum, 1953 World Champion in Kayak Slalom, would be the next individual to paddle the length of the Grand Canyon in a kayak. His initial challenge was to overcome the reticence of the NPS staff in issuing him a permit. National Park Rules instituted in the mid-fifties stated that; "Foldboats, canoes, kayaks, or conventional rowboats are considered unsafe on this section of the river." [Colorado River within Grand Canyon National Park and Monument.] Finally proving his skills to the satisfaction of Park Superintendent Dan Davis, he departed from Lee's Ferry in June of 1960, in the company of Ted Hatch guiding a pontoon raft and Tyson Dines in a motor-powered, 18-foot freight canoe. I would surmise that the motor exempted the latter from the Park's prohibition on canoes. Like Grant's, Kirschbaum's kayak was homemade, 16'-8" long with a 19" beam, fiberglass hull and fabric deck. The trip took six days, ending at Temple Bar on Lake Meade. Crystal did not exist as a major rapid and Kirschbaum took a left-side route at Lava, avoiding the "worst section, where a kayak would definitely be lost."[20] Complimenting his early Grand Canyon run, Kirschbaum is also credited with the first kayak descent of the Black Canyon of the Gunnison. He died in an accident at his Los Alamos home in 1972.

In October of 1963, Ulrich Martins and Les Jones made a seventeen-day descent of the Colorado from Lee's Ferry to Lake Meade, likely the first kayak descent without the accompaniment of support boats.

[19] From Zee Grant's personal account in American Whitewater, Summer, 1958.

[20] From Walter Kirschbaum's personal account in American Whitewater, November, 1960.

Ulrich's kayak was similar in construction to the one run by Walter Kirschbaum (glass and fabric), while Jones' home-made, all-aluminum, oar-powered boat (17'-6" length x 19" beam) resembled a racing shell, although he referred to it as a kayak. Lake Powell was filling and the river was running only 1000 cfs, making it necessary to line or carry around a number of rapids, including Lava Falls. Despite bringing repair materials on the river, Ulrich's boat was so badly damaged that he hiked out to Grand Canyon Village for more fiberglass before continuing the trip. From the photographs[21] that accompany Jones' account, it appears that life jackets were optional, and they speak of the proposed Grand Canyon dams as if they were a foregone conclusion. With the low level of Lake Meade, the pair had hoped for a run of Lava Cliff Rapid, reputedly the Grand's most difficult, but find it silted in. Jones makes mention of being on the Colorado the year before, but gives no details of that descent.

Eastern hard boaters appeared in the Canyon in June of 1968 on a trip organized by the Canoe Cruisers of Washington, DC and described in the previous chapter of this book. Due to the hesitancy of the guides, all of the hard boats were strapped to the rafts for the run through Sockdolager. "Five of our paddlers ran Lava — John [Newdorp], Mark [Fawcett] and Jim [Raleigh] in C-1 and Dan [Sullivan] and Chris [Hawkesworth] in K-1. All came through the rock strewn left side..." as Jean Dunn reported in her detailed account.[22]

By 1970, it became obvious that the word was out — the Colorado River was one of the ultimate whitewater destinations. In June of that year, a second trip from the East was organized by the Buck Ridge Ski Club (Pennsylvania) which included hard boaters Matt Lauck, Bill Jenkins, John Berry and Cay Hathaway, with Dan Sullivan and Mark Fawcett returning for their second run of the Canyon. This time the group would run Sockdolager, but take the left side of Lava again. Cay describes it.[23] "Lava Falls Rapid on the ninth day lived up to its reputation. The rafts lashed their motors and rowed furiously, accepting the first hole, but avoiding the second. This second hole should be missed to be appreciated. And, as cameras clicked, the small boats took a sneak route."

Our run of the Canyon followed two and a half weeks later. Sneak Lava Falls? I might have, if I'd known those paddlers who were my long-time whitewater heroes — Dan Sullivan and John Berry — had chosen

---

[21] Grand Canyon at Low Water, Leslie Jones, American Whitewater, Summer, 1965 and The Colorado at Low Water, Leslie Jones, American Whitewater, Autumn, 1965

[22] Cruiser (the monthly newsletter of the Canoe Cruisers Association, Washington, DC), July, 1968.

[23] Cruiser (Monthly newsletter of the Canoe Cruisers Association, Washington, DC), August, 1970

that route. But that thought never occurred at the time. With many prayers and drawn up sphincters, Frank and I just went for it. By some strange stroke of timing, it appears that we may have been the first kayakers to run the heavy side of Lava Falls.

Five days after we left the river, Walt Blackadar, the river-running surgeon from Salmon, Idaho, would arrive for his first kayaking run of the Grand Canyon, with a large entourage of top-notch paddlers plus an additional group that would fill four of outfitter Loren Smith's 22-foot rafts. It was his first experience in water that big, but he, also, was game for the right side of Lava, rolling on each of four attempts.

It soon became commonplace for hard boaters running the Colorado to take the hair route in Lava. Blackadar would return to the Canyon twice in the next five years, each time with a film crew. With Blackadar's national publicity, the release of the film Deliverance, and the ascent of slalom kayaking to the Olympics all occurring in the early seventies, the Colorado "wilderness" experience — and particularly the ability to easily schedule time in the Canyon — would cease to exist.

But my heart is in the Canyon still. It beats with the thunder of Horn, Crystal and Lava; it longs for the stillness of the hidden side canyons. In the heartbreak of a lost Glen Canyon, it follows Ed Abbey through an endless maze of sandstone passages, swims naked in the sculptured pool with Katie Lee, and swells with joy under the same star-filled desert sky that inspired Terry and Renny Russell to pen these words:

> *The weed will win in the end, of course.*
> *Time is on our side boys, time is on our side.*
> *Thine alabaster towns will tumble, thine engines rot into dust.*
> *Man will break his date with the future,*
> *No matter how long he wants to play outlaw,*
> *no matter how long he wants to gallop through town*
> *shooting like a madman*
> *and hooting at the laws of nature's god.*
> *It is not they that he has made obsolete, it is himself.*
> *This knowledge is called wisdom.*

24 From *On The Loose,* Terry and Renny Russell, 1967, Sierra Club Books, with permission from Renny Russell, who has retained all rights to *On The Loose.*

Paddling South

In the summer of 1970, immediately following our Colorado River expedition, all traces of boat building had disappeared from the basement of my Howard County home. So had I. Western Electric was moving its Product Engineering Control Center, of which I was a part, to Atlanta, Georgia. By this time, Carl Flynn, with the assistance of Fred Vigeveno and Ron Eike, had become skilled in laying up both boats and paddles, so the Maryland Post was by no means left in the lurch at my departure.

During the previous spring, I had made a trip south to view possible new homes for the family. Accompanying me was not Roberta, but John Morar, the "Sundance Kid" of Colorado River renown. John, besides helping me look at houses, had his own reasons for checking out Atlanta. He would be starting at Georgia Tech, my own alma mater, that fall. Amid a two-day downpour that made a whitewater run of Claremont Road a distinct possibility, we checked out houses and rivers. The Chattahoochee was so far out of its banks that several mega-buck riverside mansions were being manhandled by the river with no respect whatsoever.

Our search of homes took the real estate agent into strange territory. "You know," she finally commented, "I've had folks that make the kitchen a priority, or maybe a living room with a fireplace, but I've never before seen anyone look at basements first." I'm sure she had suspicions of a prospective moonshine operation or worse, but when we finally found the perfect basement in a house nearing completion in the Dunwoody section of northeast Atlanta, we let her in on the secret. Boat building. Our epoxy brew would be far more potent than a little backwoods moonshine.

This particular home was built on a steep slope and had a grade level entrance to the basement even though the ceiling was fourteen feet above the slab. "Wow," we said as our eyes lit up at the possibilities. "We can stand a kayak on end in here." Thus we could perform the vertical operations, such as plugging, without having to go outside. And the voluminous overhead space meant we could hoist and store boats and molds out of the way above us. This was it. Of course, it had to meet Roberta's approval of the living space. It did.

"And can you put that big exhaust fan in the basement?" More of a stipulation than a question. I could and did.

Fortunately, this was a company-paid move. I wouldn't have wanted to wrestle with the 55 gallon drums of hardener and resin, rolls of fiber-glass, multiple molds and boats, and above all, the question of moving them safely in the same truck with our somewhat more respectable household furnishings. Somehow the professionals accomplished it — though the crew remarked that they had never quite done this before — and soon my dream basement was ready for action.

~

Despite the stress of a family move, intertwined with the responsibilities of the Colorado River expedition, I tried to hit the ground running. Armed with movies and slides of kayaking the Colorado, and full of enthusiasm, I was soon running rivers and meeting with the GCA (Georgia Canoeing Association) folks. At that time, the club[25] was meeting at what they considered a centralized location, the Atlanta Federal building at Piedmont and Peachtree Roads — later the meetings would be held north of Atlanta at Camp Chattahoochee in Roswell, courtesy of camp owner Horace Holden and his family.

[25] There was a stalwart core of folks in the Georgia Canoeing Association — as there always must be — dedicated to leading the river trips; seeing that meeting programs happened; organizing the races that were emerging; providing basic instruction for newcomers; and, of course, writing, typing, mimeographing, stuffing, stamping and mailing the newsletter. Not so different from today's chores, except that the newsletter process is now a bit more streamlined, thanks to the wonders of modern word processing.

Along with founders Jody and Horace Holden, and Sandra and Bill Crawford, those early GCA paddling pioneers of the sixties and early seventies that come to mind are Jan &

Horace Holden and Bill Crawford, with help from other boating friends, were largely responsible for bringing the GCA into existence in 1966. The club, as I knew it in 1969 and 1970, emphasized family paddling, camping and good companionship. One of my first GCA trips, led by Bill and Anna Belle Close, was on the Class II Toccoa River, with Cricket and David (ages 8 and 6) in my canoe. Only a few of the 85 members ventured into the more extreme realm of whitewater challenges, but with trips to Section IV of the Chattooga, the Tellico, and the Little Rivers of both Alabama and the Smokies, the flames were being fanned.

The Nantahala River, from Patton's Run to the bridge at Wesser, is regarded as Class III, meaning that it is of moderate difficulty, suitable for paddlers with intermediate skills. However, just below the Wesser Bridge, the river suddenly drops twenty vertical feet over a jumble of sharp rocks before resuming its journey to Lake Fontana. This unnatural drop, known as Big Wesser Falls, was created in the forties when the river was rerouted to avoid construction — so I had thought — of two bridges on the railroad that parallels the Nantahala. The rerouting isolated a loop in the river that remains a wetland today.

When Payson read the draft of this book, he noted that there was more to the rerouting of the river than I had known. His comments follow:

"The actual story is a bit more complicated and interesting, I think. At Wesser the river made almost a complete loop around a hill. The builders blasted through the hill, shortening the distance the railroad had to travel but requiring a bridge over each end of the river loop. When Fontana Reservoir was built during World War II, a new bridge for the railroad to cross the reservoir was required but steel was in short supply. The engineers realized that by blasting a deeper channel through the hill parallel to the railroad the river could be straightened out and the spoil used to block off each end of the river loop. The railroad could be routed over the filled area and the two bridges dismantled to be used in constructing a new longer bridge over Fontana Reservoir."

Marvin Albitz, Nancy Barker, Gwen Bergen, Radine & Dale Bergen, Hugh Caldwell, Judy Canipe, Annabelle & Bill Close, Forrest Cole, Nancy & Buddy Collins, Phyllis & Bill Crowley, Jerry Davy, Ellie & Gary DeBacher, Don Downing, Bill Dunlap, Mary & Hoppy Eager, Mary & Jim Fletcher, Roger Fortin, Bronwyn & Carter Fowlkes, Jean & Dave Garrity, Bob Goeke, Lou Greathouse, Claude Grizzard, Tom Hamby, Jack Hart, John Helmlinger, Polly Heyward, Jim Hobbs, Murray Johnson, Susan & Wes Jones, Aurelia & Payson Kennedy, Hank Klausman, Eileen Lange, Helen & Dan Langston, Allen Lewis, Tom Lines, Rodger Losier, Jeanette & Craig Lyerla, John Mathiew, Maureen Maloney, Ken McAmis, Carol & Franz Menge, Earl Metzger, Nina & Jim Morrison, Falma Moye, Roger Nott, Fritz Orr, Jr, Scott Pendergrast, Scott Price, Michael Rainey, Kathy & Carlton Shuford, Jane Snow, Dot & George Stephenson, Ken Strickland, Cleve Tedford, Miller Templeton, Betty & Claude Terry, Dave Truran, Margaret Osborne Tucker, Mark Warren, Joan & Bill Webb, Jack Weems, Delores & Paul Wiens, Elizabeth & Ross Wilson, Thorne Winter, Roy Wood, Clyde Woolsey and myself. There were, of course, a host of paddling youngsters within these families.

Big Wesser, from a whitewater standpoint, is probably no more than a Class IV in difficulty. But the rocks below the surface, blasted to make a channel through the adjacent cliff, raise the difficulty to "life threatening" because of the chance of entrapment or serious injury when encountering their un-rounded edges. This was a rapid that we had examined — with and without water — many times, but we had always walked away from it.

There was a tale that had circulated, origin unknown, of a fisherman in a rowboat being swept over the falls, tumbling into the rushing river, and emerging at the bottom with a broken leg. As far as we knew, however, no one had ever run Big Wesser intentionally. Nevertheless, it called to some of us.

On Friday, April 9, 1971, several GCA paddlers joined forces with a handful of boaters from Tennessee for a satisfying run of the Nantahala. But we weren't really satisfied. Reid Gryder, Bob Keller and I walked down to Big Wesser and, looking it over from all possible angles and trying to remember the location of the most hazardous submerged rocks, began to discuss the best line for a successful run. Then, hearts pounding, and with Payson Kennedy among the witnesses, the three of us ran it.

The next day we paddled the Oconaluftee near Cherokee, but returned to the Nantahala in the afternoon. Payson, Claude Terry and Paul Wiens had also decided to run Big Wesser. Claude wanted me to follow him down with my deck-mounted movie camera.

As we approached the lip of the falls, I yelled to Claude, "Hey, that's not the line!" Too late.

Oh shit, I thought, I've got to follow him anyway if I'm going to keep him in the camera's field of view. As Payson would report in the next GCA newsletter, "Claude earned the distinction of being the first person to make a successful Eskimo roll in [Big] Wesser Falls." The rest of us, including the movie camera, reached the bottom without incident. Though I haven't watched it in twenty-five years or more, somewhere in my dusty archives is the film from that run as well as the one that took place the next day.

Sunday morning we were off to new territory — for us, at least — and the next North Carolina challenge. The rivers were still full and we were all stoked by a morning run on the Little in the Great Smokies National Park, stopping to take out short of the Sinks, a seventeen foot drop just downstream of the Little River road bridge. Most of us did, that is. Cathy Kennedy just couldn't resist running those last inviting ledges above the Sinks, to end up perilously close to the big drop. As it turned out, the more I looked at the waterfall, the more convinced I was that I could paddle it and survive.

The Sinks has been run many times since that day. But when a drop has not been run before, which, as far as we knew, was the case with the Sinks that Easter Sunday, all kinds of doubts race through your mind as you consider the worst possibilities. Payson Kennedy's words, as he described the day for the GCA newsletter, take you back to the feelings we had that weekend.

> *"On crossing to the west side of the mountains we were all happy to see the streams and rivers full from the runoff of melting snow. We met at the Sinks of the Little River which everyone carefully studied and decided was impossible to run. Doug then ran it — a feat which we still regard as impossible but fortunately recorded on film. You have to see the film to believe it. We then ran from the Sinks on down the Little River in what was one of the most beautiful, exciting and fun runs ever. We all agreed that when it has enough water this is a near ideal river for decked boats."*

Payson Kennedy on the Oconaluftee River in North Carolina, April, 1971

Another Easter weekend, a year later (April of 1972), also stands out in memory. The hard-core of GCA paddlers had gone to the Smokies again, the rivers running full from rain and snow melt, just as they had the previous year. Snow still covered the ground beneath laurel and rhododendron and, as the main party of us arrived at the rendezvous point, we immediately found ourselves in a barrage of fire from the woods bordering the parking lot. Rodger Losier had arrived before us, he and several of the Scouts having prepared a chilly snowball ambush.

The majority of the group had decided that they would run the Tellico on Saturday and the Little on Sunday, or at least parts of those rivers. The Tellico was new territory for us. A few paddlers from the Knoxville area had ventured onto these waters and given us good feedback, but as far as I can recall, no GCA boaters had as yet experienced them. Several of us running kayaks put in below Baby Falls, which was nameless at that time, and were joined by the rest of the group, including a couple of open canoes about a mile downriver. It was an exhilarating descent, as challenging first runs usually are, and we were stoked as we reached the take-out.

Late afternoon shadows were creeping into the gorge as we returned to the put-in to retrieve vehicles. I was intrigued by the rushing fourteen foot drop that seemed to beckon to me and the longer I stood there, the more evident it became to the others what was running through my mind. Maggie Tucker edged up beside me. "Don't do this thing. We all love you too much."

Claude Terry, of course, would have a caustic comment. "Don't be an idiot. Nobody runs drops like that. We don't want to cart you home to your family in a basket. Come on, let's go." And with that, they all drove out of sight. That is, all except Rodger Losier, who knew that I was going to do it anyway and already had his camera out. By the time I had my kayak at the river's edge, the others had returned shaking their heads, but were busy setting safety below the falls. The run was quick, smooth and anti-climatic.

Today, Baby Falls is considered a training run for those who aspire to the free-fall aspect of whitewater paddling. Rarely does the play-boater of today regard the falls with the apprehension that we did that chilly afternoon thirty-four years ago. At the time of my own run, creek boats and playboats did not exist, so we all negotiated the drops and tight turns of these small rivers in the much longer (13'– 2") glass boats of that era.

As often happened on trips to rivers in neighboring states, we would be joined by paddlers[26] living closer to the area. On this particular weekend, we were privileged to not only share the local whitewater expertise of Beverly and John Hiscox, but also to enjoy the hospitality of their home between river runs. Some twenty-five of us, rather than braving an icy night camping in the Park, stretched sleeping bags out on any available piece of floor for a much cozier repose. A huge spaghetti dinner required every available pot from Beverly and John's kitchen, and we all

---

[26] Paddlers in other localities were often as active with the GCA as were boaters in the Atlanta area. Many times we relied on their invaluable knowledge and advice when running rivers in neighboring states and always enjoyed their good company. Some of the stalwarts, along with Beverly and John Hiscox, were: Martin Begun, Murray Evans, Reid Gryder, Roger Scott in Tennessee; Bob Benner, Jeannie Brackett, Ed Weatherby in North Carolina; Gordon Howard, John Pilley in South Carolina; Martha & John Krickel, Carter Martin, John Tryon in Alabama. There were many others, of course. I built kayaks for both Carter Martin and John Pilley in the early seventies, since at that time there was no other source for epoxy boats (superior in strength to polyester) in the South.

contributed whatever food we had along, either to go into the sauce or serve as a side dish. Enough tossed salad to feed all was mixed in a large garbage bag.

~

Our standbys, of course, were the rivers closer to Atlanta, doable not only on weekends, but also in an evening. Claude Terry and I always kept a finger on the pulse of local stream flows, particularly when storms were raising water levels. We each drove VW Campers, his with Georgia license plate "KAYAKS," mine with "KAYAK," boats racked on top and clothing and paddling gear inside. Already prepared, we could be at some rivers within minutes of a "water alert."

A dreary January day in 1972 found me laboring away, trying to put some life into the rather unstimulating manufacturing instructions that I was writing. Winter rain was pounding outside, I knew, even though my isolated engineering cubicle had no windows. Then the call came in from Claude's Emory University office.

"I've checked in Douglasville and the Dog River is out of its banks. The weather's breaking and you know how small that watershed is. The water level's probably on its way down already. Can you slip out early?"

I pictured it in my mind. The Dog was a small river with a steep descent, about an hour west of Atlanta. We had run it once at a much lower level, enjoying a series of Class III+ rapids. At this volume, those would all be IV's, maybe more.

"When?"

"Right now!"

"Where?"

"At Briarcliff High. Grab Mark, Reid and Hugh as they come out of the school. I'll get Butch and Michael."

"Right."

I wheel into Briarcliff High, just as school is dismissed, the boat-laden vehicle a beacon to our paddling teens. The trio immediately comes running.

"Do you want to run the Dog?" I yell, much to the bewilderment of nearby students and teachers.

"You bet!" as they pile into the van.

"Claude has got your boats and gear."

Rocketing west on Interstate 20, we observe that the Six Flags parking lot — adjacent to the Chattahoochee River — is under water. We arrive at the put-in, noticing that the river level has already dropped a foot from its high water mark. But the Dog, the color of Georgia red clay, is still roaring past. We run a fast shuttle.

Quickly we're in our boats. There isn't a whole lot of daylight left and we aren't about to miss this mid-winter gift. The river bears little resemblance to our memory of it, but is all that we had hoped for. Each rapid has at least doubled in length and the waves are irregular exploding monsters. New routes have opened up. Not all of these are wise choices as Claude finds out after being stuck in a humongus hole for over a minute while doing some exploratory paddling.

Claude's younger son, Michael, already a competent kayaker at age ten, gets blasted in a long Class IV just ahead of me. He misses his roll and swims to a small island. I manage to bump his boat into the flooded trees but the paddle is long gone.

"What do I do now?" he wails. "I'm in the middle of the river, huge rapids all around and ahead of me, and I've lost my paddle!"

I hand him mine. "Never let it be said that you were stuck up the creek without a paddle." He's off in a flash.

I search the island and the best replacement I can come up with is a small uprooted tree about fifteen feet long. Hey, if a long pole could give Karl Wallenda the balance to walk a cable from rim to rim at Tallulah Gorge, surely this tree can help me make it through the several Class IV rapids that remain. I find the balance point and peel into the main current. Well…I don't think the style will start a new trend in slalom racing, but I do manage to follow my lines and stay topside for the rest of the run. The others are grinning as I arrive, a new tale to tell, except for Michael, who is pissed that I haven't flipped.

Hugh Hilliard on the Chattahoochee, February, 1972. Hugh was part of the small group of kayakers that caught the Dog River in flood a month earlier.

~

For the Georgia Canoeing Association, as well as the greater paddling community, 1972 would be a watershed year in slalom competition. It was an Olympic year, and for the first time in history, paddlers from around the world would be gathering to test their slalom skills as part of the Olympic Games on the recently constructed white-water course at Augsburg, Germany. But before the U.S. Team could be selected, trials would be held on Maryland's Savage River. And before the paddler could enter the trials, she or he must turn in qualifying performances in designated slaloms.

These "qualifying slaloms," as they came to be known, were run according to strict ICF (International Canoe Federation) standards and were well attended by aspirants to the U.S. Team. Unfortunately for the emerging competitors in the Southeast, there was no sanctioned race in the entire area. In fact the American Canoe Association's slalom chairman, Noble Enge, lived in Florida, 500 miles from the nearest whitewater, and was largely a flatwater paddler. In December of 1971, Noble wrote to me, asking if I would be willing to take over his job. I agreed, and ACA approval was quickly forthcoming for the task that I would assume for most of the decade.

The Georgia Canoeing Association had also asked me to be chairman for the fourth annual running of the whitewater races on the Nantahala. I had been a helper during the three previous races, where I

Familiar faces at start and finish, Jean Dunn, left, and Rosemary Bridge, right, were well-known for their dedication and hard work at eastern U.S. whitewater races throughout the sixties and seventies.

had seen communication and scoring problems become more severe as the number of competitors multiplied. I also felt that the previous course locations — Delabar Rock the first year and Patton's Run the second — did not offer the challenge of some of the established races in the Northeast and the West. There was definitely room for improvement.

And to some paddlers not familiar with the southern Appalachians, our area was a no-man's-land when it came to interesting rivers. I had corresponded with Margie Arighi about Oregon's Rogue River in November of 1971 and happened to mention our activities in the Southeast. In her reply, she exclaimed, "I didn't know there was ANY whitewater in Georgia!" I suspect her opinion changed when *Deliverance* hit the national movie screens the next year!

We needed to get our race on the map and show that we could do as good a job as anyone else. Changing the slalom site would be the first step. I had mulled this over since last year's races and felt that centering the slalom around Nantahala Falls was the only move that would put us on a par with the competition. The reaction from some of the GCA members was less than enthusiastic.

"No way!"

"Far too difficult!"

"You'll eliminate all the open canoe competitors!"

"Why plan a race that may kill someone?"

But Claude Terry and Mark Warren thought it was a great idea and agreed to design the course. Maggie Tucker and Claude Grizzard officially supported the change for the GCA. After the hubbub subsided, we decided to give it a shot for the '72 Races and talk again after the body count.

Now that we had cranked the race difficulty up a couple of notches, we needed a classier title.

"How about Dixie Division Championships?" came the first suggestion.

I had already run that one through my mind and hit a snag, even in 1972. "I know that 'Dixie' is the official title of our ACA Division," I replied, "but that word now has a connotation that is regarded by some as racist. The ACA goes back a bunch of years and our division was probably named a long time ago. How about Southeastern U.S. Championships?"

"Sounds good to me."

"I like it."

We agreed that it sounded cleaner, had status, and identified our region.

"Let's go with it!"

Maggie Tucker wrote the letter making our case the next day, asking ACA sanction for the Southeastern U.S. Championship Canoe and

Kayak Races, to be held on the Nantahala River over Fourth of July[27] weekend. Approval was quickly forthcoming and the Nantahala Races would henceforth be known as the "Southeasterns."

We had made some changes, but our region still didn't have a "qualifying slalom" for Olympic hopefuls. Mark Fawcett, one of the Olympic Committee members, and I had spoken by phone that winter about the prospect of the Nantahala becoming a qualifier. Mark was of the opinion that our race should prove itself for at least another year — until it was run well enough to attract top competitors. Silently I agreed that we did have some problems in '71. But it wasn't an idea that I could just abandon for another year.

I was watching the approach of the spring racing season closely, but for what, I wasn't quite sure. Then it hit me. I had been corresponding with Benny Robertson, a Missouri kayaker who had just won the K-1W Class at the Wolf River in Wisconsin. She told me that her St. Louis paddling group had set the dates for Missouri's St. Francis River races — the only Olympic qualifier without controlled water releases — for the weekend of February 18 — 20. Some of us planned to make the drive and compete there, in what would be the first qualifying race of the season.

But as I stayed in touch with Benny, I learned that the St. Francis Races had been postponed to the following weekend due to lack of water. Then to the weekend after that. Finally the slalom evaporated completely. One less race for Olympic contenders, and what would have been one of the closer ones for us.

I got in touch with John Sweet, a top C-1 competitor and a voice that was listened to in the whitewater racing community.

"John, can the Nantahala take the place of the St. Francis as an Olympic qualifier?" I outlined the changes we had already made and our vision for the future. John agreed that it was a workable idea. I called Sandy Campbell, Mary Nutt and several other contenders that I knew. Their response was similar to John's.

I sat down at the typewriter and gave the Olympic Slalom Committee[28] my best shot.

"...The slalom will be run completely in accordance with 'International' standards. The race will be staffed by forty non-competitors (already selected) who will undergo two training

[27] The Nantahala Races had originated on the Fourth of July weekend so that competitors would have an extra day for travel — or to slip over for a paddling day on the Chattooga after the races were over. It didn't take many more years before the hazard of holiday traffic, added to the race congestion at a river with limited parking, became apparent. The races were subsequently backed into June, and later scheduled in mid-spring to avoid summer traffic — and the booming rafting business on the river.

[28] The 1972 Olympic Slalom Committee members were: Dick Bridge, Jay Evans, Mark Fawcett, Ted Jacobs and Tom Johnson.

sessions (including a practice slalom) a month before the race. Southern Bell will provide complete communications for judging and scoring. Controlled water flow is guaranteed by TVA.

Located at the western tip of North Carolina, the Nantahala is within range of the middle U.S. competitors left stranded by the demise of the St. Francis and is in close proximity to the competent paddlers of the Knoxville-Chattanooga-Atlanta area... Despite being in the same Eastern area with Tarrifville [CT], the Savage [MD] and the West [VT], Nantahala is a considerable distance from this northeastern grouping and can thus provide a service not offered by those races.

The July 1st slalom date would make the Nantahala the last qualifying race before the Olympic Trials and would undoubtedly attract a number of top competitors from the Northeast. John Sweet is in agreement with this viewpoint and several other Olympic contenders have stated that they would paddle at Nantahala if it were designated a qualifying slalom.

A favorable decision could still be announced in the American Canoeist a month before the registration deadline..."

That decision was quickly reached. The Nantahala was in. Oh my God. Let me reread those promises I made to the Olympic Committee. Can we really deliver?

We had our work cut out for us, but the promises weren't hollow ones. GCA paddlers, along with others throughout the U.S., were stoked that our sport had, at last, become part of the Olympics. Cruisers and competitors alike were enthusiastic about showing the "old guard" of whitewater competition that we could produce a quality slalom race in the South. There was widespread support from many willing workers.

The job of constructing new equipment fell to the Explorer Scouts. Up until now, our slaloms had contained no more than 16 or 18 gates. In order to bring the race up to international standards, we would need at least twenty-five gates, each with a set of red/white and green/white poles, as well as spacers, gate numbers and direction indicators. Poles and plywood were cut to size, then the painters went to work in earnest. Soon we had enough finished sets to give us a grand total of thirty.

Meanwhile, I had been in touch with engineer Ken McAmis, who was the advisor for a "Communications" Explorer Post sponsored by Southern Bell. Yes, his Explorers would be delighted to provide communications for our race if I would just outline the specific needs. I did, showing them how each judging station could be on-line (by phone), providing real time results to the scorers who would immediately post times and penalties on the scoreboard. They did a superb job and more than a few of this group had caught "whitewater fever" by the time the Nantahala event was finished.

After two sessions of indoor training, the race staff volunteers were stationed at a practice slalom held on Sweetwater Creek near the ruins of the Civil War Confederate uniform factory. Factory Shoals, as it was known, was a demanding whitewater run, even without a slalom course weaving back and forth among its rapids. We all had fun running the course and the judging staff gained some good experience in calling the score on tricky gate negotiations as well as situations that might not have been covered in the classroom.

A myriad of other details was handled between the time the races were advertised and the weekend that they were run. Claude and Mark, with help from the Explorers, began stringing support and control lines for the gates a week ahead of the races. Several of us took vacation from our jobs that last week so that we could make sure everything was coming together as it should. Judging stations were laid out and a couple of diabolical gates were hung right in the Falls. The course was ready for practice runs by the Thursday preceding race weekend.

We needn't have worried about support from the racing community. There were three hundred and twelve entries in the first running of the Southeasterns that July, with good participation from the top Olympic contenders. The race was well received, the final qualifier before the Olympic Trials on Maryland's Savage River would determine who[29] would represent the United States at Augsburg.

Nantahala Outdoor Center, the emerging Mecca for whitewater paddlers, as well as the river itself would not go unnoticed by members of the U.S. Olympic Team. Lyn (Carrie) Ashton, John Burton and Angus Morrison would all return to help build NOC into the whitewater giant that it is today.

I agreed to chair the Southeasterns for one more year, but only with Tommy Lines as co-chair, since I would be absent for the critical month just before the races, far away on a western paddling expedition. That year (1973), we had to deal with freak weather, rain and wind coming in gusts so strong that it threatened to blow away the scoring records. For competitors trying to avoid a gate touch, this may have been welcome, since out on the course the gates were being blown nearly horizontal at times. But with the old Explorer Scout school bus serving as a shelter, we were able to keep everything together and finish in relatively good shape.

[29] The members of the first (1972) United States Olympic Whitewater Slalom Team were: Lyn (Carrie) Ashton, John Burton, Sandy Campbell, Eric Evans, John Evans, Cindi Goodwin, Louise Holcombe, John Ho land, Jamie McEwan, Angus Morrison, Russ Nichols, Tom Southworth and Wick Walker. Jay Evans was coach; Tom Johnson, manager; and Doc Dodson, trainer.

One embarrassing incident from that race sticks in my mind. Maggie Tucker and I, racing C-2M in the slalom, were halfway down the course, attempting to get in position for an upstream gate just above the last drop of the Falls. The current was strong and we were trying to straighten the boat without being grabbed by the back-curl of the upper hole. Fifty spectators sat watching us on the riverbank below the highway. Half a dozen unproductive strokes saw us stuck in the same spot.

"Draw!" I roared from the stern.

"Damn it, I am drawing!" Maggie screamed back.

In a masterful demonstration of negative teamwork for the spectators, we lost our concentration and, with predictable results, skewed into the hole and washed over the Falls — upside-down. We didn't roll.

Even though we had help in taking down the slalom course, it was left to my cousin Mary Alice (Mouse) Woodward and me to collect and load all of the gear into the bus, as well as finishing up a number of remaining race details after having put in an exhausting weekend. As I pointed the bus south, Mouse was asleep on the hard floor in minutes. I crept across the old Lost Bridge — a one-way iron truss structure spanning the Little Tennessee River — and remembered nothing more until I pulled into my Atlanta driveway sometime before dawn.

I was so burnt out that I couldn't imagine ever having anything to do with a whitewater race again. But there was to be no rest. I had already agreed to organize the National Wildwater Championships on the Chattooga later that month.

Maggie Tucker, competing in the women's kayak singles, negotiates a gate in the first Southeastern U.S. Championships on the Nantahala River, July, 1972.

Maggie and I would compete as partners in wildwater a few more times before she moved to Virginia. We had taken third in the wildwater nationals on the Yough in 1972, but Maggie and partner Bern Collins (whom she later married) soon became national champions in the same class. In 1978, they made the U.S. Team. I rarely paddled slalom after the early seventies, but enjoyed racing wildwater with Jeannie Brackett, Janine Cheek, and Helen Johnston.

The abilities of whitewater competitors from the Southeast were still relatively unknown in other parts of the country, so as divisional slalom chairman for the American Canoe Association (ACA), one of my functions was to introduce capable paddlers to race officials in the West and Northeast. These athletes made us proud, as Claude Grizzard became the 1973 National Open Canoe Singles Champion on Maine's Dead River; David Jones[30] and Ken Strickland each won the Eastern U.S. Men's Wildwater Kayak Singles on the Gauley River in 1974, David taking the Championship Class and Ken the Cruising Class. They were the tip of the iceberg — many more world class whitewater boaters would come out of the Southeast as paddlers began to realize that, despite occasional severe winter weather, the climate of the southern Appalachians was conducive to year-round training.

∼

As a lighter aspect of the mid-seventies — the GCA would not create the Gala Canoeing Affair for another decade — we would gather at a late autumn or winter potluck for purely social purposes. The food was tasty and plentiful, and there was plenty of time to embellish old river tales before the election of next year's officers. It was here that Miller Templeton, Georgia Tech's Dean of Students, rushed up to me with a book in his hand.

"Doug, you've got to read this! I've never laughed so hard. But it's more than that — it really has a message, too."

It was Edward Abbey's *The Monkey Wrench Gang.* I did read it and, over the years of Abbey's life, I read every book and many articles that he wrote.

But another chuckle still remains from that same potluck. Most of us had finished eating when former GCA president Clyde Woolsey stood up and clanged a spoon on his glass for attention. As the room began to fall silent, he made his important announcement.

"Who baked this squash casserole? It's out of this world and I want to marry her!" Clyde was single at the time. There was general laughter as heads turned this way and that to see who the cook was. No one had responded.

[30] David Jones would go on to make the U.S. Whitewater Team in seven of the nine years between 1982 and 1990, usually partnering with Mike Hipsher in the C-2 Wildwater class.

"I'm serious," Clyde persisted, "I want to know who she is!" He had put himself in a sexist trap.

I was living on my own in a small house in an old woods, just east of Atlanta. My cooking skills were developing and I had layered summer squash with onion slices, liberally laced with butter and cream, seasoned and topped with bread crumbs. It was rather tasty. I raised my hand.

This time the ceiling shook with the roar of laughter as the color rushed to Clyde's face, high-lighting his embarrassed grin. He withdrew his marriage proposal, but stood by his compliment on the cooking.

~

Around this same time, Gary DeBacher began a series of river explorations that would continue for decades. Sometimes he would choose "mystery" creeks from maps, and other times, seldom-paddled creeks that were relatively unknown to GCA members. On other days he would explore an unfamiliar section of a well-known river, sometimes with company, often alone. His efforts have added much to the GCA's knowledge of rivers, some of those becoming today's regular runs.

The Chauga, with its two waterfalls, was one of these, a run I first enjoyed in the seventies with Gary, and other GCA old-timers Dave Garrity, Tom Hamby, Roger Nott, Fran & Ken Strickland and Jack Weems. By the summer of 1975, the GCA was able to look toward the big water of the West, scheduling its own Colorado River trip under the guidance of Jim Hobbs.

Gary DeBacher also became the GCA's first long-term newsletter editor in 1978, succeeding a series of valiant individuals who labored during the Club's first decade. The consistency and quality of the Eddy Line improved noticeably in the late seventies and eighties, and Gary finally turned the job over to Allen Hedden, another long-term editor who helped bring the GCA publication into the electronic age.

~

Mary Atkinson and her husband, Lawrence Alexander, lived in a cabin within view of the Yellow River, about a dozen miles from my house in Lilburn, Georgia. Mary had kayaked with us when she was a student at Emory University and had wanted to give Alexander (as he preferred to be called) an opportunity to kayak, also. One evening she called me at home.

"I've got a plan, Doug. If you could bring a kayak and gear for Alexander, we could meet you after work Thursday at the Yellow River, paddle for a couple of hours while there's still daylight, take out in our front yard, and then have a late dinner at our place. What do you think?"

"That sounds great. Cathy Hirsch, a good friend at work, has been wanting to paddle on a river, too, and I can check with her if that works for you. The Yellow is a good river to begin on."

"Sure, we'll look forward to it."

It was a pleasant summer evening, the water level was decent and everyone seemed to be into the mellow outing. We were about halfway down the run when I noticed someone else was enjoying the water. A small copperhead was swimming alongside my boat, trying to make shore.

I slid my hand under the snake and lifted it from the water. The underside pressure was a natural feeling for it, rather than grabbing it from above, which would resemble the action of a hawk looking for prey. It retracted sufficiently to lie contentedly on my palm and wrist.

Then the kayak bumped the bank and the snake started to glide away. It was here that my judgment went downhill. The others hadn't seen it yet and I wanted to show them the copperhead up close. I'll make a quick grab behind its head. The snake was quicker. I wasn't even close, and it sank its fangs into the bird finger of my left hand. Hey, while it's occupied, I'll just grab it with my right hand. Before I got there, the snake had disengaged and nailed my right thumb. At that point, I tossed it clear and the copperhead landed on the branch of a small bush right over my head.

"What are you doing over there?" Mary wanted to know.

"Just performing a personal snakebite experiment," I replied, back-paddling away from the bush.

"Are you kidding?" Cathy chimed in. "Where's the snake?"

"Right there in the bush if you want to take a look." I pointed.

"Which hand did it bite?" Alexander asked.

"Uh...both,' I sheepishly responded.

"Do you want to cut and try to get the venom out?" he continued.

"No, copperhead venom is the least toxic of our poisonous snake venoms and the chance of infection from the water in this river is a lot greater than any lasting damage from the snakebite," I went on, expounding some of the snake knowledge that had gotten me into trouble in the first place.

"How do you feel?" Mary was still concerned.

"The finger and thumb hurt like hell, but I think I can keep paddling. The pain and swelling don't seem to be spreading too much. In fact very little venom got into my thumb since the fangs only pierced the thin skin on top," I replied.

"Let us know if you feel faint or anything." We headed downriver.

Stomachs were growling by the time we reached the cabin and Mary's stuffed mushrooms really hit the spot. It was September 23, 1976, my fortieth birthday.

Mary and Alexander drove us back to the put-in and Cathy headed home in her car.

"Do you want me to drive you to your house?" Alexander volunteered. "Mary could bring your car."

"I'm fine, but thanks anyway. I'll give you a call tomorrow."

"No. Give us a call when you reach the house tonight," Mary insisted. "We want to know you're still alive."

"OK."

It wasn't until after I had showered and looked at myself in the mirror that I noticed the huge blue area under my left armpit. Apparently, the venom had killed blood cells in my hand and they had collected in the lymph glands of the armpit. It took several weeks for the "bruise" to be absorbed into the rest of my body.

I couldn't bend either of the joints in the middle finger of my left hand and the flesh was hard as stone. A month later, the finger would begin to ease toward normal, but in the meantime I was lucky not to get decked by someone who didn't understand that my hand wasn't really flashing him an obscene insult.

My Heart Is Stolen

I fell in love. Deeply, dangerously, without chance of escape. Payson Kennedy and Claude Terry had introduced me to her in the summer of '69. A year later I had moved to Georgia and would be close enough to see her on weekends. Only in my fantasies had such perfection been possible — but now there was the promise of fulfillment. Did Roberta know? I suspect she did.

Others loved her too. I was aware of that. But only a few knew her well and, of those, I suspected that none were intimate as yet. She welcomed her lovers without hesitation, promising joy and ecstasy. Please come back once more.

She was beautiful. But old. Much older than any of us. And she had her moods. Sometimes she was cold. Even cruel. Her temper could quickly rise and her emotions become a raging torrent. She would take the lives of two of my friends before the decade had passed.

The Chattooga River, of course, has now come to be known by thousands, but my first run of Section IV in July of 1969 still plays vividly in my mind. A handful of kayakers, a C-1 and a single open canoe made up the party that day. Several had run it before; and major rapids were just beginning to acquire names. Portages were common, even for the decked boats.

Our vehicles were pulled onto the narrow shoulder of Highway 76 near the Chattooga Bridge, barely off of the pavement. There were no parking lots or changing rooms. Only river and forest. I knew our journey was going to be in wild country.

"Let's walk up to Bull Sluice," Payson suggested. "That will give you an idea of what our run below the bridge is going to be like." The term "Section IV" had not yet appeared in local boaters' vocabularies.

We scrambled over boulders and edged our way along the crumbling bank, using laurel for handholds when we could. The last scramble brought us face to face with the Bull.

"Looks like a challenge," I remarked. "Do you usually run it?"

"Some of us do," Payson replied.

Claude stepped closer to add his comments.

"The Cherokee and Creek never ran these rivers. Their canoes were too valuable to risk. They only used them for crossing to the other side."

I knew that Forest Service Ranger "Preach" Parsons had introduced his new boss, Chattahoochee National Forest Supervisor Harold Westerburg, to Section III of the Chattooga, the intermediate stretch, the previous summer. They never made it to Bull Sluice.

Running two square-ended aluminum fishing skiffs, the pair put in at Earl's Ford with Jack and "CV," two associates from the Georgia State Game and Fish Commission. Somewhere downstream of the Narrows, after a day of being bullied by the river, the foursome had stumbled out of the woods with only the clothes they were wearing. Even their wardrobe was not intact, as Preach was missing a trouser leg and part of his shirt. His words[31] added to the growing mystique of the Chattooga.

"Before we started on that trip, everybody [in Clayton, GA] told us, "You'll never make it." We were cautious when we started out, and used fifty-foot ropes tied to the ends of our boats to let them down over big rapids. But after a couple of hours we felt like old river men and ran right through them.

Sometimes there's a straight drop-off at a shoals. Lots of times you can hear rushing water around a sharp curve, out of sight. At the Narrows, there are places where, if your boat won't bend in the middle, you won't make the curves. We turned over several times. We'd shoot some falls too straight and the front end of the boat would go over and water would pour right down in the tail.

When we lost the first boat, Jack and Westerburg were ahead of us and they carried their boat around a shoals. CV and I decided we'd shoot it. But there was a great round boulder we couldn't see right

31 From the December, 1968 issue of the Cruiser, newsletter of the CCA of greater Washington, DC.

in the middle of the stream. When we hit, our boat went straight up. CV was sitting high up on one end of it. The Chattooga got me and the boat right in the back. White water pinned the boat to that rock like cement. Nothing was holding it except the force of the river, but we couldn't even budge it with pry poles. When some Forest Service boys got it out several days later, they had to use two sets of come-alongs with block and tackle.

We lost the second boat as we carefully let it down on ropes. It got caught under a falls and nothing would budge it. We lost everything and didn't even have a cigarette.

Except where we put in, we didn't see a house. There isn't one. We saw beaver slides where the animals had cut trees to make dams. On the river you have the feeling you're back a hundred miles in the woods. You've got to ride down it to know what it's like. It's absolutely beautiful. I can see the Chattooga becoming one of the biggest drawing cards in north Georgia. I surely would like it to be protected as a Wild River."

In 1969, runs of the Chattooga's Section IV, the most challenging section of the river, were still rather rare and regarded as awesome events. Credited with the first known descent of Section IV (1964), all in shoe-keeled Grumman canoes, are Al Barret, Hugh Caldwell, Bunny Johns and Fritz Orr, Jr. The legend of Orr's canoe — lost without a trace at Sock-Em-Dog Rapid — still lives on.

For our own Section IV trip, the difficult shuttle would be the first test. The road was nearly all dirt then — "gravel" is too kind a term — full of washouts and boulders that could trash your oil pan. A stretch called "Oh Shit Hill" could turn into a quagmire in wet weather and required the highest possible speed to gain the summit — if you were one of the lucky ones.

Now we were on the river. As soon as we had rounded the first bend below the bridge, the wildness closed in around us, creating the feeling of traveling through primeval country. Unlike so many other rivers, no road or railroad had ever penetrated this remote gorge. The country was too rugged and construction would have been too costly.

For the most part we ran slowly, cautiously probing the unnamed rapids that would become known as Screaming Left Turn and Rock Jumble. As we ran through the calm at Sutton's Hole, the group had strung out a bit. Rodger Losier, paddling his Grumman and also running Section IV for the first time, was a hundred yards ahead of me, approaching the lip of Woodall Shoals.

I could see that the river dropped away steeply into a long, large rapid. Rodger disappeared over a ledge. In the next moment, his empty canoe shot straight up, performing an ender in the hydraulic below the ledge.

"I would like to have scouted this one," I thought to myself, "and Rodger, why didn't you?"

There was no time now. As I drew closer, I could tell it must be a keeper hole and I dug in for all I was worth. I could see Rodger floating to the right of the main current so I aimed for that side of the ledge. I stopped dead for an instant as the river gremlins tried to suck my stern into the hole, but I was far enough from center to break free and pull onto a low rock.

By this time, Rodger had scrambled onto some rocks below mine and we both turned to watch his canoe as it continued to do enders in the hole. The remainder of the group had eddied out above Woodall and brought a throw line down to the water's edge. At that moment, as if in disgust, the river suddenly spat Rodger's canoe from the hole where he and I were able to retrieve and empty it. The rest of the Woodall run was uneventful.

"There's another big drop not very far from here," cautioned Payson, "Let me run ahead and set up a line." It was, of course, Seven-Foot Falls.

As we approached, I could see the C-1 drawn up on river right, Payson himself standing on a large rock in mid-current. He held a throw rope in one hand and was signaling with the other. As he pointed to the steep left side drop, I zeroed in on the spot, completely missing the crossed arms and shaking head that came after the pointing finger. As I reached the lip of the drop, I could see that I was pointed directly at the rock wall on river left, no more than eight feet away. A glance at Payson as I went by showed a face frozen with dread.

It was over in seconds. I plunged deep, and my high brace became a draw as I pulled the bow around to the right and eddied out below Payson.

He was grinning now. "We've never run that side — it always looked too dangerous. We take the right chute, or carry around in low water," Payson explained.

The others had arrived and decided this would be our lunch stop. They had missed my run.

"Crazy Woodward!" Claude admonished on hearing the account. "Will you do it again so we can see?" I did.

They had all watched that second run very closely and it became the topic over lunch. One by one, each member of the group carried his boat to the top eddy and peeled out toward the left side of the drop. That big, pinching pour-over could do strange things to you when your line was off, but from that day on, the left side became the route of choice at Seven Foot Falls.

We moved on, and the seduction of the Chattooga was irresistible. Stekoa Creek Rapid, with its myriad of choices for the adventurous paddler. Long Creek entering the river just below a thirty foot falls, a liquid curtain that you could stand behind. A tightrope line as you barely held yourself clear of the huge, flat-faced boulder on your right — a giant monument, tumbled from the cliffs above, that two years later would become known as "*Deliverance* Rock."

And then every charm is revealed. In quick succession, she shows you Devil's Chute (Entrance Rapid), Corkscrew, Crack-In-The-Rock, Jawbone and Sockemdog. Danger and ecstasy.

I would, of course, be introduced to other Southern rivers, often by Claude, Payson and Rodger. But the Chattooga would remain my truest love of all. The next kayak I built for myself had a topographic map of the river and its watershed, from Bull Sluice to Sockemdog, embedded in the first layer of the deck, just forward of the cockpit.

Joe Lederle in the grip of the hydraulic at Bull Sluice Rapid on the Chattooga River, July, 1969.

Still I see scenes from those early days on the Chattooga — when the river was known only to a handful of paddlers — which play vividly in my mind. An abandoned canoe, pinned in the approach to Devil's Chute. Recovering it, and leaving it on the Georgia shore. Then deciding later that night to bring it out. Rising in the dark for a solo run of Section IV at dawn, pockets of mist and wildlife everywhere. Sunlight beginning to paint the rocks at river's edge. Then, unbelievably, no canoe. It didn't matter.

Paddling out across Tugaloo. Past Bad Creek. Past Worse Creek. Almost. Catching motion at the top of the little falls where Worse empties into the lake. Coming closer. A couple making love right in the water on top of the falls. Paddling on, looking for more wonders of nature.

There was Chester Summit, lean and muscular, running Bull Sluice in his solo open canoe, taking on perhaps a cup of river water in the process. He was a welder for six months of the year, a wandering connoisseur of whitewater rivers for the other six.

~

The United States Congress had passed the Wild and Scenic Rivers Act in 1968. Relatively unknown, the Chattooga hadn't been included. We knew that the original Act called for rivers to be managed for solitude, adventure, risk and challenge. There was no doubt whatsoever that this remote and uninhabited river valley fit the intent of the Act. But just after *Deliverance* hit theater screens nationwide, the Chattooga suddenly became one of the most sought after rivers in the country. She could easily be loved to death.

The protection of the WSR Act would be vital to the Chattooga's future. We had known this even prior to the river's explosion of popularity. Horace Holden, Billy Crawford, Fritz Orr, Payson Kennedy, Charlie Wharton, Claude Terry and others would be key players, educating those who would ultimately make the decision. The decision-makers must also get to know the river personally, and so we turned to the resources of the Georgia Canoeing Association and the Georgia Tech Outing Club. Skilled paddlers, canoes and a knowledge of the watershed would be provided to all that would come with us.

Following untold hours of groundwork, bills to bring Wild and Scenic protection to the Chattooga were introduced in both the House and Senate. The House bill was authored by U.S. Representative Roy Taylor of North Carolina and co-sponsored by U.S. Representative Phil Landrum of Georgia. Matching legislation was authored by Georgia's senior senator, Herman Talmadge and co-sponsored by Georgia Senator Sam Nunn. Joe Tanner, head of Georgia's Department of Natural Resources, and Claude Terry went north to testify before the Senate subcommittee reviewing the bill. Despite their informed testimony favoring the bill, the outcome was still in doubt.

More than twenty years later, in an interview for *The Chattooga Quarterly*, Claude elaborated,

> "He [Jimmy Carter] played an absolutely key role that, as far as I
> know, has never been publicly discussed. You see, there was a rider
> on a bill to put the Chattooga in, and Scoop Jackson [Democratic
> Senator from Washington State] didn't like the rider, and was

going to turn it down. He was going to keep the bill in committee. I called up the Governor's office and said that I needed to talk to the Governor. The Governor was not amused by the phone call, even though he had been on the river, and he said: 'Have you guys exhausted every administrative remedy that you have on this? What have you done?' I went through all that had been done to try to get Wild and Scenic status for the Chattooga. Finally, he said, 'Claude, I'm going to call up Scoop... [he had nominated Scoop for president in 1972] ...and ask him as a personal favor to get this bill out of committee. I hope you understand, you guys owe me one on this one.' Lots of folks got credit, and deserved it, but the victory was really, to a large extent, Jimmy Carter's."

The Chattooga was designated Wild and Scenic in May of 1974.

$\sim$

Although James Dickey, author of *Deliverance*, often expressed the view that the Chattooga had been destroyed by being discovered, many of us would have to disagree. Certainly the potential was there in those early years between 1972 and 1974. But a year before the river had gained Wild and Scenic status — and because of growing safety concerns, as well as overuse — the Forest Service stepped in with some of the most stringent safety and overuse controls of any river in the East. Concerned with the same issues, the paddling clubs, the rafting companies, and many individuals supported this step.

Over a decade later, the health of the Chattooga watershed was aided by a unique concept. Buzz Williams, long-time river guide and a former Forest Service ranger, had a vision for the river. Three separate National Forests (one each in Georgia, South Carolina and North Carolina) border the Chattooga. Each has its own Supervisor and staff, often making independent decisions that affect the river and its watershed. Would not the Chattooga be better served by coordination of that decision-making activity into a uniform policy, treating the watershed as a single ecological unit, regardless of arbitrary political boundaries?

Out of this far-sighted thinking came the Chattooga Conservancy (formerly the Chattooga River Watershed Coalition), formed in 1991 and supported by many area conservation groups and concerned individuals. Policy is still the bailiwick of the Forest Service, but in many ways the Conservancy became a source of ideas as well as a vehicle to promote joint, rather than autonomous, decisions within the Districts. Practical concepts, touching on anything from river corridor archeology to low-impact logging, continue to be brought up for evaluation.

~

Some watershed activities go on beyond the range of bureaucratic radar. Many writers, trying to capture the flavor of mountain life in the southern Appalachians, have referred to the proliferation of moonshine operations in Georgia's Rabun County. Few, perhaps with the exception of *Foxfire's* Eliot Wiggenton, have ever actually seen one.

In the early seventies, and on through the eighties, the only place on U.S. Highway 76 that you could buy a soda or a moon pie anywhere close to the river was the Wolverton Mountain Store. Run by Coban and Harry Moore, it sat at the crest of the long South Carolina grade that climbed up from the Chattooga where Orchard Road leaves the main highway. Section IV paddlers all passed that way.

Coban and Harry knew every "regular" who ran the river. When my kids were with me, their generosity knew no limits.

"What kind of soda do you want today? How about some chips?" And to me, as my hand would be pushed aside, "Go away, we don't want your money!" And then, "Is it all right if I give them each a pack of firecrackers?"

Some parts of the store probably hadn't been dusted in a decade. An autographed photo of Burt Reynolds hugging Coban was proudly taped to the front window, fading as the years passed by. And when Harry died of a heart attack in the eighties, a lonely and fearful Coban brought an ill-tempered German Shepherd to live within reach of the front steps of her trailer.

My closest brush with moonshine had been in the town of Clayton, when I would gas up at the Twenty Penny. The attendant had seen me often enough that I was a familiar face, and with a kayak on top of my rig, he could figure out what my business was. I guess I had crossed into his "safe zone."

"You see that propane tank over yonder?" he inquired one night. "Right. You need a drink a lightnin' anytime, they's always a jug sittin' behind the right hand end. Good stuff! No lead. Now that other hog piss'll turn ya blind."

I paid for my gas and thanked him, heading back to the river to camp on my own land. Claude and I had recently become the closest landowners to the Chattooga on the Georgia side, holding the first hill on the left, a mile up from the river. That taste of 'shine would have to wait for another day.

There was another friend with whom I would kayak the Chattooga now and then — Joe Terrell of Charlotte. A skilled paddler, he had recently been featured in *Fortune Magazine* as a promising young businessman with an unusual hobby. It's not often that a full-page shot of a kayaker, exploding through a wave, makes it into that publication!

Joe had two boys, close in age to Cricket and David, and we both enjoyed bringing our kids to the Chattooga. Sometimes we took to the woods instead of the river and this particular weekend was one of those times. We had often looked up Stekoa Creek from the river and wondered...

"Look at those drops! Do you think we could run them?"

"Maybe. I wonder if there's any reasonable access point a couple of miles back from the river? I've heard talk of a falls in that stretch, too."

So, with our group of kids, all under twelve, we would do some exploring. Leaving Clayton, often with less than optimal water quality, Stekoa Creek takes a torturous, winding route before finally dropping into the Chattooga a half mile above *Deliverance* Rock. It passes within a mile of our rear property line.

Bushwhacking can be exhilarating at times, a nightmare at others, particularly when you find yourself caught in a "laurel hell." On that day we were lucky. Following a trail-less draw downward for half an hour, we reached Stekoa Creek as we had hoped. But bushwhacking along the creek soon became more than we had bargained for, as we often had to cross to the opposite side or climb high away from the water to make any progress. In three hours, we had not reached either falls or cascades and decided it was time to turn around.

On our return, we chose a different draw to ascend. I was in the lead, just starting to come over a rise which opened into a tiny cove. The scene took a split second to register, and then I could feel the skin on the back of my neck begin to tingle. I held a finger to my lips for silence and motioned the others to stop.

There before us lay a scene straight out of *Foxfire* — a steaming tank of mash covered with tar paper; empty sugar sacks stuffed in the fire box, ready to light; fifty milk jugs tied together and covered with a tarp; the sheen of copper reflecting from plate and pipe; a donkey in a small enclosure of barbed wire, with his own supply of hay; and a length of black pipe, bringing water from a nearby branch to both the donkey and the distilling operation. All was covered with a "roof" of tarpaper, camouflaged with branches and pine needles to make it invisible from the air.

We stood motionless for a long time as our eyes scanned the scene, taking in the details, then the surrounding woods and laurel hells, all the while listening for the slide and click of a rifle bolt. We saw no one, relaxed a little, and edged closer, waiting once more. Finally, I took my camera out of the daypack and quickly began to capture the scene, one that I doubted I would ever be given the privilege to see again.

The next morning I was at the Wolverton Mountain Store when it opened.

"Harry, do you know who might be running shine back between my place and Stekoa Creek?"

"Might."

"Well, if you bump into them and they wonder whose footprints are all around their still, I'd appreciate it if you'd tell them it was just hikers and not the Feds."

"Reckon they already know."

A year later, I hiked into the same draw. There was no donkey. No feeling of danger in the forest, waiting to emerge from the shadows. Only scattered pieces of copper and plastic, already beginning to disappear under the decaying leaves of autumn.

Investigating the active moonshine still that the author found in the Stekoa Creek drainage with his children and friends, February, 1976.

~

In those early years, Crack in the Rock was considered a minor player in a run of the Five Falls, having neither the length nor complexity of its neighbors just upstream and down. It was a single drop, no matter which of the cracks you chose. The hole below Right Crack could be grabby, and new debris would sometimes appear in Center or Right. Because of its position in relation to the river's main flow, Left Crack was not prone to catching logs. In higher water, a sneak chute appeared at far right, and the whole thing was an easy portage for those who wished to carry around. We gave the rapid little attention, not realizing then that it is probably the single most dangerous place on the Chattooga.

In October of 1972, a normally dry month, and following a significant drought, I floated down to the Cracks with a chainsaw aboard. A massive log had been caught in Right Crack for as long as I could recall, but it had been pushed upward a year or so earlier, creating a hazard for those running that route. I was determined to cut it off just above the surface of the river.

There was sand embedded in the log and the chainsaw quickly dulled. I had not brought my sharpening file. The footing and balance was tricky, to say the least, and cutting with a dull blade took forever, but at last it was finished I sat down with my lunch and contemplated this spot where the whole river was squeezed through three narrow slots.

I had learned some things that day. Probing with my feet, I found that there were other logs below the surface at Right Crack, and that there was significant downward suction on my legs. Left and Center Cracks were also revealing their secrets with the low flow. I could see that Left Crack was a keyhole-like slot that could be deadly for a swimmer, and Center Crack was showing a strainer of four and six-inch logs near its base. The consequences of what had once seemed a relatively benign rapid were becoming clearer — don't swim out of Corkscrew!

At six-foot-six, Bob Goeke was an enthusiastic whitewater paddler, a professor at the University of Georgia, and a devoted family man. The Georgia Canoeing Association had just elected him vice-president. A long-time canoeist who had become interested in kayaking, he asked me to build him a kayak since he knew mine had larger cockpits and higher volume than many other designs. I did, and he was delighted with the results, trying it out on several rivers near Athens that spring. One of these was the Broad River, where he was the leader for a large group of local paddlers, and had the chance to practice his roll.

The year was 1974 and there was a GCA trip scheduled for Section IV on June 23. I would not be on the trip, but I would be kayaking the same stretch of river that day, setting safety for a rafting group. As it turned out, I was about an hour behind the GCA trip as we reached the Five Falls.

The day was warm and the river level moderately low. I had already decided to walk my group around Right Crack and slide the rafts into the eddy below. As we arrived at the Cracks, I noticed a small group of paddlers gathered on the rocks beside Left Crack, most of them familiar faces. Below the Cracks, I had the raft group hold in place as I ferried over to the South Carolina side. Payson broke free of the others and climbed down beside my kayak.

In a subdued voice he let me know the worst. "Bob Goeke's down there in Left Crack. He flipped in Corkscrew, missed his roll and tried to swim left. It sucked him down and there's no safe way to get to him."

A dark feeling washed over me and I felt that some piece of my own spirit had gone with Bob.

Payson and I talked for another twenty minutes, considering possibilities for recovering Bob's body, but in the end, none seemed really viable with the little equipment we had at hand. We both knew the tons of force the river was applying to jam the body into the slot. Most of the GCA group had already paddled out to bring in more help, and I knew I had a responsibility to my rafting group. I moved on, carefully setting safety at Jawbone and Sockemdog, yet a piece of my mind was somewhere else, already grieving for Bob's wife Oleatha and their young daughters, Robin, Janet, Laura and Karen.

Bob's body was, after many failed attempts, recovered. As I embraced Oleatha at the memorial service in Athens, she thanked me with emotion for being there. Yet there was still a little guilty voice inside me that kept asking what I might have done differently, sometime that spring, to change Bob's destiny. Maureen Maloney, writing a memorial to Bob in the GCA newsletter, summed it all up in the phrase, "We lost our gentle giant..."

During the week, my engineering job at Western Electric in Atlanta brought me into contact with many folks. Some became good friends, and a few I even introduced to whitewater paddling. Among these were Becky Brazier and her husband Bob, both avid rugby players. They were joined by Vickie Sanders, her husband Jay, and a young engineer in my own division, Lisa Sebacher.

The challenge and beauty of our area rivers quickly became a driving force in their lives. Once in a while all of us paddled together, but more often than not, we would be on separate trips. I knew that Bob, Lisa and a handful of others would be on Section IV that late spring day — it would be Lisa's first time — while I was upriver on Section III.

Full of enthusiasm, Lisa was paddling regularly and eager to challenge the toughest rapids that the Chattooga could offer. It was June 8, 1980, the weather was mild and the water level about 1.7 — a great prospect for a first run of Section IV.

My own run down from Earl's Ford had been smooth and several of us carried our boats back up for a second run of the Bull. As I started to load boat and gear, a friend walked across the parking lot.

"Left Crack got another one today."

"Who was it? What happened?"

"I don't know her name. She swam out of Corkscrew, of course, and grabbed the throw line one of her group tossed to her. Then she lost her grip on her kayak, decided to go after it, and let go of the safety line. She and the boat washed toward Left Crack. The boat went over. She didn't."

"That's terrible," I said, the words not really doing justice to the heart-breaking scenario I was replaying in my mind.

That night I was slowly eating dinner in Clayton, still thinking of nothing but the tragedy at the Cracks, when Vickie and Jay slid into the seats across from me

Never one to mince words, Vickie electrified me with, "Did you hear about Lisa?"

Before the words were out of her mouth, I knew exactly who had died in Left Crack that day. Tears ran down my cheeks as I thought of Lisa — petite, pretty, and always so full of smiles and enthusiasm. Gone. No more rivers. An empty desk at work.

Bob Brazier had been paddling with her that day and later added to the grim details. How startled they were when Lisa chose to let go of the rope, even though no one in their group was fully aware of the danger below. Seeing her wash into Left Crack and not reappear in the outflow. Getting a grip on her arm from above — at great personal risk — but not being able to budge her. I could tell how much it hurt him to recall those events.

Help was summoned from the river party negotiating Jawbone Rapid, two hundred yards downstream. Robert Harrison, an expert open canoeist with scores of Section IV runs under his boat, responded immediately. He had worked in the recovery of Bob Goeke's body six years earlier at the same spot and knew the undercuts as few others do.

Robert Harrison takes the Chattooga's Seven-Foot-Falls in stride on a run of Section IV. Robert made one of the early open canoe runs of the Colorado River through the Grand Canyon in July of 1986.

Robert quickly broached the Crack with both a canoe and kayak and, on a belay from fellow paddler Pat Nolan, was able to reach Lisa. Even so, it took two more hours and the upstream pull of more than ten persons to dislodge Lisa from the undercut rock.

More than a decade later, Buzz Williams would describe the drowning of another kayaker in Left Crack, his work in recovering the body, and the grim task of providing details to the victim's parents. In 2003, Right Crack claimed a boater's life in a similar manner, as many of us thought it could. I have been told that recent floods may have cleared the underwater logs from that spot, making Right Crack essentially the lethal twin of Left Crack.

In times of lean water, we would often explore the "bones" of the Chattooga. At Raven's Chute, there is a river-wide ledge that contains a substantial pothole at its center. We once squeezed eighteen of us into that cavity to see how many it could accommodate. I was on the bottom, of course.

In the diagonal ledge at Bull Sluice, there is a pothole that tunnels completely through the rock. We found that at lower river levels there was a large breathable air pocket, both in the pothole and behind the curtain of water pouring over the lip of the ledge. We were also able to negotiate the pothole "tunnel," swimming out just above Decapitation Rock. This once led to a hilarious incident.

It took some pre-planning, of course. A raft trip was seen approaching Bull Sluice from upriver. Two off-duty guides immediately made their way to the pothole and, lowering themselves in, disappeared into the air pocket behind the pour-over from the ledge. Another guide, young and clean-shaven, eased into his kayak above the drop.

The rafting guests were brought down to scout the rapid before running it, their guides emphasizing safety procedures and giving anyone who desired it, the chance to walk around the drop. As they stood taking in the scene, one of their guides noted the kayak waiting above.

"Good, there's a kayaker about to run. You'll get to see the proper line to take."

Dropping slowly off of the ledge, the paddler deliberately turned slightly left, letting his boat get sucked broadside into the hydraulic and held by the force of the water. All the group standing on shore could see was the hull of the kayak, bouncing about, with the paddler apparently in distress.

Meanwhile, the two hidden guides had grabbed the boat, pulling the occupant from the cockpit. While the other two assisted, one of the hidden guides climbed into the kayak, sealing his spray skirt in place, water and all. With a hand from his buddies, the new paddler rolled and broke free of the hole. By now, the kayak had been in the hydraulic so long that every eye was turned that way.

"Look! Look at that!"

"What happened to him?"

"Holy Shit! He's aged and grown a beard!"

Another unbelievable river tale to share at the dinner table.

But the same spot could just as easily become the scene of tragedy. On April 12, 1981, Skip Holmes, an experienced boater from Atlanta, leaped from his canoe to make a course correction at the top of Bull Sluice. Probably thinking he would find solid footing on the ledge, he disappeared into the pothole. At one point, his forearm appeared and he was able to grasp a line that was immediately thrown to him. The rescuers were not able to extract him, however, probably because they were unable to get enough upward pull on the rope. Others attempted to reach him on the ledge, and approximately half an hour later his body appeared in the hydraulic, having apparently washed through the tunnel. CPR was immediately initiated, without success. It is guessed that Holmes was unaware that the pothole had a lower exit, and quite possibly did not know that the pothole even existed.

My own Chattooga experience is not without its share of close calls. On one of the early trips, a raft from the Georgia Tech Outing Club had become stuck in the hydraulic at the top of Woodall Shoals. Successfully abandoned by its crew, we waited for it to break free on its own, but it would not.

"I can get it," I said. "Just give me that line." I figured to hold the rope in my teeth while I surfed the hole out to the raft, abandoned my kayak, tied the line off, and had the rest of my party pull the raft and me to shore. "Please retrieve my boat after I climb into the raft."

Surfing to the raft was no problem. Neither was the exiting of my kayak. But right there, all resemblance to the original plan came to a screeching halt. The raft was not a platform that could be boarded. All rigidity had disappeared. Constructed of yellow, vinyl-impregnated fabric, it had been steadily leaking air and, under the forces at work in the hydraulic, had turned into a limp, undulating blob of material. Hanging onto what was once an air chamber, there was so little buoyancy left that I was continuously being pulled down into the hole, then circulated to the surface again. The rope I had held in my teeth was long gone as I gasped for breath.

But an even more serious problem presented itself. The Tech group had tied spare paddles to the raft, each on a six-foot length of rope. These were now trailing in the water, whipping about in the turbulence, and each time one of my legs came close, it became wrapped in several coils of rope. It was a major effort to cling to the raft — much of the time underwater — and I felt my strength quickly ebbing away. With my head and eyes, I frantically signaled Rodger Losier to throw the rope as I tried to extricate my right leg from the restraining coils that held it fast. It all happened in seconds. Suddenly I was free of the coils, the line sailed across my shoulder in a perfect toss, I wrapped a couple of turns around my wrist and collapsed, using my last bit of energy to simply hang on.

Like a beached fish gasping its last, I lay a long time in the spot on shore to which Rodger had pulled me. Gradually, passing time and a warm sun restored my energy and I was able to continue. The raft? It later lost enough buoyancy that it washed out on its own.

Don Downing of the Georgia Canoeing Association makes a successful open canoe run of Sockemdog Rapid on the Chattooga River, October, 1971.

Twice I experienced vertical pins in the Five Falls. The first was in the center of Devil's Chute (Entrance Rapid), running with my son David while he was still a young teen. I was able to rock the boat free within about two minutes.

The second came as I peeled out of the top eddy into Jawbone, inadvertently loading weight too far forward with an aggressive lean. Fortunately, I was paddling a first-generation River Chaser, made before Tom Johnson's production crew began roto-molding with cross-linked polyethylene. The bow caught and jammed, immediately breaking free of the rest of the boat about a foot behind the grab loop. My bow float bag was tight enough that I was able to run the rest of Jawbone without mishap. In about five minutes, the missing bow cone came floating by. I taped it back in place and moved on to Sockemdog.

Sockemdog, on another day, was the site of a hair-raising pin. The water level was pushy, I had come off slightly right of the launching pad, and was sucked back into the hole. The kayak and I did a short dance in the hydraulic, and shot backward toward the Georgia shore. I rolled up with such a snap that I went past center and had to throw out a brace to the left. At the same moment, I felt something solid pop my spray skirt and force its way into the boat between my legs. I was impaled on the end of a twenty-foot log protruding from the eddy! Stuck fast on my side, I could breathe but I couldn't move. Nearly doubled up with laughter, Maggie Tucker and Claude Terry climbed down to free me, inquiring if I still had all my personal equipment!

As the years passed, and we came to know the Chattooga in so many of her moods, we became almost smug in our attitude that we could handle her under any conditions that she might dictate. Then, as more years passed, and she took the lives of paddlers whose skills were not so different from our own, our confidence became tempered with a new respect. We had never been invincible after all.

But wild and beautiful she remains. The Chattooga. My true love for nearly forty years.

The Teens Take Over

From my trip to the Nantahala and Chattooga Rivers in 1969, I knew that Claude Terry and Payson Kennedy were working with a Scout Troop (Troop 312) at the Unitarian Church. It seemed that the three of us were each thinking, "How about a whitewater Explorer Post?" Within weeks of my move to Atlanta, we had determined to make it happen and the GCA had agreed to be the sponsor. Troop 312 provided the nucleus of Scouts, and soon teenage gals and guys from around Atlanta were drawn to the adventure that whitewater paddling offered.

Payson and Claude were also in the experimental stages of boat building. They had built one kayak — for Aurelia — so far, and that had a range of about one quarter mile before sinking from severe pinhole problems. Problems of technique were solved and Claude and Payson were soon contributing their own ideas to the process of laying up kayaks and canoes. Always a fount of creativity, Aurelia used that first kayak as a giant salad bowl at a Post potluck, greens and veggies flowing forth abundantly from the cockpit in cornucopia fashion.

With most Scouting units, beating the bushes to find a competent leader or two is the most difficult part of start up. Payson, Claude and I were already in that leadership role, but what came next with Post 49 was rather mind-boggling. Not only did the GCA sponsor this group, but a good dozen of the club's most active paddlers also became active in

Post activities. Why? Was there an overwhelming altruistic urge toward the would-be paddling youth of Atlanta? Perhaps. Or was there something more immediate and tangible? There was.

Being associated with Explorer Post 49, either as a Scout or an adult advisor, became an avenue toward building your own kayak at cost. Plastic kayaks were unknown — it would still be several years before Hollowform in California would begin roto-molding Tom Johnson's first prototypes. Our fiberglass K-1's and C-2's were among the best available — strong (epoxy was our resin of choice), lightweight (24# for a 4/3 K-1 lay-up[32]), strategically reinforced (bow & stern, hull under seat and deck behind cockpit), and with our own design of adjustable foot braces.

Eighteen boats were built in my Dunwoody basement the first year (1971) of the Post's existence. Twenty-one were popped from molds the second year. Often there would be from three to five kayaks in various stages of completion at any given time. Anyone associated with the Post could build a kayak for $140, slightly more than the cost had been in Maryland. However, each person who did so had to help the next two persons build their kayaks. This served to lighten my load a bit. Activity was so fast and furious that long-time friend Les Bechdel was once sent south by High Performance Products, Tom Wilson's fledgling company, to see if our operation might be commercial and, if so, what molds we were using.

In the early and mid-seventies, it was the Explorers who shared much of the service load with the GCA. When basic canoe and kayak classes were taught (both in spring and fall), the majority of instructors were Scouts or leaders from the Post. The Dogwood Festival downriver races were planned and carried out by the Post, as were two years of Stone Mountain races. When the Southeasterns moved to Nantahala Falls in '72, it was Post 49 that designed the first slalom course and handled the scoring. Another Post, sponsored by Southern Bell and led by longtime GCA member Ken McAmis, set up the first phone reporting system for gate judges that year.

We continued to meet at Camp Chattahoochee, which later became the Chattahoochee Nature Center. Rolling instruction, English Gate practice and drownproofing courses (Georgia Tech/Fred Lanoue type taught by Lanoue's longtime co-instructor, Charlie Wiggin) were held at Keywaden pool, also in Roswell, during the winter months. We paddled during that season, too — I can still remember a fifteen degree trip on Alabama's Little River (February, 1971) where I could hardly see Payson

[32] A lay-up of 4/3 refers to the number of layers, four in the hull, three in the deck. The layers would differ one from the other according to function: the outer layer using a glass weave that would give the most perfect surface; a fracture-resistant layer (usually woven polypropylene, but later Kevlar); and the remaining layer or layers of a glass weave that would use less epoxy and thus reduce total weight of the kayak.

Kennedy's face through the icicles hanging from his helmet! My beard was solid ice! (At that time, Payson was clean-shaven and I was fuzzy.)

Our adventures could occur on any river that we felt was within driving range. August of that first Post year found us back in my old stomping ground, camping for a week at Pennsylvania's Youghiogheny River. By this time, however, construction of the riverfront park had begun and camping was no longer permitted in the area that my Maryland Explorers had used for so long. But Bob Marietta, a lifetime native of Ohiopyle and joint owner of the Yough's first homegrown rafting company, generously let us stay the week at his company's base camp. The week was all that had been promised, with many runs of the "Loop" and side trips to the New and Castleman Rivers. Our gang consisted of seventeen kayakers, one decked canoeist (Payson) and six rafters.

Sometimes it appeared that adults[33] outnumbered Explorer Scouts. But for all the apparent adult presence, it was the Explorers who took

A new crop of Explorer Post 49 kayaks rises from the field. From left to right, the builders were: Mark Reimer, Reid Dowdle, Johnny Stephenson, Maggie Tucker, Claude Terry and Mary Atkinson. Author Doug Woodward squats behind his boat.

33 The adults who worked with the Post during the seventies were Mary Atkinson, Harry Brown, Harry (Buddy) Collins, Melanie Dixon, Ruth Gershon, Claude Grizzard, Horace Holden, Aurelia and Payson Kennedy, Tom Lines, Rodger Losier, Falma Moye, Denise Siegel, George and Dot Stephenson, Claude and Betty Terry, Pat Tomeny, Dave Truran, Margaret Osborne Tucker, Barbara Walmsley, Mark Warren, Julie Wilson, Mary Alice (Mouse) Woodward, Clyde Woolsey, Boni Zucker and myself. There are many others, of course, who will have memories of those times.

most of the responsibility for planning and carrying out events — and it was done well. The Post newsletter was called the Rapid Express and had a string of able editors — Cathy Kennedy, Ronnie Cohen, Butch Terry, and Greg Mohr.[34] Although paddling was our primary activity, there were many others — camping on Georgia's Cumberland Island, backpacking in North Carolina's Linville Gorge, and rock-climbing at Alabama's Little River Canyon. But it was Claude Terry who often appeared to have an inside track for getting whitewater into the spotlight, whether it was taking the late Harry Chapin and his family down the Chattooga on an overnight raft trip, or arranging for NBC to film their *Go Show* around a Post river trip with a paddling safety theme. Cathy Kennedy was the star of that one!

Cathy Kennedy, left, prepares for another run of the Chattooga's Bull Sluice as the NBC Go Show cameramen get set to shoot.

Something like this always seemed to be happening. The autumn (1971) after Payson, Claude and I had worked with Warner Brothers on filming *Deliverance*, one of our Explorers, Steve Kohler, was called to do a national Wheaties TV commercial that had whitewater paddling as its theme. At age fourteen, he was chosen to be the "son" of his older tandem paddling partner — not one of us — for the cameras. Steve was out of school for several days, and when he returned to Briarcliff High, found that his locker had been filled with Wheaties! Fellow Explorers had actually used corn flakes because they were cheaper.

Returning to West Virginia for the Petersburg Races was particularly special for me since it brought my old and new Scouts together. Almost everyone in the two Posts would enter one of the wildwater races, many competing in slalom as well. We had worked out a scoring system

34 Other Scouts who were active leaders in the Explorer Post were Cathy Brown, Tracy Chapple, Reid Dowdle, Laura Greiner, Hugh Hilliard, Charlie Holden, Rick Howard, Gretchen Hund, Helen Johnston, Frances Kennedy, Steve Kohler, Harry Kustick, Bruce Loehle, Lisa Pieper, Mark Reimer, Helen Stephenson, John Stephenson and Charlie Woolsey.

between the two groups and purchased a trophy, but it was a friendly rivalry. Camping and eating together helped cement many new friendships for those teenage paddlers.

One April we arrived at Petersburg in the old green and yellow school bus. Post 49 had purchased it from their Maryland counterparts in anticipation of a western trip of their own. My new scouts weren't about to let me off the hook on leading an expedition that would be equivalent to the Colorado adventure of 1970! But getting to Petersburg in the bus could be as tough as taking it west.

We leave Atlanta in high spirits, traveling on the bus as a group for the first time. We'll pick up Jeannie Brackett and her kayak near Greensboro, North Carolina. Twenty boats are already racked overhead. A dark curtain has been rigged behind the driver to eliminate distracting light from the main portion of the bus where eating, reading and card games are taking place. Behind the wheel, as night closes in, I have the first hint of trouble as the intensity of the headlights begins to change from time to time. The charge indicator is also rising and falling. We pull over and I tighten the belt on the generator.

That doesn't solve the problem, but otherwise we still seem to be running normally, whatever that may be for this contrary beast. We need gas, so I pull into a station and head under the canopy, the only unoccupied pump space.

"It won't clear!" yells Harry Kustick from the rear.

"Optical illusion," I reply, just before broken fluorescent lamps shower down on the bus and the pump area becomes a little darker.

"I'm afraid we took out some of your lights," I tell the attendant as I pay for the gas. "We need to give you something for them."

"How about five dollars?" he responds. I lay a five on the counter, we quickly re-board and are on the road before he can reconsider.

Up the highway in Kernersville, North Carolina, we find a chilly and forlorn Jeannie Brackett still waiting for us in the dark with her boat and paddling gear. Fortunately, she has had enough experience with the Post to not despair when she finds us running two hours behind schedule. We tighten the generator belt once more and roll on north.

As we pull into camp by the river in the wee hours, the generator decides that it won't charge at all. An early morning examination shows one side of the slotted bracket to be broken, and several of us take off in the bus to find some place that can make a quick welding repair. Good fortune smiles — momentarily — as we pull into an ancient and oily repair shop that will do it.

The repair takes longer than advertised — the race starting times are drawing nearer — and I head for the rest room. I swing open the door only to find the throne already occupied by fellow paddler John Mathieu.

I mumble an apology for the intrusion, but before I can leave, my eye catches a sight unlike anything I've seen before. John is holding a flaming match at seat level, seemingly about to light up his private parts. I quickly close the door and withdraw.

I'm still mulling over what I've seen, trying to make some sense of it, when John appears five minutes later.

"Doug, I need to explain. You must think I'm a real weirdo!"

"Well...I'll have to admit, I haven't figured it out yet."

"It was a tick — really attached. It took me most of a pack of matches, plus scorching myself a bit, before it finally backed out."

"That makes sense," I agreed, glad that self-mutilation wasn't part of John's bag of tricks after all.

Deni Siegel was a relatively new advisor to the Explorer Post and this was her first trip out of Georgia with the gang. As such, she drew the lot of planning food for the trip, which she performed with considerable competency. But at lunch we find the flaw.

"Smooth peanut butter? Where's the crunchy?"

"Smooth peanut butter? How could you?"

"Smooth peanut butter? What kind of taste do you have?"

Everyone gets into the act until she finally cracks.

"Fuck you all!" she screams and walks away. We soon forget about it. She doesn't.

After a great weekend on the water, we point the bus toward home. By this time, we know that the bracket repair has not solved the problem and the generator is dead. I, of all people, should have known, from the Colorado River adventure, that this bus eats generators. We have no spare and no way to get a replacement on the weekend. Bathroom stops are postponed and gas stretched as far as possible as we put maximum miles behind us before dark.

This only postpones the moment of truth as darkness overtakes us somewhere in southern Virginia. We stop at a station that can charge our battery as we gas up and take care of personal needs. As we head south once more, only our running lights and flashers turned on, we try to attach ourselves to a point vehicle whose speed we can match. Many pairs of eyes crowd behind the driver to watch the road. Headlights are briefly flipped on as the situation demands and we stop once more for a charge. We breathe a collective sigh of relief as we reach Atlanta at last.

I replace the generator that week and drive the bus to the Post meeting at Camp Chattahoochee. After the meeting is over, I slide into the driver's seat in the dark to take the bus up the hill to its designated parking spot. Too late, I smell Deni's revenge. The steering wheel, gear shift and driver's seat — where I now sit — have been covered with peanut butter. Crunchy.

~

Having raced both slalom and wildwater when I lived in Maryland, it was natural to continue the competition and to try to enthuse others about that aspect of the sport. When I first arrived in Georgia, I had an edge by way of experience over most of my fellow paddlers. But as they gained experience of their own, there was no longer any gap. Payson Kennedy, Claude Terry and I would often be grouped within seconds of each other in the final results, the order changing from race to race. Soon our own Explorer Scouts, particularly Reid Dowdle, Hugh Hilliard, Cathy Kennedy, Frances Kennedy, Steve Kohler, and Mark Reimer were leaving us in their wake. Too young for the Explorers, Mike Terry, Butch Terry, John Kennedy, Jr. and Stuart Kennedy were also making their mark.

The paddlers of Post 49 were becoming a factor in every race they entered. The 1971 Hiawassee Races were typical as the Explorers and advisors, running wildwater, took first and third in K-1 Senior, second through ninth in K-1 Junior and first in C-2 Open. In the slalom, we were first and second in every class, Aurelia, Cathy and Frances Kennedy, in that order, making a clean sweep of the K-1W class. And, as if having the Post walk away with most of the medals wasn't enough, I won a new Mohawk canoe in the race raffle drawing!

In June of both 1971 and 1972, Post 49 helped plan and supervise the flat-water races at Stone Mountain Lake. Even though it wasn't our usual paddling fare, the Post cleaned up as usual. In 1971, there were photos of Bruce Loehle and Steve Kohler in the *DeKalb Neighbor*, their local paper, for their winning performances in the junior kayak division. The races didn't generally attract the whitewater crowd, but the serious flatwater paddlers in Florida often made the trip. The next year at Stone Mountain Lake, I would win the kayak open class, edging out Olympic women's paddler Sperry Rademaker (actually paddling in K-1W) by eight seconds. Of course, Sperry's being eight months pregnant at the time had nothing to do with my win! She and her husband, Jack, would even things up at the 1973 Dogwood Festival races by edging out Maggie Tucker and me by thirty-one seconds to take first place in the C-2M class.

Cathy Kennedy was the Post's first newsletter editor through a year-and-a-half's whirlwind of whitewater instruction, cruises, and races, as well as backpacking and technical climbing events. She might have continued her fine job with the Post had not another event taken her to a different river. She gives a clue in her last issue (April 25, 1972) as editor of the *Rapid Express*:

> *"Horace Holden has bought the Tote and Tarry Motel on the Nantahala River. This summer the Kennedy family will be living at*

Nantahala and running the Tote and Tarry (which will have another name). Some of our other Explorers will also be working, which will mean a chance to run the river in [their] spare time."

"Another name," of course, became the Nantahala Outdoor Center and "summer" turned into a lifetime for the Kennedy family. So, in 1972, both the Post and the GCA "lost" the Kennedy family to their new project on the Nantahala, John and Stuart not yet having reached Explorer age. Cathy would later marry Jimmy Holcombe, a superb whitewater paddler and instructor from Maryland. It is little surprise that their son, Andrew, has become a world-class competitor.

At that time, water releases on the Nantahala were not reliable and GCA members were urged to write to TVA, requesting more frequent and longer running releases. In order to hold a race on the river, arrangements for water had to be made months in advance, confirmed closer to the weekend of the event, and even then the race chairman might have nightmares of slalom gates hanging over a dry riverbed.

Beautiful Ferebee Park, near the midpoint of the Nantahala run, did not exist in those days. On the opposite side of the river, the quarry was in operation — albeit smaller — but the spot that is now Ferebee was a mud and gravel parking lot, full of pools of oil and other vehicle fluids, scattered parts and an array of inoperative heavy machinery.

The river flowed more regularly, the Nantahala Outdoor Center blossomed on its banks, and others rushed in to imitate them. Throughout the seventies, and even into the early eighties, the rafting business remained unregulated, and many outfitters set up shop in the Nantahala Gorge. By the time the U.S. Forest Service stepped in to take control in 1983, there were seventeen competitors on the river. All were grandfathered in by the Forest Service, although "guest days" on peak weekends were limited according to each outfitter's business history on the river.

~

As I sift through old newsletters, I'm overwhelmed by the pace of Post activities — it was off to a race or river almost every weekend, and on long weekends we might be as far away as the New, Gauley or Yough. But as we've often said, the road is more dangerous than the river. The following is an excerpt from the *Rapid Express* of March 7, 1973 (I was filling in for editor Ronnie Cohen).

"As many of you already know, Ronnie Cohen, together with Mark Gavron, Gretchen Hund, Ken Kohler, and Laurie Lassiter were involved in an auto accident on I-85 returning from the Chattooga River Sunday night. Briefly, Mark's van hit a flooded portion of the Interstate just south of I-285 [the complex I-85/I-285 interchange

was under construction then and proper drainage was a big problem], skidded, flipped and then [exploded and] burned when it was struck by a second car a short time later.

Without any attempt to make a judgment on an accident which occurred in an extremely hazardous section of highway — at least four other accidents were reported in this same spot on the same night — I offer these comments. First, the quick thinking and action by Mark was able to change the direction of the initial skid, avoiding the concrete barrier and almost certain serious injury to the three front seat occupants. Second, immediate action and an unbelievable lift by Gretchen, Laurie and a passing motorist freed Ken from under the van seconds before it was struck from behind. All five are now at home, mending well, and thanks to some very cool heads, a tragedy that might have been ... never was."

The 1973 Dogwood Festival Races on the Chattahoochee drew nearly 200 paddlers and were run on a rain-swollen course. Not only did the Post handle planning, advertising, registration, timing and all the other mechanics of the event, but Julie Wilson — bless her heart — made by hand, 138 medals (we had *a lot* of categories!), each one a copper disc which she had enameled with a dogwood blossom and suspended on a leather thong. These medals would be collector's items today.

As if a full Saturday of racing were not enough, we were off to Section IV of the Chattooga the next day. We were hosting Walt Blackadar and several other western paddlers to give them their first taste of southeastern rivers. As luck would have it, the Chattooga was 3.5 feet and rising. At that level, Five Falls is pretty continuous; sneak routes appear in a few rapids, while some of the normally easy runs become far more difficult. Raven's Chute was one of the latter.

Nothing looked familiar except the towering cliff above us. The main ledge had turned into a river-wide stopper and the pothole that eighteen of us had once squeezed into was nowhere to be seen. The Chattooga roared over the lunch rocks to the left and created intimidating holes in the large cracks.

I had paddled with Blackadar in Colorado. Once, when I came out of my kayak in the "Numbers" section of the Arkansas River, he had admonished me by saying that I still had plenty of air and time for more roll attempts — despite the beating my head was taking from bumping over rocks. I knew of his reputation in Turnback Canyon on the Alsek and the upper Susitna, both in Alaska. He *never* came out of his boat. That day, at Raven's Chute, he did. Running the line that he chose, the river became a bully — it physically separated him from his kayak — it was not his choice. Walt was a good sport about it, running competently everything that came before and after — and had naught but praise for the Chattooga ever after.

Walt Blackadar, whitewater legend, in the Five Falls of the Chattooga, April, 1973. The river level was 3.5 Feet on the US 76 Gauge. Two months later, Walt would host our group of Georgia paddlers on the Selway and Lochsa Rivers, near his home in Salmon, Idaho.

We were paddling well, too, but there were some hair-raising moments in the Five Falls. Hugh Hilliard and I had stationed ourselves with a throw rope on the large boulder above Left Crack to spot one of our rafts coming through Corkscrew. It needed us. The occupants of the raft snubbed our line to a D-ring, and Hugh and I hung with all our weight on a belay over the top of the rock as we fought to hold the raft out of the Cracks.

At that moment, Payson, running C-1, which was his boat of choice in those years, came out of Corkscrew — upside-down! Not to worry, like Walt, Payson *always* rolled. But with the river now at a probable four feet, there was only a space of seconds between the bottom of Corkscrew and the top of the Cracks. Payson rolled once, twice… three times, but on each attempt, he was flattened again by a wave with a mind of its own. Ten feet above the Cracks he exited, but it was too late. He flushed through Center Crack and disappeared. Hugh and I watched as we still clung to the line that had been unavailable to Payson. Had we known then what we would learn the next year — that the Cracks could so easily pin and kill a swimmer — our safety set-up would have been much more extensive.

After what seemed an eternity, Payson surfaced, nearly halfway to Jawbone. An Olympic swimmer could not have gained the Georgia shore more quickly Our group of about fifteen Explorers and western guests reassembled below the Cracks. Jawbone and Sockemdog were successfully run by all, but with great respect. A high water center route in Sockemdog actually made the run much easier.

~

Within two months, nineteen Explorers were heading west, in the old school bus that bore 13 kayaks and two rafts on its roof, for what would be the biggest adventure ever for the Atlanta Post. Our rafts had rowing rigs and would be manned by Explorers Pat Tomeny and Charlie Holden. Four newer Scouts would go as raft passengers, while the rest would paddle kayak. It was in the waning days of cheap gasoline and we were incensed to find a station in Grand Junction charging *40 cents per gallon!*

We arrived to camp beside the rain-swollen Arkansas River at night and it really looked scary in the bus headlights. The next day we ran the section above Cottonwood Rapid, then the Numbers and finally Brown's Canyon. Pat and Charlie had never run rafts with oar-rigs before, but they were good at reading whitewater. Local paddlers bet that at least one of our rafts would flip in Brown's. Neither did.

Enjoying a barbecue outside the Blackadar home. Left to right at the table, Mark Reimer, Butch Terry, Julie Wilson, Maggie Tucker. Pat Tomeny standing.

Our warm-up continued on the Colorado north of Grand Junction and then it was on to Idaho — more or less! The bus was showing an increased reluctance to run, so in Price, Utah, we stopped to rebuild the carburetor and replace solenoid, battery cable and fuel pump. To get back on schedule, the adults took turns driving through the night. Somewhere in the black hours of early morning, Julie made a wrong turn and we were shortly surrounded and stopped by three government security vehicles. After interrogating us and finding out that those long pointy things on top of the bus weren't missiles, we were promptly escorted to the boundaries of the Atomic Energy Commission proving ground!

Walt Blackadar met us in the town of Salmon and took us to his home high above the river and town, snow-capped peaks in the distant background. He, his wife Shirley and two of his daughters — Lois and Sue — hosted all nineteen of us with an outdoor barbecue! We spent a bright moonlit night camping in their front yard.

Early the next morning, we were off for the Bitterroot Wilderness and the Selway. Walt had made arrangements for shuttle (a long one) and obtained the permit for running this outstanding river before we arrived. The experience was all we had hoped for — impressive whitewater (many Class IV's), an untouched mountain wilderness of vast dimensions, back-rubbing circles around the nightly campfires, water so clear that sunlight danced off the riverbed a dozen feet below our kayaks, and a bond of shared adventure that each of us would carry with us for

Entering Jim's Creek Rapid on the Selway River, northern Idaho. Charlie Holden at the oars, Carolyn Rich and Cathy Brown aboard, June, 1973.

the rest of our lives. There was sadness throughout the group as we reached the take-out and our four river days came to an end.

We treated Walt to a restaurant dinner that night, camped, and prolonged our Idaho paddling by one more day. This time it was the Lochsa — not wilderness, but superb big water paddling. All too soon, it was time to point the bus toward Atlanta — more or less!

But our month was not yet over. Our next stop was to catch good water on the Gallatin River near the border of Montana and Wyoming. We ran the section above and below House Rock, the trickiest part being the avoidance of downed power lines that were dragging in a heavy rapid!

Camping that night by the Yellowstone River at the turnoff to Springdale, we were startled out of our sleep at dawn by a sudden thundering sound. Several hundred head of cattle were being driven across a wooden plank bridge and heading right for us! It was the quickest breaking of camp we had ever seen as everyone came awake, scooped up sleeping bags and made a mad dash for the bus!

The following day, at Wyoming's Tongue River, we hiked far up into the sub-alpine meadows, alive with wildflowers, and swam in the icy waters of snowmelt. Later, we carried and dragged our boats up the canyon trail until we were well within a Class IV section of the Tongue. The run was worth it!

Left, Mary Alice 'Mouse" Woodward separates a rattlesnake from its skin. The snake was found dead in our campsite on the Selway. Right, The old green creeper is loaded for the road once more, with an elk rack added to the roof load.

As had been the case with my Maryland explorers, we were traveling under an approved National Tour Permit and thus had the privilege of stopping at military bases for food and shelter.

We had chosen Warren AFB in Cheyenne as our break from camping and cooking on the return leg of the trip. Upon arrival, Lieutenant Dan Thorsen, who had been assigned to meet us, seemed a bit taken aback by the fact that we were co-ed. "You'll sleep in the gym tonight, but we have only one set of facilities," he apologized.

"No sweat," we replied. Actually, having been on the road in the bus in mid-summer for two days since hitting water, we had quite a bit of sweat! The first thing on our mind was showers — we shed our dirty clothes and all piled in together without a second thought. As we left Cheyenne the next morning, we passed a billboard that read, "Scouting Today is More Than You Think!" The whole bus roared with laughter!

From Cheyenne, the driving days became long and the old school bus cantankerous, but on the evening of July 4, we finally chugged into my Dunwoody driveway to the incredulous stares of neighbors! It had been a month we would never forget!

Claude Terry on the Lochsa River, northern Idaho, June, 1973

~

Within days of our return, I received a frantic call from Sandy Campbell in New England. The Post had helped Sandy hang a nine-gate mini-slalom between Bull Sluice and the U.S. Highway 76 bridge earlier in the year.

"The Kayak Wildwater Nationals have fallen through up here. They're not going to give us a water release [on Vermont's West River, if I remember correctly], so we have no race. Can you do the Nationals on the Chattooga?"

"When?" I asked.

"In three weeks," Sandy replied.

"Well, with a cushy lead time like that, why not?" I laughed. "Let me check the Forest Service and I'll get right back to you."

Somehow I managed to convince the District Ranger at Walhalla, SC that the impact would be minimal and we had confirming letters in the mail that week. The Explorer Post went into a frenzy of activity — writing up releases and applications to go out immediately to whitewater clubs, arranging for safety (no small task), getting timing clocks shipped from the supplier, gathering volunteers, and performing the dozens of other tasks that go into race planning.

On July 29, the Nationals were indeed run on the Chattooga, starting above Bull Sluice and ending in the Sockemdog pool. Water level was at 1.75 feet on the US 76 gauge. Tom McEwan of Silver Spring, MD was 1st, Ken Cooper of Oak Ridge, TN 2nd, and John Holland of Fair Oaks, CA 3rd. Locally, Jim Shelander, Payson Kennedy and David Jones were 5th, 6th and 7th, respectively. Julie Wilson was 3rd in K-1W. Paddlers from Post 49 took five of the first six places in the Junior Division, with Steve Kohler and Hugh Hilliard taking 1st and 2nd. The next day, we typed, copied and mailed the results. We had pulled off the nearly impossible! A year later the race would have been impossible, with the designation of the Chattooga as a Wild & Scenic River.

Exactly two months later, on September 29, 1973, we received a same-day call from our paddling friends in Tennessee, telling us there would be a first-ever release of water into the dry river bed we knew as the Ocoee. We thought the run could be a good one and about 15 of us scooped up our gear and sped north. We arrived about a half hour before the water was due to be turned off, so it was find a spot on the shoulder to park, slide down the bank and hop into our boats — no chance to scout!

It was a run that had us all in smiles. The release was 2600 cfs that day and our adrenaline was pumping! I approached the old bridge[35] at the powerhouse and Johnny Stephenson, one of the Scouts who hadn't paddled that day, was motioning at me and pointing to a huge wave train directly below. It looked like a great ride until I came over the second wave and saw the size of the powerhouse hole. I disappeared for most of

[35] The "old bridge" at the powerhouse, since replaced by the unsupported single span that now crosses the river, was supported by two large concrete pilings that rose imposingly out of the water. The piling on river left center-split the wave train that I rode that first day on the Ocoee.

a minute and when I finally made shore, they told me Johnny was still running east on US 64! The Ocoee, of course, became a favorite for the Explorers, as it did for so many others.

Some years later, on October 23, 1982, a piling below the old bridge was the scene of an impressive rescue when an open canoe was pinned against the upstream concrete face. The canoe had flattened and the paddler, John Norton, was trapped in his thigh straps, rapidly losing the strength to keep his head above the surging current.

The witnesses on the bridge and the paddlers at Hell Hole were frantically trying to come up with an appropriate course of action when Karen Berry, a raft guide for High Country, ran onto the bridge with coiled ropes, gave quick instructions to her companions and, being the lightest of the group, was immediately lowered down the piling. Looping a second vertical line under the nearly unconscious paddler's armpits, she had her helpers on the bridge exert enough pull to stabilize the victim's head above water. Then, working carefully below the surface with her knife, she cut the straps that were binding the paddler to his boat. After rigging a more secure harness, she gave the all-clear signal and the paddler was hoisted up to the bridge. Photos of the rescue made the front page in several southern papers the next day.

～

Our friendship with the Blackadars was to continue and many in the Post would return individually and in small groups to paddle with Walt. Julie Wilson was one of these and had become like another daughter to him. In the spring of '74, Julie, Rodger Losier and Boni Zucker had gone west, Julie to paddle, Rodger and Boni to backpack.

Blackadar had been the first to run Idaho's Upper Bruneau and longed to share the wild beauty of this canyon with his friends. Julie was included in this handful of paddlers as they made their April 27 descent through Class IV waters turned treacherous with sudden snowmelt. In a rapid where each paddler could concentrate on only his or her own survival, Julie was lost.

Driven by grief, Walt paddled the river that day and for the week that followed, hoping against hope that Julie might have crawled out on some rock or beach downriver. Her life jacket and broken boat were found and as time passed, the last glimmer of hope faded. Rodger and Boni hiked the canyon daily, searching.

Walt flew to Atlanta three weeks later for Julie's memorial service and to be with her parents, Elizabeth and Ross. Julie was twenty-six that year, a second generation GCA member, her folks having been active in both paddling and service to the club. At the memorial, Dave Truran, Julie's closest companion, played guitar and sang *Will Ye Go Lassie Go?*,

Blowin' in the Wind and others. I don't know how he did it — I couldn't hold back my own tears. The same hour that we in Atlanta were sharing memories of Julie, her body was found by Rodger Losier, trapped beneath a submerged tree 100 feet from where she was last seen by Walt. With her parents' permission, she was buried overlooking the Bruneau and the rapid that bore her name — *Julie Wilson Falls.*

Julie was the only child of Ross and Elizabeth and they became close friends of the Blackadars after her death, visiting their Idaho home and the spot where Julie died. Thus it was Ross who called me four years later to drop the bombshell that now Walt had drowned, trapped in his boat under a log in Idaho's Payette River. The whitewater community had lost a legend, and those of us who knew him well felt the absence of a generous and caring friend.

But that was not the end of it. In May of '83, Rodger Losier, who had found Julie's body, died on the Toccoa River. He knew the trails of the southern Appalachians as few people do, was a capable open boater, and had started his own rafting company on the Ocoee River. Most of all, we missed him for his practical jokes and boisterous good humor!

After we lost Julie, it seemed that the shadow of death was never far away. Adrienne Orr was one of the newer Scouts on our western trip and went by raft. Her family was enthusiastic about paddling, though, and shortly afterward was on the Nantahala for an outing. Again tragedy struck. Her dad, wading into the cold water to help someone who had spilled in the Falls, collapsed and died in the river from a heart attack.

Greg Mohr, the Post's last newsletter editor, was killed in an automobile accident while in Florida. He too, left a void in the hearts of family and fellow Post members. The *Rapid Express* was never published again.

Only three of these deaths were of Post leaders or members, but they all affected us deeply. The losses seemed far too great for the few years during which they occurred. We continued to paddle and do things together, but by the end of the seventies, Post 49 was fading into memory. Individually, many of the group stayed active in whitewater and most still paddle today.

Dark River of Deliverance

James Dickey changed my life. He never knew that. And at the time I didn't even know it myself. But as surely as Dickey could put swashbuckling thoughts to paper and then morph them into his own persona, his words also became a part of who I was.

I met him only once. It was on an intimate fall evening in Atlanta, at Lewis King's Buckhead home. Dickey's friend since their early twenties, King was, in many ways, the real life model for the Lewis Medlock of *Deliverance*. He had the skills — canoeist, archer, guitarist, athlete of note during his years at Georgia Tech. He had already lived the role. But there were differences. With a tough, wiry body, piercing blue eyes and silver hair, King bears little resemblance to Burt Reynolds, who portrays Lewis in the film version of *Deliverance*. And where the movie character comes across as macho and flamboyant, dominating his companions, King is modest in the extreme, making little of his personal accomplishments.

There were six of us at the table that night — King and his wife Joan, Dickey, Payson Kennedy, Claude Terry and myself. Payson, Claude and I had been running whitewater rivers together for years, but it was Claude's friendship with King that had brought us there.

That week, Claude had asked me, "Have you read *Deliverance*?" I had, of course. It had caught my eye earlier that year, while I was still living in Maryland, since it appeared to be a tale of wilderness canoeing. It wasn't quite an uninhabited wilderness as it turned out, and the action wasn't all of a whitewater nature. But I read it through, at the time not having the slightest inkling of how my life would be drawn into that tale.

"Well," Claude continued, "Warner Brothers is going to film that story down here and they're looking for a river. There's a chance, too, that we might get involved in some way. Can you make it to dinner this Friday? Great! Bring your Colorado films and projector. Oh, by the way, James Dickey will be there."

Around the King dinner table, with rising excitement, we discussed logistics, equipment and sets as if we were the filmmakers ourselves. The Chattooga was the river we all knew best — the rapids, the obscure access points, where to find the right scene ("down there that river climbs them walls like a monkey") — but we concluded that Alabama's Little River would better fill the bill since it had both the rapids and the towering cliffs needed for a death-defying climb out of the canyon. North Georgia's precipitous Tallulah Gorge was briefly mentioned, but we considered it too difficult a venue for practical filming. Warner Brothers thought otherwise, and in the end, both the Chattooga and Tallulah would be chosen, each becoming a portion of Dickey's fictitious Cahulawassee River.

Following dinner, I set up projector and screen to take the group a bit farther west. Running the rapids of the Grand Canyon by kayak had been the highlight of my year and one by one, the Colorado's big ones — Hance, Hermit, Crystal and Lava — lit up the screen. There were some oohs and aahs as angry brown water exploded in fifteen-foot haystacks and our tiny kayaks flitted here and there. But it was only an interlude to the hopes and feelings that were being given substance that night. The lights came on. Dickey and King passed a guitar back and forth, strumming a few tunes, each deferring to the other.

Dickey was an imposing figure of a man, and his presence filled the room. But it was much more than physical. There was a mystique about him — of things hidden, perhaps ominous — that he enjoyed perpetuating. There were references to the canoe trip which he and King had taken years before with another close friend, Al Braselton. The trip that had spawned the imaginings which would eventually become *Deliverance*. Dickey would not describe details of that canoe trip. With a knowing smile, he would simply say, "There's a lot more truth in the story [*Deliverance*] than you might think."

King was more candid. We knew that they had canoed the Coosawattee[36] River in northwest Georgia. Truth now eerily imitating fiction, the Coosawattee was in the process of being dammed and the valley behind it would slowly fill over the next two years, drowning all traces of the history of those whose lives were once intertwined with the river.

King later supplied what we came to regard as the facts of that river trip, now long faded into the mists of time. First, he had emphasized, "You may think of the southern Appalachians as being wilderness now, but in the thirties and forties that country was really wild. A man that was perceived as a threat to the mountain folks might just disappear — permanently. Murder was always a viable option, because few outsiders were going to go snooping around those forests looking for the missing man."

It seemed that the canoeing that day was actually done by Dickey and Braselton, while King went looking for a place downstream where he could meet the pair. Finding no road to the river, he parked and started down a path leading through the woods. Like yellow jacket sentries guarding their nest against danger, two armed men suddenly appeared and demanded to know his business. King's tale of a canoe on its way through the rapids of this river seemed absurd to the mountain men, and they thought it was far more likely that he was a revenue officer looking for their moonshine still. The older of the pair told the younger to take King to the river and "stay with him, son," words — along with their sinister undertone and unspoken meaning — that King has never forgotten.

Unsure of his armed companion's patience, and almost overwhelmed by the thought that Dickey and Braselton might already have passed that point, King waited and sweated and prayed. The canoeists had run into serious difficulties themselves in the rapids upstream, but finally hove into sight as daylight was beginning to dim. At that point, the demeanor

---

36 In the period between the filming of Deliverance and the filling of the lake behind Carter's Dam, there was a flurry of activity among regional paddling groups to run the Coosawattee before it was gone. Cleve Tecford of the Georgia Canoeing Association advertised one such trip as follows:

"From Mountaintown Creek to Carter's Dam, the Coosawattee is a continuous series of long Class II runs through some of the most beautiful wilderness in North Georgia. There is one spectacular 30-foot waterfall that we will portage. Inundation of this area by Carter's Dam Reservoir will begin sometime this year. The total length of the run is just over 20 miles. Due to the length of the trip and the inaccessibility of the take-out which requires 4-wheel drive transportation, there will be a limit of ten boats. Written reservations are required on a first come-first served basis; however, the leader reserves the right to arbitrarily and discriminatorily (sic) reject any applicant. An incorrect appraisal of your physical condition and canoeing skills could make this trip a personal disaster for you and spoil the day for your friends. Meet at the Dairy Queen in Ellijay on Ga. Highway 5 at 8:00 a.m., Saturday morning, February 24." [1973]

In April of 1976, Gary DeBocher, Marion Barker, Earl Metzger and Carlton Shuford put in on the Coosawattee below GA 5 to see what was left of the river after the lake had filled. They found flatwater, a series of Class II rapids, prevailing westerly winds, and a lake already clogged with powerboats. The waterfall, as we all knew it would be, was silenced, for our lifetimes at least, beneath the deadening waters of the lake.

of the mountain men changed completely. Shotguns disappeared, and there were smiles and kind words as they helped carry the canoe and gear up the hill to the truck.

Deliverance had been a Book-of-the Month Club selection early that year. Dickey had rewritten it into a film script that he had just sold to Warner Brothers. Now, in King's living room, he held a copy in his hand. He turned to me, motioning with the script, and asked, "It's a good book, don't you think? Do you really like it?" I was startled. How could such a powerful writer, so widely acclaimed and honored, need assurance from us? As he tossed down more alcohol and the evening wore on, the question was repeated, until it became embarrassing.

Nevertheless, we left in high spirits, hoping against hope that we could become part of the adventure to come — the actual filming of *Deliverance*. Dickey and King knew that we were competent canoeists, that we knew the Chattooga, Little and other area rivers as few others knew them and that we would be good technical advisors on equipment and scenes. But they were not Warner Brothers, even though they might be in touch with them. And so that night we left with a caution born of realism.

~

We kept working our jobs at Emory, Georgia Tech and Western Electric, paddling rivers every weekend, but in our hearts we waited. No word. Then a glimmer of hope. Warner Brothers needed some heavy-duty rafts for getting the filming crew down the river. I knew where to get them, so Payson and I drove north in his Ford van to pick them up from Lance Martin, whose commercial rafting operation on Pennsylvania's Yough was in its infancy. One raft was an eighteen-foot military assault boat with full sponsons and inflatable floor. What a bear! It was all the two of us could do to wrestle it into the van. We dutifully delivered the rafts to the Warner Brothers equipment area in Clayton and waited. Again.

Filming had started in mid-May, and we knew that many of those early days would be spent shooting scenes away from the river or events at the river that did not require canoeing. But May faded into June and June was fast dwindling away. We began to hear rumors through Lewis King. The crew was already filming on the river, but it was not going well. A canoe had been trashed — not purposely — and a support raft had capsized near the start of Section IV, expensive camera equipment going to the bottom. As far as we could tell, that loss took place between Screaming Left Turn and Rock Jumble.

"For Christ's sake, find somebody who knows how to handle this river!" Director John Boorman, stringy red hair flying free beneath the brim of his witch-like hat, was not a patient man. A proper Englishman, he was still adjusting to life in the Southern Appalachians.

Reinforcements were brought in, but we were not. Ralph Garrett, a professional stuntman, who had come from California to take the fall from the cliff, was paired with a local fisherman who "knew the river like the back of his hand." Neither had any canoeing experience, but they would try their skills first on Section II, the "family" stretch of the Chattooga. At the end of the day, the pair stumbled ashore at Earl's Ford, bruised but wiser men.

It was Ralph's turn. "We've heard that you have some guys who really know this river and are good in a canoe. Get them up here. You need them!"

The call came to Claude and he relayed the news to Payson and me. "It's happened. They want us. In fact it sounds as if they need us." All of our normal work came to a sudden halt as the three of us activated the leaves of absence that we had prearranged.

We had our orders at last. "Check into the Heart of Rabun Motel in Clayton Sunday night. There's a room reserved for each of you." (The stars and top staff, of course, were quartered at the Kingwood Country Club, two miles away.) "We can't classify you as stunt men — you'd have to join the union, which would cost you more than you'd make in this short time period. No film credits. You'll be listed as stand-ins and paid accordingly." Hell, we were so stoked, we would have run naked down Clayton's Main Street if they had asked us to, and done it for nothing!

"Report to the makeup trailer at seven, Monday morning. See Bucky Rous, wardrobe master, for your clothing. Terry and Garrett (the professional stuntman) will be made up as Ed (Jon Voight), Kennedy and Woodward as Bobby (Ned Beatty). We don't need doubles for Ronnie and Burt, since they've already been killed and injured at this point in the story. Donoene McKay will color your hair, then Mike Hancock will apply the cuts and bruises."

By the time we were called to appear in July of 1971, Warner Brothers already had most of the cabin, camping and archery scenes in the can. They were ready to concentrate on the river. So were we.

On some days — at First Falls, Corkscrew, and Jawbone — we were called on to be doubles. We would report to the makeup station at seven, just as we had that first morning, and repeat all the dressing and makeup procedures. But instead of Burt Reynolds lying in the bottom of our Grumman, it would be his dummy, known affectionately as "No Balls," for the large void in the hinged crotch area.

On "Five Falls Days," we often did not return to Clayton until 10 P.M., where we would grab dinner and stumble to our rooms at the Heart of Rabun Motel. On other days, we might act as demonstrators, running the easier rapids several times until the principals felt they could do the run themselves. By this time they were beginning to acquire some basic river skills out of necessity.

Or again, we might be called on for technical advice, such as, "Where can we find a rock face with a swift current running past, that Jon Voight can be clawing at for a finger hold — and where we won't lose him downriver!" Thus the naming of "Deliverance Rock," where that scene was shot repeatedly.

Left to right: Claude Terry, Payson Kennedy and the author. Claude doubled for Jon Voight; Payson and Doug for Ned Beatty in some of the rougher canoeing scenes in Warner Brothers film adaptation of James Dickey's novel *Deliverance*.

Our advice was not always accepted. Claude and I were made up as doubles for Jon Voight and Ned Beatty, respectively, and kneeled in a green Old Town canoe awaiting instructions from director John Boorman. Actors Burt Reynolds and Ned Beatty waited in a Grumman canoe. Claude had just paddled the Old Town through several rapids,

Doubling for Beatty and Voight, with "No Balls" (Burt Reynolds' dummy) aboard, the author (bow) and Claude Terry (stern) head into Shoulderbone Rapid, trying to imitate the paddling style of the principals.

fighting against the flat-water keel and the load of waterlogged gear to keep the boat on track.

"What they (Warner Brothers) ought to do", he expounded, "is rip the keel off of this canoe, substitute Styrofoam for the camping gear, cover it with a tarp and stick the bow and arrows on top." A good suggestion from an experienced canoeist, but spoken in a moment of frustration.

Reynolds had heard the remark. He swiveled around in the stern of the Grumman, fixed his eyes on Claude and snapped, "Look Candy-ass, you don't go into a scene driving a Greyhound bus and come out riding a bicycle!" The silence that followed was profound. Normally eloquent Claude chose to let the moment pass without a reply.

Lewis Medlock (Burt Reynolds) writhes in agony on the bottom of the canoe as Bobby Trippe (Ned Beatty) paddles for his life to escape their Cahulawassee nightmare. Photography Director Vilmos Zsigmond captures the close-up on camera as the Warner Brothers crew keeps the canoe and raft on track.

Later that same week, I was to get my comeuppance in Jawbone Rapid. I was ferrying the Grumman and No Balls to the next shooting site and dropped into the large top eddy on river left. However, I had violated a cardinal rule of paddling any craft — never take to the water with loose rope in your boat! There was a tangle of perhaps eighty feet of three-eighth inch line in the bottom of my canoe, tied to a thwart and tossed in with unnecessary haste.

As I peeled out into the surging current, I leaned hard on a left draw and as my paddle took my weight, it snapped completely in two, plunging me headfirst into the "jaws," the canoe on top of me. In the next moment, as I was taking my lumps from the rocks, I realized that No Balls, the Grumman and I were all still connected by rope.

Fortunately, *very fortunately*, we passed to the left of Hydroelectric Rock, an undercut death trap, but the canoe was still hell-bent on running Sockemdog, the last of the Five Falls. It was only through a well-timed assist from Claude that we made the eddy above and I was able to get enough slack to slip the coils of rope from my ankle.

The Warner Brothers crew was also exceptional in looking out for our safety, as well as that of the principals. They had been hand-picked for fitness and their desire to work in a remote setting away from the usual conveniences. When we were making hazardous runs, there were constantly alert eyes and ready arms tucked out of camera view along our route. "Jerry the Fish" had a knack for always being where he was needed.

Not all days were as long or as tedious as the ones worked in Five Falls. Often we would sit for an hour or two while Boorman and photography director Vilmos Zsigmond decided how a particular scene would be set up. One such day ground to a halt at Dick's Creek Ledge while the pair climbed to the top of Five Finger Falls to discuss the next take. Beatty clowned around in his movie hat while Voight frolicked nearly nude in a small pour-over. Ralph Garrett and Claude got into friendly water fight that ended up with a rolling tussle over the ledge and into the river. By the end of the afternoon, the only footage captured was a portage scene where Beatty and Voight drag the canoe over Dick's Creek Ledge.

If the day ended at a reasonable hour, we would be invited to Kingwood Country Club to see the rushes (the previous day's shooting). Evenings there had a party atmosphere, as Reynolds would loudly try to draw others into a hot game of skittles, usually with substantial wagers. In contrast to a day of shooting a men's movie, this was the time when the women would appear. Marcheline Bertrand, soon to marry Voight, and Belinha Beatty, Ned's wife, were there and it seemed that Reynolds could never be seen without an admirer at hand. Some of the wives or partners of crew had also come.

We would hear tales of incidents that had taken place before we arrived. In Tallulah Gorge where, in the story, the rope breaks and Ed (Jon Voight) plunges from the cliff face to the river, a local man had agreed to take the fall. After viewing the spot from below, he told Zsigmond that he needed to see it from the top of the cliff. The next day, when they finally found him again, he had "remembered some errands that my wife asked me to do that day." It was then that Boorman decided to bring in Ralph Garrett, a professional stuntman out of California.

The stunt itself was far from routine. Ralph was lowered by rope to a steeply sloping ledge, probably two hundred feet above a small pool in the Tallulah River. While sliding on the ledge, he had to kick out from the cliff to make sure he cleared rocks directly below and hit deep water. There would be only one take. To everyone's relief, he took the fall flawlessly.

We worked almost daily with Ralph who was, by that time, doing the same job that we were. He was quick to learn, and we shared what canoeing skills we could in the time available. His wife Donna, we were told, was also employed in stunt work, doubling for Raquel Welch in many of her films. By the end of the *Deliverance* filming, we had become good friends. And at the wrap party, amid other hilarious presentations, Ralph was given the "cliff-hanger award," a coat hanger which had been spray-painted gold.

There appeared to be a growing discontent, at times even hostility, as residents of the surrounding area became familiar with the story of *Deliverance*. Not all were cooperative. Warner Brothers had found their "perfect" backwoods cabin and gas pump location for shooting the "That river don't go to Aintree!" scene. When they returned a week later to start fine tuning the set, they were met by the owner who quickly sent them packing with, "I just read the book and you're not shooting that filthy story on my place!"

It was interesting to see how locals were brought into the filming, even after the crew had begun work. It may be that Boorman had determined to do this before ever arriving in Rabun County, but then again he may have been trying to stem the rising tide of resentment against how the mountain folks were being portrayed by Dickey's novel. A Rabun County man who had been hired to drive cast and crew to various locations, caught Boorman's eye and was slipped into a deputy sheriff's role. Louise Coldren, who fed river paddlers for so many years at her Dillard Motor Lodge, played a similar part, serving food to guests in a scene near the end of the film. And for the dueling banjos scene, the boy, Billy Redden, was found waiting tables in Clayton. The local jail was even used as a source for one of the Griner brothers, the tough looking one who exclaims in disgust at the ignorance of the foursome from the city, "It ain't nothin' but the biggest fuckin' river in the state."

There were those who helped in other ways. Frank Rickman was one. When Warner Brothers needed visually disturbing characters for minor roles, Rickman was the person who knew where to find them. A strange upside-down tree gracing his Clayton front yard, Rickman is to the bulldozer what Stradivarius is to the violin. A craftsman supreme, but with earth and rock, he can sculpt a scene of beauty out of a hopeless mess. Or, he can do the opposite.

During our weeks of waiting to see if we would be summoned to the *Deliverance* set, Claude, Payson and I would often come north to kayak the Chattooga on weekends. This is a river that each of us loves deeply and at that point we were already involved with the proposal to give it Wild and Scenic status. On this particular day, we were eddying out on the South Carolina shore after an exhilarating run of Woodall Shoals when we were struck by a depressing sight. Car bodies were half buried at the water's edge. Stoves and refrigerators littered the small beach. The junk and litter just went on and on. "Shit! What S.O.B. could have done a thing like this!" was our collective thought. We were depressed for the rest of the trip. A couple of weeks later, when the beach was again spotless, we realized that it had been a temporary set for the movie and was Frank Rickman's work!

The major characters, of course, were cast well ahead of the film crew's arrival. Herbert "Cowboy" Coward, hailing from the ghost town of Maggie Valley, North Carolina, where he worked as a gun-slinging cowboy, played the scary mountain man that Voight waits for atop the cliff. Bill McKinney, a California tree surgeon and folksinger, played the other depraved mountaineer, who is skewered by Burt Reynold's arrow. He had originally tried out for the role of Lewis, ultimately filled by Burt Reynolds. In a near-perfect piece of casting, the large, imposing Aintree County Sheriff is played by James Dickey himself.

During the early part of the filming, Dickey was on hand, giving advice to actors and crew. Some of this was helpful, but he apparently went beyond limits that Boorman considered appropriate, and was asked to leave the set.

What took place in Tallulah Gorge was a tribute to persistence and ingenuity. Besides the cliff scaling scene, it was here that the two canoes collide and the Oldtown breaks apart. Having picked their ideal spot high in the Gorge, the crew, under the direction of special effects coordinator Marcel Vercoutere, set about building an artificial rapid of boulders and logs, taking care to not make it into a lethal strainer. A track was constructed so that the Oldtown would slide into a broached position in the rapid, the canoe having already been rigged to separate into two halves when a cable was pulled from shore.

Those who have hiked or paddled Tallulah Gorge will appreciate the difficulty of getting boats, camera equipment and related gear to river level — not to mention getting them out again. This was accomplished with a cable and pulleys, a Grumman canoe being the "basket." The system ran from the top of the climbing cliff down to the south shore of the Tallulah, 300 feet below, a section of the river upstream of today's boating run. The process was slow and physically demanding, but no comparison to the alternative of lugging things in and out by hand!

When the artificial rapid was ready and safety crews set in place (including us), the director would radio Georgia Power for perhaps three quarters of a gate of water to be released from the Tallulah Falls dam to make the rapid come alive and hide any signs of construction. "*Too much! Too much!* Reynolds and Beatty have swamped! Give us half a gate!" and his bullhorn would go sailing into the river. It took several takes to finally get it right.

This same hundred yards of river in the early part of Tallulah Gorge — upstream of the section that boaters paddle today — was a hot spot of activity, as two other significant scenes were filmed here. Marcel and his crew had constructed a catapult, which consisted of one of the Grumman canoes hinged in the center and mounted on a ten-foot tower. A rope attached to the bow was quickly pulled by half a dozen crewmembers, throwing the stern into a vertical position and ejecting the occupant. No Balls made the first try with great success.

Reynolds, a former stuntman, insisted on doing the scene himself and took his place in the stern. Rocks behind him were hosed down to look darker to the camera. As with all the scenes, darkness — life jackets spray-painted green to cover the original orange, shooting under cloud cover — was used to create a somber mood in the film. With a neat diver's tuck, Reynolds sailed thirty horizontal feet, doing a full gainer in the process. Only one take was necessary and that scene was later spliced in sequence with the canoe break-up scene to make them appear as one.

It is also in this stretch of river that Drew (Ronnie Cox) is lost as he lurches from the bow of the canoe in one of the big uncertainties of the story. Was he shot or not? It's a difficult task for Cox to bring off to the satisfaction of Boorman. The cameras roll six times on this one before a real-life injury halts the shooting. On the sixth take, Cox dives squarely into an underwater rock, nearly dislocating his shoulder. He's unable to continue that day, so the crew will deliver what they've got to film editor Tom Priestley.

It's interesting to recall the scene where Drew's body is found in the eerie garden of slanting rocks on Section III of the Chattooga. The sight of his arm grotesquely twisted behind his head is not a photographic trick. Cox's shoulder joints are so flexible that he was able to get into that position on his own. Perhaps that is why his shoulder never actually dislocated in the Tallulah mishap.

All of the Tallulah Gorge filming took place directly above an intimidating sixty-foot falls. A single safety line spanned the river no more than ten feet from the brink, while Claude, Payson and I took turns standing by in a canoe in the pool below, just in case anyone washed over the drop. Amazingly, no one ever did, although at one point Claude had Burt Reynolds and two crew members — would-be rescuers who had succumbed to the current — clinging to the end of his throw line. With the water-borne trio pulling him along the shore, he was finally able to snub the rope around a tree, arresting the progress of the group just above the falls.

Jerry the Fish, always in his wetsuit, worked his way back and forth on the line, snatching each actor from the swift current at the critical moment. On the last take of the day, when Cox injured his shoulder, it took two additional crew members to get him safely ashore.

Working in the shadow of the principals was a good learning experience and a lot of fun. Burt Reynolds was relatively unknown at the time, fresh from his first "exposure" as *Cosmopolitan's* centerfold. He had a quick wit and plenty of self-confidence. Already an accomplished actor of considerable reputation, Jon Voight was also a caring person with class. Ronny Cox was down to earth and a pleasure to listen to with guitar and song.

Ned Beatty was my favorite. Most of the cast and crew had gone to Underground Atlanta to party one weekend. The bus returning to Clayton left early Monday morning and Beatty, with two others, missed it. When Boorman learned that he was absent, he asked if I would fill in for Ned in a non-canoeing scene. It was simple enough — one of the early film scenes — following Reynolds and Voight in their jeep, and driving the station wagon with Ronny Cox as we "head for the river," negotiating the hairpin turns above Betty's Creek. When Beatty arrived that afternoon, he took time to track me down and personally thank me for filling in. His sincerity touched my heart and made a lasting impression.

~

When the filming of *Deliverance* began in May, James Dickey's son Chris was hired as a stand-in. He was nineteen at the time and the spectacle of seeing his father's novel come to life in the mountains of North Georgia had a profound effect on his relationship with his father. Nearly thirty years later, he wrote *Summer of Deliverance*, a poignant and, at times, brutally honest memoir of the most defining years of his life.

Chris had been called to the set the day the homosexual rape scene was to be filmed. He was to "stand in" for Beatty at all the critical marks — climbing the leafy bank, bending over the log — so that the camera crew could focus precisely, prior to the actual shooting. The somber, sickening mood of the day followed him and he felt the film taking a twisted turn that threatened to overshadow all else. In *Summer of Deliverance* he describes his thoughts, and a conversation with his father:

> *"...I didn't think my father understood what had happened that day filming by the river. In the book you can read the rape scene and know it happened, but you get around it and go on, and get*

other things out of the novel. In the movie — it was becoming what the movie was about, it was the thing everybody was going to remember. 'Squeal like a pig!' Not Lewis's survivalism, not the climb up the cliff, not Ed's conquest of his own fear. It was all going to be about butt-fucking.

'You're wrong, son,' my father said."

Ultimately, I think they were both correct. The scene with Bobby and the perverted mountain man broke new ground for mainstream films and usually is the first image that comes to mind when *Deliverance* is mentioned. However, the feel of wilderness and the lure of river running also emerged in a big way.

Indeed. At times, the rush to conquer the "*Deliverance* River" seemed totally out of control. Nineteen people drowned on the Chattooga in the three years following the filming and more would follow. There were exceptions, but the usual scenario saw young people who had floated the relatively benign Chattahoochee in Atlanta in two discount store rafts, one filled with people and the other with a couple of coolers of beer, bringing the same equipment to the Chattooga. It just didn't work.

A similar scenario was being repeated on river after river across the country, and soon a new term for the driving force behind these ill-prepared adventure seekers had been coined — the "*Deliverance* Syndrome." The original phrase has been attributed to Claude Terry, but it spread so rapidly in those early years — both among river guides and in the mainstream press — that it is difficult to pinpoint its origin. Even *Esquire* Magazine picked up on the term, as Jerry Bledsoe wrote an incisive and sobering feature article that probed the reasons behind the alarming rise in river-running deaths that followed the release of *Deliverance*.

Deliverance premiered in New York in August of 1972, a year after the filming had been completed, and was shown in Los Angeles at almost the same time. My brother John phoned from California. "I just saw it and it's a thriller. People are lining up outside theaters here. I think it may be a good one."

We had to wait another agonizing week for *Deliverance* to reach Atlanta. It opened the Atlanta International Film Festival on August 11 and, of course, we were there. So were Jimmy and Rosalyn Carter, James Dickey and Burt Reynolds. By the time the Film Festival was over, *Deliverance* had taken the top award, the Golden Phoenix, over twenty-nine competing films. The cast and crew cleaned up, also — John Boorman, best director; Jon Voight, best actor; Ned Beatty, best supporting actor; and Tom Priestley, best editor.

In his September 21 *Atlanta Journal* theater review, Editor Terry Kay predicted that *Deliverance* would be seen by a lot of people, make money in the process, be considered one of the finer technical and artistic efforts of 1972, and give a tremendous boost to the careers of Reynolds, Voight, Beatty, Boorman and Dickey. He was correct on all counts.

The film was soon in theaters across the country. My mother called from Maryland. "You know, Doug, I've been telling friends at church for a year that you're in *Deliverance*. But I just saw it last night, and I don't think I'll tell anybody else!"

∿

A few years later (1975), our friend and fellow paddler, Mark Warren, wrote a hilarious play titled *Son of Deliverance*[37], as a Georgia Canoeing Association fund raiser[38] for the defense of river navigation rights. The Nacoochee section of the Chattahoochee River and the Turner's Corner

[37] The all-star cast of this one-night stand included:
The mountain boys:
   Clem "the brain": Claude Terry
   Bubba "the jock": Mark Warren
   G.W. "stupider than a can of tomatoes": Doug Woodward
Highly pissed land owner:
   Carlton Shuford
"How're y'all" rafters:
   Margaret Tucker and Tom Moye
Raft race "How'd you boys find such authentic costumes?" official:
   John Mathieu
The bikini-clad "uh, almost clad" Miss Raft Race:
   Falma Moye
Used car "how much ya got?" salesman:
   Clyde Woolsey
Woman "I warn you, I've got gas!" motorist:
   Margaret Tucker
Urban "one of the Grimey Brothers" slob:
   John Mathieu
Log flume "you'd better believe it's safe!" attendant:
   Miller Templeton
Prowling Atlanta rapist:
   Barbara Walmsley
Secretary "Ms. Wall of Ice" to Mr. Flags:
   Tracy Chapple
Mr. Flags "So tight you couldn't drive a ten penny nail up his butt with a six pound hammer":
   Ross Wilson
Gas station "It's only the biggest frikin' fun park in the State" attendants:
   Jack Weems and John Mathieu
Director:
   Betty Terry
Technical Director:
   Tom Lines
Lighting:
   Butch Terry, Mike Terry, Skip Tucker
Props and costumes:
   Melanie Dixon
Written and Adapted to the Stage by Mark Warren

[38] It seemed that most of the GCA had turned out for the theater performance and by the time the receipts were tallied, the River Rights Defense Fund stood at $2,987.90. Skip Tucker at Green, Buckley, DeRieux & Jones was engaged as counsel for the Club's case.

to Grinnel Bridge section of the Chestatee River had just been closed to canoeing and kayaking by the private landowners along those rivers.

Mark's story was a reversal of Dickey's tale, as three mountain boys make an epic journey down the Chattahoochee River from the mountains to the big city for one last ride on the Six Flags log flume before it is inundated by the new West Point Reservoir. Hurriedly escaping from an irate landowner with their raft-load of moonshine, they find themselves in the midst of the annual Chattahoochee Raft Race where they ultimately win the prize for "most original costumes."

After being wowed by the voluptuous Miss Raft Race, they at last wander bewildered into Atlanta, where they are soon swindled by a fast-talking used car salesman and threatened by a nervous lady wielding a tear gas pen. At Six Flags, they're intimidated by the log flume attendant and insulted by Mr. Flags. One of them drowns in the log flume and as the battered survivors scramble to escape, they are robbed and raped by an Atlanta streetwalker.

As Mark described the play in the benefit invitation, "The journey becomes a nightmare of adventure that would wilt Burt Reynold's cigar. In this performance, you'll see some of the top names in Georgia canoeing ruined — the giants of whitewater degraded to a ship of fools." ... And so our own journey down the river of *Deliverance* continued.

~

Our screen time could be measured in seconds, but the effect that the film had on our lives was far-reaching. That same summer, Claude and I started Southeastern Expeditions, running folks by raft down the Chattooga while still hanging onto our jobs in Atlanta. Payson and his family took an even bigger leap as they broke all Atlanta ties and threw themselves into transforming the old Tote-N-Tarry Motel in Wesser, North Carolina into one of the premier whitewater communities in the world, the Nantahala Outdoor Center.

I had taken 35-mm slides and my own 8-mm movies during the time that we were working on the *Deliverance* set. When I was busy with a Warner Brothers scene, either Claude or Payson would pick up the movie camera and shoot, since two, never three, of us were called for any given sequence. We ended up with some interesting footage. When our time on the river came to a close, I took the slides and movies back to Atlanta and edited them into a show.

Both the Georgia Canoeing Association and our whitewater Explorer Scout Post were eager to see what had been going on up on the Chattooga, so they were the first to see what I had put together. Word of mouth took over from there. The Atlanta Ski Club called for a showing. The Sierra Club, both in Atlanta and Athens. There were groups that

I had never heard of that wanted to see the show. The same thing was happening to Claude, first at Emory and the University of Georgia, then almost anywhere.

The Birmingham Sierra Club wanted to see the *Deliverance* show. Carol Retan called to tell me that they would pay for my airline ticket, feed me and put me up overnight. "I'm not anybody that special, Carol," I tried to tell her. "Just a river bum that happened to be in the right place at the right time." But I went.

The Warner Brothers crew catches a few thrills of their own as their raft pounds through the Chattooga's Jawbone Rapid.

In Baltimore, I visited my long-time friends Pat and Jim Holechek[39] and shared the experience with them. A few weeks later, Jim sent me a copy of the *Baltimore Sun*, containing my photo and the article he had written from my description of the *Deliverance* filming.

So the myth took on a life of its own. A dozen years after the filming, my oldest son David, now on the cutting edge of whitewater play-boating, was graduating from Rabun Gap Nacoochee School in the mountains of north Georgia. School staff wanted to see "The Making of Deliverance," as my film had come to be known, and so itwas shown to the full assembly of high school students.

---

[39] Jim Holechek, having spent a lifetime writing articles and authoring books, is also a competent paddler. He canoed the length of the Susquehanna, from its New York headwaters to the Chesapeake Bay as a young man, then repeated the trip in 1971 with his son Mark, a teenager at the time. He has a standing challenge with his five grandchildren to duplicate the voyage, a challenge which none has yet accepted. He and his lovely wife, Pat, have been "family" to me for forty years.

I had taught kayaking clinics for two successive years to David's classmates at the school and what I saw there brought a chuckle. When Warner Brothers left Rabun County, they had donated to the school the six original Grumman canoes used in the filming — or what was left of them. With hammers, drills and come-alongs, rivets and pieces of aluminum sheet, Des Oliver and his shop students had somehow restored the twisted and dented hulks to serviceable condition.

A decade later, with a move to the North Carolina mountains, I saw a chance to leave behind some of the *Deliverance* intensity that had followed me for so many years. Perhaps I could be defined in a more balanced way — by the house I might build, the words I might write, and an appreciation of the value of every person I might come to know.

This was not an active quest for change. It was more passive. My four younger children never came to hear of my part in *Deliverance* — from me, at least — until the oldest entered her teens.

Later, my sister's daughter, Emily, emailed her mother from college, "Hey, I'm writing papers on the book *Deliverance*, and we also just watched the movie in class. The movie was filmed on the Chattooga River in Georgia. Did Uncle Doug ever raft it? Just curious."

I smiled to myself when I read that forwarded email. Time and distance enough, I thought. Then I filled her in with a bit of material for her class.

More than thirty years have passed since Boorman and his crew brought Dickey's novel to life on the screen. For me, the old intensity is gone and now it's just fun to get into it once in a while when someone happens to mention *Deliverance*. But sometimes I look back over all those years — how I became linked to the legends of the film and the river, the whitewater rafting business that Claude and I founded, the evenings spent behind the projector as folks clamored for candid glimpses of Reynolds and Voight — and think to myself, "if not for James Dickey..."

Sharing The Myth

"These days won't come again, you know."

It was Claude Terry, the philosopher, speaking. And I knew what he meant. We were in our late thirties, our river skills had been honed to a sharp edge, and we had the years of experience to go with them. Almost every weekend we were cruising or racing on rivers from Alabama to Pennsylvania with fifteen or twenty enthusiastic young men and women. Sunlight danced on our waves.

I also knew that Claude's words meant something more. We had often discussed it while waiting for the Deliverance cameras to roll. There was a need, an obligation and an opportunity, all tied to the Chattooga. The need arose from the growing interest in this river and the lack of experience of many who would come to raft it. There was an implied obligation on the part of those of us who knew the river well to help those who needed and desired it. The opportunity was obvious — a rafting business where none had previously existed.

We knew, as well, that Payson, with help from long-time friend and fellow paddler Horace Holden, was already poised to make the leap from Atlanta to the mountains of North Carolina. Payson's wife, Aurelia, could hardly contain her enthusiasm. We had heard her describe her vision of how they might entertain a small group of guests on the Nantahala River.

The raft group, guided by Payson of course, would stop for lunch about half way down the river. Aurelia and her two teenage girls (Cathy and Frances) would step from the trees, long dresses swirling, and spread a tablecloth on the grass before the famished paddlers. From their baskets would come all manner of mouth-watering delicacies, prepared that morning by the lovely women who would serve them. Ah, the beauty of those early dreams.

"We need to do it," I replied, as I envisioned our own rafting operations on the Chattooga.

Some of the groundwork had already been laid. When Warner Brothers purchased the rafts for getting the crew into the Chattooga and out again, Lewis King, at our request, had made a buy-back clause part of the written agreement. Once the filming was finished, Property Manager Syd Greenwood released the rafts to Claude and me for about one-third of the initial cost. That was a start.

Following the release of the film **Deliverance** in 1972, would-be river runners flocked to the Chattooga. Many were inexperienced and woefully unprepared for the challenge of Class IV rapids. By the time three years had passed, nineteen persons had died trying to emulate the **Deliverance** characters.

To get the feel of taking groups down the Chattooga, we even ran a couple of freebie trips on Section IV late that summer (1971) for our Explorer Scouts and some Emory University students. The operation worked, but the Chattooga was definitely not the Nantahala. With changes in water level, each run would be different from the one before, requiring decisions from the head guide as to how a given rapid would be run, or even if it should be run.

Another difference is access. The Nantahala is paralleled by U.S. Highway 19, put-ins and take-outs convenient, whereas Section IV of the Chattooga is remote, and the cramped take-out, two and a half miles down Lake Tugaloo could hardly be termed convenient.

But while Payson and his family were consumed with transforming the motel, restaurant, gas station and old stone dwelling at Wesser, North Carolina into a rafting business, Claude and I had no local base of operation as yet. With our equipment in tow, we were making the long drive from Atlanta each weekend that a trip was scheduled.

Business looked promising after several small trips that next spring. Claude and I had already ordered more rafts. One Sunday night, we were heading home after an exhausting but satisfying weekend on the river. A hundred times or more in the past, we had driven by the Whispering Pines Music Park. Located on U.S. Highway 76, a mile from the Chattooga, it had stood derelict for years.

Claude suddenly braked to a stop.

"Do I see what I think I see?" he said, excitement creeping into his voice. I followed his gaze to where a small card was tacked to the boards at the back of the stage, a hundred feet from the road. We were both out of the van in a flash, sprinting through the weeds.

"It is!" I cried in delight.

Claude's hand reached out and pulled the *For Sale* sign from the wall. "We'd better take this with us," he smiled, not wanting someone else to beat us to the land. The phone number was local.

"But it's Sunday. We shouldn't call tonight — it might set them against us." Claude had grown up in the mountains, his mother a lay minister in the local church. He would be the first to think of such things.

We called the next morning and yes, the Whitaker family would meet with us that evening. We left work early and made the long drive north again through Alto, Cornelia, Demorest and the other small north Georgia towns — GA 365 did not exist in those days — and found the Whitaker home on U.S. 76 about a mile from Whispering Pines.

Now, just who were we? This was important to them.

Well, we lived in Atlanta. A minus.

We worked with Scouts. A plus.

We knew and loved the Chattooga. A maybe.

"That's a good-looking Blue Tick you've got out there."

Claude had seen the hunting hound as we came to the door. A smile flickered for an instant on Allen Whitaker's impassive face. The ice of cautious formality was beginning to thaw and Claude seized the moment to establish his mountain roots. Whitaker responded by recalling folks that had performed at Whispering Pines and how much that place meant to them. But, hard as it might be, the time had come to sell.

"How much land do you have over there?"

"'bout fifteen, twenty acres, I reckon."

"All the open land around and behind the music pavilion?"

"Lot's more. They's woods, too. 'Specially all up that hill from the branch."

"Your price seems fair." Claude's eyes met mine as I nodded imperceptibly. "We'd like to buy it, Mr. Whitaker."

"Now you boys think on it. Walk the lines. You can tell 'em right off 'cause the Government land runs with it and they's splashed red paint all on them line trees."

"We'll do that, Mr. Whitaker. But we'd like to buy your land. Tonight."

Claude pulled a roll of bills from his pocket and counted out two hundred dollars in twenties. The cash would mean the most to the Whitakers. I wrote a check for the same amount and handed it to Whitaker. The check would be important for our records.

"You fellows wantin' a receipt?" Whitaker asked.

"No need," Claude replied. "Your word is better than a piece of paper."

Whispering Pines Music Park, 1972, just before it became the base for Southeastern Expeditions' Chattooga River rafting operations

We returned on Saturday to explore the property, line up a surveyor, and set a closing date. Serendipity perhaps. But we had, indeed, found our ideal base of operation.

At about that same time, we came to an agreement on a company name. We chose Southeastern Expeditions (SEE), so that our name would not limit us to a single river. The next year (1973) we would formally incorporate. Claude designed a T-shirt with our name on the front and his drawing of a raft running a rapid on the back.

As we purchased more equipment and gradually began to convert the music park into a rafting camp, other needs became apparent.

Transportation was a big one. We had been running private vehicle shuttles (including our guests' cars!) down the tortuous road to the cramped lake take-out, squeezing them into almost non-existent parking spots.

"We've got to have a school bus." Claude agreed and so I went looking. There was so much junk, but I finally found a '58 Ford that seemed to run reasonably well, for five hundred dollars. The owner, who rode with me on the test drive, seemed tense, as if waiting for something on the vehicle to fall apart. Nothing did. At least on that day.

We used the bus almost every weekend that summer. One Saturday found me working at the base camp while Claude did the river trip. He was late coming off the river and it was after dark by the time he burst through the door.

"Woodward, you son-of-a-bitch, where do you turn on the headlights on that piece of shit you bought? I just had to run these folks all the way back in the dark!"

"Oh." We hadn't needed the lights before. "There are two wires under the dash, where the switch used to be. You have to twist them together to get the headlights to come on. Sorry."

I had never seen Claude so angry, but I could forgive the blast I had endured when I thought of the four miles he had just driven on U.S. Highway 76 in the dark.

Then it was my turn to be whooped up on by the bus. In spades. I was driving, an empty bus fortunately, to the take-out where I would be followed shortly by one of our guides who would shuttle me back. Not far past the apple packing shed, the road turned to red clay, with almost continuous washboards.

Half a mile into this stretch, there was a disturbing "clunk," mixed with other unwelcome noises, and the rear of the bus vaulted into the air, landing four feet to the side of the track it had been on. I fought for control, as the steering wheel seemed to have a mind of its own, and finally brought the bus to a stop just before dropping down an embankment. I was skewed at a strange angle, nearly blocking the entire road.

As I climbed down from the bus, I noticed a long furrow had been plowed in the clay behind me. Then I saw what had happened. Unobserved, the large bolts that secure the leaf springs to the body frame had departed. This allowed the right side of the rear axle to move backwards until the drive shaft fell out of the front universal joint. As the forward end of the shaft hit the road, the bus performed its pole vault trick.

Unbelievably, the spline at the end of the shaft had not been damaged and, with the help of my shuttle guide, I was able to reattach it to the U-joint. There were enough odd parts and baling wire in the bus to cobble up a repair to the rear springs until we were able to find the proper bolts. I drove the Class V take-out road like the proverbial little old lady that day, especially as I returned to base camp with my river guests.

NOC (Aurelia and Payson's Nantahala Outdoor Center) was also running Section IV trips on the Chattooga. They would descend the last torturous mile to the lake in a stake-sided flatbed truck, where they would load their deflated rafts and other river equipment, then pile the guests on top until they could deliver them to their own vehicles. Although we had a friendly rivalry going between SEE and NOC, both would bend over backward to help the other out in a pinch, either with rafting equipment or vehicles.

On one particular day, having just brought my guests down the river and across Lake Tugaloo, I arrived at the take-out to find that our infamous bus had been trashed. Whether through a Deliverance-like attitude toward the rafting companies, or simply a bad day of fishing, someone had fired seven bullets into the front of the bus at point-blank range. It was dead. Without hesitation NOC stepped in to haul our guests back to the SEE base camp. Later I dug a slug out of one of the bus's front tires and delivered it to Rabun County Sheriff Marley Cannon, where it was dutifully labeled and filed without comment.

That was by no means the most serious incident to occur. There was a third company operating guided trips on the Chattooga, albeit over a somewhat different section of the river. Wildwater Limited, started by Jim and Jeanette Greiner of Danville, Virginia, had located their operations in the Old Schoolhouse at Long Creek, South Carolina. They felt the risk of mishap was too great for them to offer Section IV trips, so they chose Fall Creek on Section III as their put-in, taking out at the top of Woodall Shoals on Section IV.

In those days, river guides with Chattooga experience were in short supply. The majority came from our Explorer Scout Post or the Georgia Canoeing Association. Three of our Scouts, Steve Kohler, Johnny Stephenson and Steve Reimer, were employed by Wildwater that summer.

On the afternoon of July 30, Reimer and two other guides were nearing the end of their trip with a party of guests from Atlanta when a local group of about a dozen men and one woman in inner tubes started a run of Woodall Shoals. According to witnesses, the local group had been drinking moonshine and the woman fell out of her tube as she started down the rapid.[40]

Steve Reimer came to her aid, then started to criticize the group for drinking on the river and running without safety gear. They immediately began pelting him with rocks until he withdrew out of range. The group then turned on a second guide, pushing him down in the water and repeatedly banging his head on the rocks. He was later taken to the hospital in Clayton with a concussion. As some folks tried to defuse the situation, another tuber took a swing at Mrs. McClung, one of the rafting guests, breaking a bone in her face and sending her sprawling five feet to the rocks below.

At this point, there was a tense standoff as some of the rafters raised paddles, ready to use them as weapons, and two of the tubers had knives in hand. Tempers subsided only when Reimer returned quickly to offer an apology to the local group. Georgia Governor Jimmy Carter asked for reports on the incident to come to his office as Mrs. McClung considered prosecution of the attackers, who had been identified at the scene.

Eleven days later, Claude and Betty, Payson and Aurelia, and Roberta and I sat in Symphony Hall of the Atlanta Memorial Arts Center, watching the dignitaries file in for the Atlanta premier of *Deliverance*. Many of the river guides were there too. Claude leaned over and nudged me.

"Do you see who's sitting over there?"

"Sure," I replied, "The Carters and the Dickeys."

"No, not there. Look about ten rows back. It's two of the guys who attacked the Wildwater group."

"Are you sure? How do you know that for certain?"

"Steve Reimer. He saw them come in and slipped over to tell me."

"Well, if that doesn't beat all. I guess they wanted to check out the movie to see how they should have done things back on the river!"

We later learned that tickets to the Atlanta premier had been freely given out for the asking in the Clayton area while those of us in Atlanta had had to buy our own.

～

That summer we had the first Southeastern Expedition brochures printed by Claude Grizzard, an Atlanta printer who was a skilled open canoeist and long-time friend. They really gave our outfit a professional look, except…the name of the company read Southeastern Exhibitions! Not only was the error in the main heading, but also appeared again in the disclaimer. "Due to the hazardous nature of these exhibitions, we

[40] Tubing on any section of the Chattooga has been prohibited since the USDA Forest Service began regulation of the river in 1974. Woodall Shoals, where several drownings have occurred, is considered one of the more dangerous rapids on Section IV, both because of its "keeper hole" in the first drop and its easy accessibility to those on foot.

ask..." Grizzard was apologetic, but we thought the whole affair hilarious and used the brochures anyway.

Whether Freudian slip or genuine error, there might have been more than a grain of truth in our exhibitionist reputation. One Saturday, in the dark of the late summer moon, my six guides on duty for the weekend and I decided to liven things up and run a naked nighttime raft trip (guides only) from Highway 76 to Woodall Shoals. I would accompany them by kayak.

Some of our Sunday river guests were enjoying time around the campfire before heading for the sack. I walked over wearing only my spray skirt to tell them what we were doing and that we'd be back before midnight.

One gal said, "Don't give us that line. I know you're wearing shorts."

There were peals of laughter from the group as I walked away and they saw I was for real.

Under the highway bridge, we realized just what a challenge this escapade was going to be. Not only was the moon in its new phase, but the thick cloud cover kept all starlight from illuminating any back curls of whitewater. Navigation would be totally by sound. Nude we were, but at this point we all donned our PFD's.

True, this wasn't the most difficult part of the river, but it did contain Screaming Left Turn and Rock Jumble, as well as a host of little drops and chutes that weren't even noticed by a paddler in daylight. River level was a benign 1.4 feet.

Suffice it to say that the trip was smooth — no one came off of the raft (it was turned bottom up for some reason unknown to me) and I stayed upright in my kayak. Even now, I can recall the intensity of navigating by sound and memory, running the footage in my brain forward and backward in the dark, trying to identify the water and rocks that were creating each new river voice.

When we reached Woodall, we were not yet home free. First, there was the climb, with raft, kayak, and paddles down the ledges on the South Carolina shore, stumbling around in inky blackness until my old pickup truck was located. Then came the biggest challenge of all — driving the eight miles back to camp on a Saturday night, four of them on a U.S. highway, six nude river rats standing in the back of the truck, without being stopped by a state trooper. Well, we made it, but the couple of cars that did overtake us that night surely went home with a story to tell!

Nightlife in Rabun County revolved around the Clayton Dairy Queen and the Tiger Drive-in Theater.[41] The Tiger showed grade B films that

41 The Tiger Drive-In Theater, closed for many years, reopened to a new life in 2003. It once again is popular, drawing patrons not only from north Georgia, but South and North Carolina as well. It now shows first-run features.

were so bad they were actually good entertainment. As we waited all that summer for *Deliverance* to appear, we couldn't help but wonder if it would be the same kind of movie and we'd end up laughing and watching it at the Tiger some night.

Our rafting business was growing, but always operating on the edge those first couple of years. If we had a large trip, we might borrow a raft from NOC or Wildwater, then do the same for them when the need arose. We were always counting paddles and PFD's, sometimes calling in panic Thursday night for more to be purchased and brought up from Atlanta.

Keeping our vehicles running was a continuous challenge. Not able to afford a full-time mechanic, we did the best we could on our own. When the task was beyond us, it was off to John Canup's place deep in the woods near Walhalla, South Carolina. Warner Brothers had missed this one during the *Deliverance* filming. They wouldn't have had to add anything to the set.

If you visualize a spider's lair that has existed for a very long time, the hollow shells of sucked out insects littering the ground beneath it, that is the way you might feel as you approach the Canup home. You would thread your way in among the empty hulks of ancient automobiles, axles, seats, tires, gas cans and wheels until at last you arrived at the front porch of a habitable house. It was there, however, that all resemblance to *Deliverance* ended.

Whatever your vehicle problem, Canup could fix it. Maybe in the barn. Maybe beside the hog pen. Certainly not on a lift. And don't expect factory parts. The methods were definitely unconventional, but the result was dependable. And if you came by at dinnertime, you were not going to leave without being fed. It would be an insult to the family. And, as you might guess with the obviously low overhead, Canup's rates were quite reasonable.

Our raft trips that first summer were sometimes on the far side of the moon, too. We were limited only by our equipment — what we owned and what we could borrow. One such excursion included some sixty guests, ten rafts, and guides for only half of them. It was a rather overbearing procession to put on Section IV, the lead raft often out of sight of the sweep. Two of us in kayaks were worked hard that day. Helen Johnston would station herself at the top of a rapid to instruct the unguided folks while I would pick a strategic spot farther down to setup safety.

At Woodall Shoals, Seven Foot Falls and the Five Falls, we slowed down for extensive instruction and additional safety precautions, of course. There were no self-bailing rafts in those years and swamping was often a problem, despite frequent stops to dump water. On this trip, our old eighteen-foot assault raft completely filled and stuck fast on the approach to Devil's Chute (Entrance Rapid). It took us half an hour to free it and get it river-worthy. The inflatable floor had developed a leak and taken on a couple of hundred pounds of water. We retired the beast at the end of that season.

An early Southeastern Expeditions commercial raft trip on Section IV of the Chattooga. Jeanine Cheek guides from the stern.

We were by no means unaware of the ecological impact that large numbers of people could have on the river. Lunch spots, despite scrupulous clean-up, would begin to look well trodden. Vegetation fringes would be pushed back. There were other factors as well. Small private boating groups would be outraged if there were no end to the string of rafts passing by. Safety of guests could easily be compromised if numbers were too great. We had often talked about this among ourselves and already begun to move in the direction of reasonable, uniform trip ceilings before the Forest Service stepped in with their regulations.

Nationally, the year 1972 saw a surfacing of safety awareness throughout the paddling community. With Olympic whitewater slalom being seen on national television, and the series of drownings that began to follow the release of Deliverance, the wearing of PFD's had at last gained universal acceptance. The Safety Code of the American White

Water Affiliation had been revised and updated so as to better prepare paddlers for the hazards they might encounter on swift water.

Charlie Walbridge, an experienced Pennsylvania paddler, noted the disturbing rise in fatalities among competent boaters. Spurred by the drowning of Gene Bernardin, a C-2 competitor at the Icebreaker Slalom on Ouleout Creek in New York State where Charlie was also competing, Charlie wrote an extensive analysis of the accident for a subsequent issue of the AWA Journal. He would continue in that vein, not only as our sport's national safety voice, but as a designer and manufacturer of innovative safety equipment for whitewater paddlers.

Claude and I knew we were treading thin ice any time that we let a raft go with us unguided. This was sharply driven home one day when we had moved a trip to Section III because of high water. We were a guide short and asked if there were those who didn't mind paddling on their own with direction from us in the critical spots. There was no shortage of raised hands.

With the higher water, our group moved right along and we were approaching the strange slanting rock garden where Drew's body is found in *Deliverance*. I was running kayak sweep for the trip, twenty yards behind the unguided raft, pleased to see how well they were handling the river.

Ahead of them, a rock in river center had collected several trees and I saw the paddlers on the left side begin to draw to avoid the spot. Good, I thought, when suddenly I noticed that the paddlers on the opposite side had started to draw *right*.

I was already digging hard when their raft hit the mess and flipped. Quickly catching the downstream eddy, I leaped onto the rock. Two paddles floated on the surface, but not one head was in sight! The raft was solidly pasted against the strainer, one tube almost submerged in the force of the current. My river knife was out in a flash, cutting the raft's outside safety line, which had snagged on a branch, holding it in place. Throwing my weight against the upper tube, the raft reluctantly became horizontal once more, spinning to the side.

"Thank God," exclaimed a shaken woman as she emerged from the water. All four had been pinned against the logs by the raft and the force of the current, some able to breathe, some not. It still remains one the strangest entrapments I have ever seen.

I was shaken, too. "What if I had not been running a proper sweep and had passed them for a bit? What if I had not had a knife on my PFD? What if...?" It was the last time we would run an unguided raft on a commercial river trip.

Other incidents served as warnings and became part of our promotional literature and pre-trip briefings. There was the 300-pound gentleman who wrenched his knee at Sockemdog and had to be carried from the lake to a van by another guide and myself. When we would trip and fall, he would scream, and since he fell on us, we would scream!

"We ask that all persons joining us on the river be in reasonable physical condition..."

And there was the diabetic guest who had changed his insulin dose and skipped breakfast in a rush the morning of a Section III trip. A mile down the river he collapsed in his raft. Fortunately, there was a friend with him who knew those details, and I had had some previous treatment experience with one of my Maryland Scouts. Determining that it was insulin shock and not diabetic coma, we got enough sugar into him from the lunch Cool-Aide powder to bring him back to a semi-conscious state.

With three volunteer guests, we laid him in the bottom of a raft and split for the take-out. It was probably a record for a raft run of Section III, and certainly a thrill for the guests who got to run Bull Sluice blind! By that time, our horizontal passenger, probably having been prodded by rocks through the raft floor, was completely conscious and insisting that a hospital visit was unnecessary. I took him anyway.

"Please inform your guide at this time if anyone here has a medical condition or is carrying medication of which we should be aware. We will be glad to place it in..."

In those early years, the guests were expected to paddle their rafts two and one-half miles down Lake Tugaloo, from the spot where the river quietly gives up its life at Opossum Creek, to the tiny take-out on the steep South Carolina lake shore. The task took about an hour, added to the remote feel of the river, and was a way to wind down from the adrenaline rush of the Five Falls. If the day were hot, our shuttle driver would have a chilled watermelon sliced and waiting at the take-out. Now a chugging motorboat meets the rafts as they exit the last rapid. One more amenity for the tired muscles of the guest, but also a piece of wild experience lost.

I don't know whether Aurelia ever tried out her riverside picnic vision, but I do know that her energy, as much as Payson's, took NOC in many directions never even imagined. Today, Relia's Garden Restaurant graces the hilltop behind the Stone House, guests wending their way up the entrance pathway between beds of herbs, greens and other vegetables that they might be enjoying at their dinner table half an hour later.

NOC's story is worthy of a book in itself, but suffice it to say here that they stand head and shoulders above all others in the whitewater business. With the financial help of Horace Holden, Sr. in 1972, and a handful of staff — mostly the Kennedy family — NOC has grown in size and stature to an organization that is known worldwide. And the driving force behind the vision has been the energy and enthusiasm of Payson and Aurelia, who have created in NOC a community and business that had no model or predecessor to emulate. The Nantahala Outdoor Center filled the void and became that leader.

Payson and Aurelia Kennedy, with daughter, Cathy, on a 1971 Explorer Post rock climbing trip to Alabama's Little River Canyon the year before they founded the Nantahala Outdoor Center.

In 1973, the Forest Service, having watched with concern the rapidly expanding river activity, began to take a keen interest in the Chattooga and called a meeting of all interested parties. They were alarmed by the rising death toll as well as myriad close calls by uninformed and unprepared river adventurers. We first met in March in Gainesville, Georgia at the offices of the Chattahoochee National Forest. By the May meeting, it had been determined that regulation of the Chattooga would fall to the Sumter National Forest Supervisor since most of the river access came from the South Carolina side of the river.

I had participated in a similar meeting in Pennsylvania in December of 1969, when over a hundred individuals representing thirty interested groups had braved a heavy snowstorm to voice their views on regulation of the Youghiogheny River. That meeting was hosted jointly by the Pennsylvania Department of Environmental Resources and Ralph McCarty, a local outfitter. It would be useful, I thought, to give my friend Ralph a call, as well as Clayton Kritschgau, Planning Coordinator for Pennsylvania's parks. I had my original notes from that meeting, but I wanted to find out what their experience had been since the rules had been introduced at the Yough.

As might be expected, there were ideas that had worked well, and a few which had not. Visitor days on the Yough had skyrocketed from 165,000 when we met in 1969 to 829,000 during the 1972 season. Other valuable information had also been sent, but preventing excessive use of the Chattooga and creating a safe river experience were the primary thoughts in all of our minds.

In this context of use and safety, we, as outfitters, did not object to the limits put on the size and frequency of our trips. We could work happily within the rules, even though we knew that some of our trips the previous summer would not have been acceptable. And the Forest Service realized the role that commercial outfitters with trained staff could play in providing a safe river experience.

Private groups would also be limited in size. Tubing would be prohibited and PFD's required. Access points would be improved and safety education promoted through warning signs at all put-in points. By September of 1974, camping had been prohibited at Burrel's Ford, Earl's Ford and U.S. Highway 76, three stinking, eroded, and over-used areas often strewn with disposable diapers, garbage and human feces. The health of the air, water and adjacent forest began to improve. In May of 1975, registration of all private trips became mandatory, primarily to keep track of river traffic, since no usage fee was involved. Construction of parking and toilet facilities was started in 1978. Most of the rules formulated at those two early meetings[42] remain in effect today.

Based largely on the commercial experience at the Youghiogheny River, additional rules were developed for the three Chattooga outfitters. We were required to submit bids to the Forest Service for the privilege of operating on the river. Although the bidding process is open to anyone,

---

[42] It is worth noting here the individuals who contributed their knowledge, ideas and time to help keep the Chattooga experience what it is today. Those who came together in 1973 were: Clemson University: Gordon Howard, Stuart Johnson; East Tennessee Whitewater Club: Ed Brockelbank; Explorer Post 49: Steve Kohler, John Stephenson; Georgia Canoeing Association: Tom Hamby, Tom Lines, Cleve Tedford; Georgia Department of Natural Resources: Ken Kohler; Georgia Game & Fish Commission: Robert Carter, Lamar Robinson; Nantahala Outdoor Center: Aurelia Kennedy, Payson Kennedy; Sierra Club (Greenville, SC): Ann Snyder, Ted Snyder, Kirk Stone, Randolph Stone; Southeastern Expeditions: Claude Terry, Mike Terry, Doug Woodward; U.S. Bureau of Outdoor Recreation: Margaret Tucker; U.S. Forest Service: Jim Barrett (Walhalla), Max Gates (Clayton), Robert Harper (Gainesville), Vaughn Hofeldt (Gainesville), John Ore (Columbia), Earl "Preach" Parsons (Clayton), Dave Rosdahl (Columbia), Jack Wolfe (Atlanta); Wildwater: Kitty Culp, Jim Culp, Jeanette Greiner, Jim Greiner, Rory Hodge, Scott Hubbard, Steve Reimer; Unaffiliated: Holmes Marchman (Atlanta). At the May meeting, Dot Jackson of the Charlotte Observer was on hand to report the proceedings.

The following March (1974), we met once more with the Forest Service to consider the alternatives which had been developed for a Chattooga Wild & Scenic Management Plan. Tom Hamby, Scott Price, Cleve Tedford, Claude Terry and I all made recommendations at that time.

so many factors such as experience on, and knowledge of, the Chattooga are considered, that it would be highly unusual for one of the present outfitters to be displaced unless they were in gross violation of Forest Service rules. I prepared the original bid for Southeastern and at that time the Forest Service wanted to permit only two operators. We stood fast, maintaining that the agency had already assured a quality experience by limiting our trip size, and that a single commercial trip passing a point one time in the day was less disruptive to the wilderness experience than random private rafts, appearing all day long. The Forest Service backed off, keeping three outfitters on the Chattooga.

~

Being on the river was soothing to my spirit, but days at home were tense. The difficult process of divorce had started, and knowing that Roberta and I were separating at my request made it no easier. Cricket was eleven and David nine. One day as I was moving a load of boat-building materials out of the basement, David came down to help. As we finished, he turned toward me, tears running down his cheeks. "Dad, why can't it just be like it used to be?" I couldn't answer. There was a lump in my throat and my own face was wet as I held him close. Cricket kept much of what she felt bottled up inside.

There was a parallel with Southeastern. The early years were difficult, and Claude and I used to joke about which of us would give the other his half for Christmas. "No, no, don't give it to me!" Finally the time arrived and I did sell my half to Claude.

Despite the sadness inside, there came a freedom that I had never felt before. As much as can be, my life was now my own. There was time to reflect and plan, time to make new friends, time to reach out to my kids. Cricket and Dave and I hiked, camped and paddled on weekends. Roberta, to make those days possible, stayed on in Atlanta when she could have gone west to further her medical career.

My friendship with Claude would continue and he never ceased to surprise me. There was the night he called me to ask if I was available that weekend. "We'll be taking Jimmy Carter, with some of his family and friends, down the Chattooga Saturday. Would you paddle one of the canoes?"

Ship of State

Jimmy Carter, I was about to find out, was a person of genuine warmth. Down-to-earth and approachable, he also has a deep caring for places wild and beautiful. When he first came with us to the Chattooga, that river had already been made famous by the movie *Deliverance*. But to the average theatergoer in Philadelphia or Seattle, Georgia's Governor, James Earl Carter, had not even reached the status of "Jimmy who?" Yet the course of the river and the path of the man were about to coincide long enough to produce a feat of unusual daring and skill. Soon Jimmy Carter would become America's best-known paddler.

Bull Sluice is not a rapid to be trifled with. It is here that the Chattooga first gives a preview of what lies in wait on Section IV. The river hurries through boulders toward the steep South Carolina shore, then changes its mind as it becomes Georgia-bound, and with a roar of laughter drops twelve feet to the pool below. Burt Reynolds and the *Deliverance* crew looked this one over and did their filming elsewhere. A year later, an unfortunate and inexperienced rafter was tumbled from his raft here, caught by a boot, and drowned.

To the experienced paddler in a kayak or decked canoe, Bull Sluice is a challenge offering a reasonable probability of success. For the solo canoeist, paddling an undecked boat, a technically perfect run is required to remain upright and unbruised. Tandem crews are wise to put ashore and carry their open canoe around this rapid.

Jimmy Carter is not a man prone to reckless action, nor does he possess the skill of a trained Olympic athlete. On the other hand, few have proved more adept at shaping a long shot to a successful conclusion, be the challenge political or physical. And as our small party of canoeists stood in a tight knot overlooking Bull Sluice, it appeared that this was going to be one of those times.

Carter and Claude Terry, with whom he was canoeing that day, were engaged in serious conversation, inaudible above the roar of Bull Sluice. Most of the canoes had already been portaged around the rapid. Suddenly the Governor turned to me, a question mark tempering the Carter smile.

"Doug, what do *you* think the risk is?"

I must have hesitated for several seconds as my mind raced. Kayak runs of Bull Sluice were commonplace to many of us. But try as I might, I could not recall a successful run by a tandem open canoe in my years of Chattooga paddling. Margaret Tucker and I, both experienced in whitewater canoeing competition, had once given it a good shot. Running right on course, our bow had buried in the second drop, swamping the canoe and catapulting us into the last chute.

"You've probably got a one in a hundred chance of making it," I finally replied.

Carter corrected me. "No, no, that's not what I meant. What's the risk of our being killed or badly hurt?"

I smiled inwardly as I picked up his train of thought — he had already written off the probable dunking and a few bruises as part of the game. "Very small," I replied. "We'll have two strong paddlers stand by with safety ropes at the last two drops, but you'd do well to borrow a helmet from one of the kayakers."

I already knew that Carter had increased his probability of success on several counts. Claude, one of the most skilled and experienced Chattooga River canoeists at that time, would be guiding the canoe from the stern. They would be running a seventeen-foot aluminum canoe, with extra center flotation and a shoe keel, designed to maneuver well in whitewater. And unlike some political figures of the past who have been publicized as participants in the sport, Carter had taken the time to practice and prepare before ever dipping his paddle into the Chattooga.

I picked up my camera and went to check on the rope tossers. The Governor had turned again to Claude, and I heard his optimistic, "Let's do it!" as the pair headed around the bend toward their canoe. I knew they were going to swim.

The constant roar of Bull Sluice dominated the scene, making the rest of us feel very small. A quarter of a mile from the end of our trip and easily accessible from Highway 76, this rapid is made to order for a TV crew or a group of press photographers. But Carter, as we were finding out, was there to run the river.

We were learning to recognize his casual but confident manner. No state troopers had accompanied him to the river that morning, only a few close associates from the Georgia Department of Natural Resources. At the Earl's Ford put-in on the South Carolina shore, a ranger from Sumter National Forest, perhaps with mild surprise, had taken note that Georgia's governor was out canoeing today.

Satisfied that our safety coverage was in good order, I chose my vantage point for shooting. It appeared that I would be the only photographer, and I cursed under my breath at finding only one unexposed frame remaining on my only roll of film. Normally, I could squeeze off four or five shots during a Bull Sluice run. But since we were all paddling tandem in opens, I had tried to finish my film upstream at Keyhole Rapid, figuring that we'd portage Bull Sluice.

I nestled into a comfortable spot in the massive rock on the Georgia side, directly opposite the diagonal ledge where the canoe would face me for a brief moment. Here I could catch the pair still upright, but could abandon my camera and scramble over to assist with rescue at the first throw-rope position should I be needed.

Bull Sluice presents several technical problems to the whitewater paddler. First, the proper route cannot be picked out from your boat at river level. You approach through a wide rock garden, with several immense boulders blocking the view of the actual drops. Even old-timers still scout this one because of the surprises caused by a slight change in water flow.

Second, as the river narrows, its velocity and depth increase. The paddler, straining for a glimpse of the big drops ahead, may tend to ignore the nasty hole and stopper wave that suddenly appear under the boat. This is actually the start of the Bull Sluice descent, and it can send the unwary paddler on a premature and hair-raising swim.

The diagonal ledge is the third and most demanding of the rapid's problems. Normally, it is considered good whitewater practice to keep your boat lined up parallel to the flow in a well-defined current, adjusting as necessary with a strong draw stroke. So much for the general rule — this is Bull Sluice.

At the diagonal ledge, the edge line of the rock is crossed by the current not at a ninety degree, but at about a forty-five degree angle. The paddler who lines up with the flow will find his boat immediately turned broadside, sucked into the base of this small falls, and subsequently rolled in a most undignified manner. To avoid this kind of misadventure, you turn your boat at a right angle to the ledge and drive hard, directly toward the Georgia shore.

The run ends with a final drop of six feet, the main flow being further constricted by "Decapitation Rock" on the left. No problem, if you're exactly where you should be, but the seven-foot wide chute will not let you sneak through if your alignment is sloppy.

We must have all tensed just a bit as "Here they come!" sounded above the water's roar. Perhaps another minute passed as Terry and Carter wove their way through the maze of preliminary chutes and boulders, still hidden from view to those of us crouched by the rapid's edge.

Our eyes were fixed on the entrance drop, framed by dark granite, laurel, and rhododendron. The canoe appeared and cut through the stopper wave with authority, both paddles biting the water together, the mark of an experienced canoe team. No trouble here, but then, none had really been expected.

The real test was but moments away. I raised my camera and framed the canoe as Terry and Carter strained to get into position for the diagonal ledge. Teeth clenched, Terry put everything into a last-second draw stroke. It was just enough. They would come straight off the ledge.

But a current that strong hitting your canoe obliquely from the side is always potential trouble. The boat dipped sharply toward the right, creating a feeling of tightrope balance. Carter started to react with a corrective paddle brace, realized that there was nothing but air beneath him, and grabbed the gunwale in a moment of uncertainty. Then, in the instant that the canoe was half on and half off the ledge, Claude crossed over for a saving brace on the right side.

It was this scene that my camera recorded: the moment of hesitation, the outcome still in doubt — even the smile vanished. But it was not typical.

Then-Governor Jimmy Carter and Claude Terry making a rare tandem open canoe descent of the Chattooga's formidable Bull Sluice.

Now came the moment of truth. The bow of the canoe dropped beneath the surface. Water breaking over his head, Carter reached forward with a strong stroke to maintain momentum. The bow rose. Water poured off the midship flotation. And the canoe still floated high as it slid toward the final drop. They'd made it!

The rest was anticlimactic. Their position was perfect, and though the last drop is steeper than the diagonal ledge, there is less of a tendency for a canoe to bury at the bottom. Three quick strokes and they were clear, turning into the narrow eddy below the chute, Jimmy Carter and Claude Terry grinning together.

Smiles everywhere. The rope tossers relaxed and a mixed feeling of relief and admiration ran through the group. They had accomplished what few people in that day would attempt. Even now, tandem runs of Bull Sluice are still problematic.

~

This was the first of three Chattooga River paddling trips Carter would take while Governor, not to mention the firsthand familiarity he gained with other rivers, such as the Chattahoochee and Flint. A major decision concerning the Flint, perhaps best reflects Carter's consideration of environmental values.

The Flint River rises near Atlanta and flows unrestricted through Georgia's Piedmont region for nearly two hundred miles. Plans for a massive impoundment at Spewrell Bluff by the Corps of Engineers had been completed, and the dam seemed a near certainty despite the opposition of many concerned citizens and organizations. Construction would provide many jobs in Carter's home area of southwest Georgia and the project received his support while he was a state senator.

But as Governor, Carter asked for additional economic and environmental studies of the project. After a careful review of the facts, he termed the project unnecessary and wasteful, and used his executive power to de-authorize the dam. This move infuriated proponents of the project and invoked much verbal abuse from certain members of the State Legislature. But Carter's decision was firm, and typical of the thorough way in which he investigates the facts before making difficult decisions.

Earlier in his term as Governor, Carter had given close attention to the Chattahoochee River controversy, which had been periodically resurfacing over a period of several years. This conflict involved a portion of the river close to metropolitan Atlanta, with particular scenic values and relatively high water quality. Certain groups wanted to see the natural characteristics of the river corridor protected by limiting development in the flood plain and on steep slopes, and by setting aside public areas for state parks. Other parties, with a financial interest in these properties, seemed bent on maximizing their profit before any such restrictions could become law.

Carter himself requested the opportunity to see the Palisades Cliff area from the river, as well as investigating the manner in which development was taking place. Several canoe trips added much to his firsthand knowledge of the situation. This was in sharp contrast to his predecessor, Lester Maddox, who had declined several invitations to examine the area by canoe during his term as governor.

During the winter following the appearance of *Deliverance* on the screen, it became apparent that the whitewater bug had bitten Carter. He developed an interest in kayaking, and began to appear with us at rolling practice sessions in Georgia State's indoor pool. We were delighted, to say the least, to see a genuine desire to learn and prepare for the river sport. There was no shortage of volunteer instructors, and by the third session, Carter had learned both the extended and screw roll to about seventy percent reliability.

In May we set up a kayak trip on Section II of the Chattooga, a good beginning test for Carter's kayak skills. The majority of the nine mile run is Class II water, with a couple of good Class III rapids thrown in for entertainment. Mountain laurel would be in bloom and the river would be clear and full.

The week before the trip, the Governor's office informed us that Carter's Sunday schedule would not permit him to attend, and that subsequent weekends looked equally busy. When Carter himself learned of

Claude Terry and Governor Jimmy Carter running Keyhole Rapid (Painted Rock) on Section III of the Chattooga. Claude had lent his PFD to Carter that day and was without one himself. The photo received widespread national publicity, causing Claude to lose his position as Safety Chairman for the American Canoe Association.

the plans, the conflict was quickly resolved. A Friday call from Claude Terry informed me that the trip was on again.

At the Highway 28 put-in, our small group of kayakers, perhaps half the size of the group on that earlier canoe trip, wriggled into spray skirts and life jackets. Both Carter and his oldest son, Jack, would be paddling kayaks. Safety gear and lunches in dry bags were stowed behind the seats, and one by one we peeled off into the current.

The trip was smooth and the group was loose; conversation came easily. We knew that Carter intended to run for President, and that he had already begun laying the groundwork. What impressed us most was his candor. He was completely willing to talk about the difficulties of his administration as well as the successes, the problems and advantages of his massive reorganization, why the Chattahoochee bill had failed on several occasions, even his views on the kind of person the President of the United States should be.

Carter shows perfect form as he runs Big Shoals on the Chattooga River during his first kayak trip.

As we relaxed for lunch on a small island at the head of Buck Shoals, the conversation turned again to the Presidency. Watergate was almost daily news, but Nixon's resignation was still three months in the future. What seemed to bother Carter most was the inaccessibility of the Presidential office, not just to the ordinary citizen but to many of the President's own advisors. Things would be different, he said with a grin, when *he* occupied the Oval Office.

In Georgia, Carter's environmental credentials were already mounting. Laws strengthening air and water quality enforcement, coastal marshland protection, and solid waste management had been passed early in his term of office. His Heritage Trust Commission had already acquired for the people of the State, twenty-nine sites of unique historical, cultural, or ecological significance.

Even while he was Governor, Carter's thinking would be felt at a broader level. Attending the National Governor's Conference the following year, he would introduce a resolution urging the Administration and Congress "to study, redefine and improve the role of the Soil Conservation Service." In this resolution, Carter would note the detrimental effects of stream channelization, and would emphasize that "Flood plain management and land use controls are now seen to be the most desirable methods of reducing flood problems, with structural and engineering approaches utilized as a last resort."

Lunch finished, we turned our attention once more to the river. Launching from the head of the island, we gained paddling room, and one by one slipped into the narrow opening at the top of Buck Shoals. Both of the Carters took the Class III run in stride and turned smartly into the eddy below the island. Neither had any hesitation or balance problem. Prior training was paying off.

By mid-afternoon, we had reached the take-out at Earl's Ford, with time to reflect and relax again. Here Jack Carter took half an hour's cold water rolling practice under the guiding hands of Rodger Losier. The rest of us loaded up our gear and changed to dry clothes.

Sharing thank-you hugs with his Chattooga guides, Governor Carter expresses his appreciation to Maggie Tucker, left, and Barbara Walmsley, right.

We saw the Governor next on Section IV of the Chattooga, running by raft with several of us guiding and providing safety in kayaks. It was here, of course, that much of *Deliverance* was filmed, amid some of the most demanding rapids the Chattooga has to offer. Rosalyn Carter paddled next to her husband, showing much of the same determination.

In fact, it was she alone who remained in the raft after the twisting plunge over Seven-Foot-Falls. Smiling all the while, she helped the kayakers pull Carter and two others from the churning water below the drop.

~

It has now been thirty years since the Chattooga has seen the Carter paddle, but I still like to recall the "wild rivers" part of his soul, even as the former President's many other dimensions continue to shape our world, from "Habitat" housing for those in need, to international conflict resolution through the Carter Center. He is a man of extraordinary vision, but one who has never lost the common touch.

Arctic Adventure

"You've got to come to Alaska," Joe urged. "The best wilderness rivers you'll ever kayak are up here. Bring Cricket and Dave and we'll all run the Noatak this summer. I think I can even find boats for you in Kotzebue."

My friend Joe Terrell had been working out of Kotzebue, Alaska, a hundred miles north of the Arctic Circle for the past four years. His offer was tempting.

I ordered sectional topographic maps — there were no large-scale maps of that region — and spent evenings studying the river and the surrounding country. I talked about the expedition with Cricket and Dave as we devoured books that pictured the Alaskan North Country. The trip and its time frame were cleared through Roberta, and my three weeks of vacation were appropriately scheduled for late July and early August.

I called Joe on his satellite phone in Kotzebue to tell him the good news.

"Uh, Doug, there's something you should know. I can't go with you. A job has just come up at King Cove out in the Aleutians, too big a job to pass up.

"Oh."

"But the three of you can still paddle the Noatak. Use my Folbot and inflatable, and I'll borrow another inflatable for Cricket or Dave. You can sleep and eat in the construction trailer and Cliff Hyatt will arrange for your bush flight."

"That sounds workable, but we're sure going to miss you."

"I might see you at the end of your trip."

~

Joe had not run the Noatak himself, but knew a few who had. He passed on what information he could. Our trip would be over four hundred miles long and in tundra north of the timberline for the most part. It was now the rainy season. The river had no rapids rated higher than a Class III. There would be abundant wildlife and the possibility of bear encounters. We were warned to keep our camp and clothing free of food odors, particularly fish. There was no human habitation anywhere near our route with the exception of a tiny Inuit village about fifty miles from the mouth of the river. No one would come looking for us until we were at least a week overdue. It was the summer of 1978 and we were on our own.

My diary notes tell the story best:

August 1

Morning comes much too early after a late night of final packing — transferring all gear to the waterproof river bags. We ride to the construction trailer with Cliff Hyatt (who has done more than we could ever ask to make this trip go) for a last hot breakfast of ham and eggs and fruit.

Then it's out to the airstrip to load our mountain of gear, if possible, into Baker's Cessna 185. The mood at Baker Aviation is somber. Yesterday they lost their other 185 and pilot, Jeff, when he flew into a mountainside in bad weather, just east of the continental divide and Noatak headwaters.

Our pilot, Greg, looks at our gear and shakes his head, but somehow it stows behind the seats, with only a kayak left over to ride on Cricket and Dave's laps!

The weather is close in with a ceiling at about 1100 feet and drizzle as we hop across ten miles of ocean to the mouth of the Noatak River and its impressive delta. From here, we snake our way along the twisting river, taking shortcuts over mountains, often no more than fifty feet off the ground to avoid the clouds.

Greg would like to land us at the junction of the Noatak and Cutler Rivers, since he has never flown beyond that point. However, that would put us about eighty miles short of the high mountains and the most beautiful part of the trip.

Greg flies on, but of course the final decision will be his - we're flying with wheels and will have to find a suitable gravel bar for landing. Also, the valley begins to narrow as the mountain walls become more impressive.

At a bend just below Otkurak Creek, we catch a glimpse of brilliant blue. No doubt another floater's tent — we saw one party camped at Nigikpalvgururvrak Creek about twenty miles downriver. But as we fly closer, we see it's not a tent but a downed plane.

Greg puts the 185 in a tight spiral and we drop quickly, making several passes just over the wreck. He remembers now that a DeHaviland Beaver — which this is — went down on the Noatak a week ago. Overloaded, it tried to take off from the gravel bar and couldn't clear the riverbank, plowing into the tundra and breaking apart without a fire. No one was killed.

We fly on, rain pounding the windshield and ragged clouds filling the valley. We're almost to the river's source as the glaciers on Mt. Igikpak suddenly appear through a break in the clouds.

"Far enough," says Greg, and puts the Cessna into a 180-degree turn to look for a suitable gravel bar. Most are small or irregular, but finally one meets with his approval. We make two trial passes and on the third, despite the choppy wind and rain, Greg sets the load down as easily as a mosquito landing on your hand.

We quickly unload, Greg taxies to the end of the bar, waves, and is airborne. For what seems an interminable time, he flies straight at the mountainside to gain airspeed and at the last second pulls up and banks to the right. A wiggle of wings and he's gone.

We are alone on a gravel island, over 400 miles from the nearest human habitation. Whatever we have with us must do for the next two to three weeks.

Joe has graciously loaned us two boats and Cliff, a third. Two are inflatable kayaks (German Metzelers) and the third is a two-person Folbot. We spend the next two hours assembling and inflating, as the case may be. After a few pictures in the drizzle, we load the kayaks and shove off. I'll be paddling the "barge" (the Folbot with almost all the gear — probably 300 pounds!) and Cricket and Dave, the inflatables.

We're six hours west of Atlanta time (Bering Standard Time) and still feeling it, so we make camp early after stopping to investigate the downed plane. The river current is strong, but no rapids yet, making the paddling easy.

Camp is set up in a grassy tundra area on the south bank — actually a little bit marshy. Mosquitoes are out in force — the bush hats with netting are life savers. Clouds begin breaking up in early evening and by

Our bush pilot leaves the three of us on a gravel bar island in the Brooks Range, far from human habitation. The sixteen-day Alaskan odyssey down the Noatak would cover 430 river and ocean miles, ending at the village of Kotzebue, just east of the Bering Sea.

8 PM it is definitely clearing. Sunset begins about 10:30 PM and lingers. It's gotten quite chilly. We fry up a delicious salmon given to us by Jan Cabanis, who cooks for the construction crew back in Kotzebue. She was delighted by a gallon of Tupelo honey that we had left for her.

August 2

Early morning clouds on the mountains give way to sunshine and brilliant blue skies. A small taffy-colored animal works its way along the far riverbank — about the size of a marmot. It is a marmot! Moments later, a red fox (arctic foxes are blue or white) makes an appearance in the same area.

The river level has fallen almost a foot — we don't know yet whether this is a daily cycle from the snowmelt or a permanent drop following the rain. If it stays down, it will probably mean trouble for the barge on the shallow gravel bars.

I feel lousy — bad headache, nausea and chills all afternoon. Three aspirin seem to knock it out and I'm feeling better as we make camp. We find enough dead wood for a good campfire — even toast marshmallows. The sun is down at 10:30 PM, but sky stays light, even to read by, all night. Hard to sleep!

Bite/Swat score: Mosquitoes — 83, Dad — 11.

August 3

We wake up several times — to bright sunlight at 4:00 AM and again about every hour. I'm up at 8 AM — let Cricket and Dave sleep 'til 9. Water level has dropped another three inches, so we're evidently losing the rain effect.

As we pass the junctions of the Kugrak and Igning Rivers, we have the choice of taking dozens of water channels, some not rejoining others for half a mile or more. About noon, we paddle down on a caribou swimming the river from the south to the north bank, head and antlers held impressively above the water. He then turns and trots toward us along the north shore after a vigorous shaking. I take a quick shot with the 50mm lens, then scramble for the telephoto, dropping my lens cap in the river. The caribou takes an amazed look at us and is gone.

We make camp on a sandy bar on the south shore with a stand of that beautiful springtime green grass. The place is evidently a favorite of others, too — we pick out the tracks of bear and wolf, as well as many smaller animals. Some large leg bones lie in the sand.

Today we make 15 to 20 miles, the best yet, but still below our required average of 25 to 30. Taking it slow to enjoy the high country and get the muscles used to paddling is probably the best bet at the beginning.

We treat David's thumb again (each evening) with alcohol and antibiotic ointment. (David cut his thumb rather badly in Kotzebue just before we left.) The spot where the flesh is missing, about as big as a fingernail, is looking better — no sign of infection.

At mid-afternoon we come upon an unusual looking object in the middle of the river far downstream — unusual, because the river is very predictable so far — no rapids, gravel bars, strong currents, no large rocks. But as we come closer, we can see the fuselage of another bush plane — upside down with the tail and wings visible beneath the water. He's in line with a long gravel bar that should be good enough for take-off and landing, but obviously was not — at least for this pilot! This crash looks older than the first — but hard to tell, being in the river. I wonder about the life expectancy of a bush pilot.

We stop for lunch on a gravel bar — also skinny-dipping and rock hunting.

August 4

We're underway at 11:15 AM — mornings are still slow. We paddle three hours before lunch, but with the Folbot you can nibble as you go since things are convenient in the cockpit.

Rocks are larger now (one and two feet in diameter) and I have to be even more precise to avoid damage to the Folbot skin. Many marmots watch our river passage with interest and I pull ashore, trying to creep up on a caribou for a picture. I don't get very close, but pick a handful of blueberries while there.

By noon it starts to rain and stays with us off and on for the rest of the day. We surprise several caribou on a sandbar and they bolt away on thundering hooves.

Just beyond the sandbar, we find that Midas Creek loops around to almost touch the Noatak before actually joining it a mile downstream. Paddling in the rear, Cricket is viewed for a long while by a curious red fox keeping pace with us along the riverbank.

There's a break in the rain, we make camp, cook dinner and climb into the tent. The rain settles down in earnest.

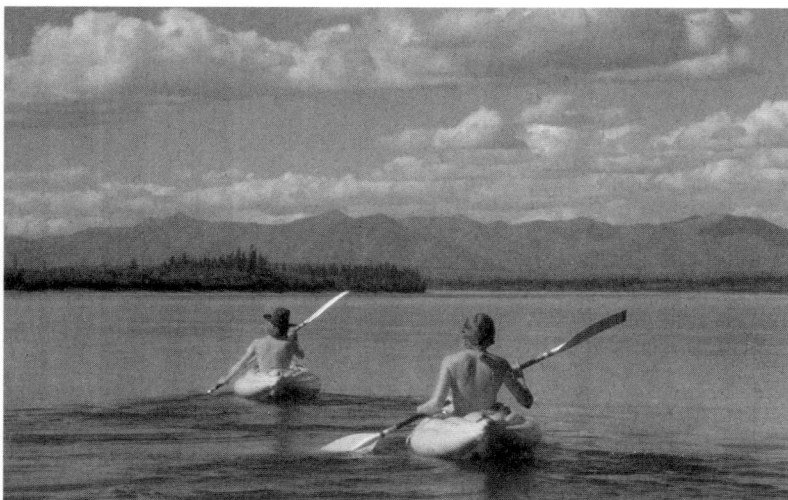

David, 13, and Cricket, 15, paddle toward a stand of fir on the Noatak's south shore, some of the first trees we had seen since the start of the trip. Most of our journey took place a hundred miles north of the Arctic Circle.

August 5

The light never goes out! Three in the morning and it's light enough to wake up — of course the pouring rain helps too. The tent is as dry as the palms of our hands after four days on the Noatak! It's a North Face Dandelion, lent to us by Joe Terrell along with the boats. The pouring rain continues into morning, making us just snuggle down tighter in the sleeping bags. Finally it subsides about 9:30 AM and we start the morning chores; later on, we may have to pack up — rain or no — to make our daily mileage.

We wind through a miniature canyon with hills and moraine slides on each side and find ourselves in a succession of Class II rapids — no sweat for the decked boats (once Cricket decides to wear her spray skirt!) but I've got to take great pains to keep the barge away from the largest standing waves.

More caribou and marmots appear on the sides. Arctic terns dart here and there, then hover in one spot over the water, flapping their wings rapidly. Toward evening a cormorant goes over with a fish in its mouth. Right after lunch we passed a mother and two young loons that kept diving to avoid our seeing them, but the mother and one went one way, the other young one going downstream in the opposite direction.

By late afternoon we're beginning to come out of the mountains and run smack into strong headwinds with a 50 °F air temperature. We make camp early behind a gravel bar — on the north shore for the first time. What a treat is in store as we sit by our campfire eating. First one, then two, and finally three red foxes put on a show for us, dancing and leaping on the gravel bar, pausing to sit and look at us from 150 feet away, all the while barking and wailing plaintively.

David found a caribou rack (antlers) today and is carrying it on the front deck of his kayak.

August 6

Sleep seems so necessary — we can't help but get nine or ten hours a night — so no early start today. We leave at 11 AM. Although it's not early, it's the best yet for us. We paddle until 8 PM, with a 45-minute lunch stop.

Today is caribou day! We first see lone bulls against the skyline, then small herds (8 or 10) crossing the river at several places. Finally, we see a herd of about fifty at the spot where we will camp (north shore again). They disappear up the bank and over the bluff as we put ashore.

But then an amazing thing happens. We are standing downwind and against the setting sun and a second caribou herd starts grazing down the shore, completely unaware of our presence. We stand motionless (except for camera) and they walk right into camp before realizing something is different and bounding out of sight.

This is the second day in a row we've seen no bush planes — just a lone seagull that had a lot to say to us. It's our best paddling day yet for distance — all three of us stuck together pretty well and covered 25 to 30 miles.

There are large bear tracks in the sand, about a day old. It's a *cold, cold* evening (snow on riverbank at one spot), beautiful sunset, warm campfire. All is peaceful at Caribou Gardens.

August 7

A *cold, cold* night — below freezing and we snuggle deep into the sleeping bags in the morning until the sun warms the tent. This also means a late start as we hit the river at noon.

We stop about 2 PM for a quick dip and to wash our hair — brrr! The day is good for paddling — sunny with fast-moving clouds racing by, but only a light wind on the river — that is, until about 6 PM, when a stiff, cold north wind comes up.

At 8 PM we pass the junction of the Cutler River and camp an hour later on the north shore, at a place shielded from the wind. Looks like another cold night, though — air temperature is already at 42 °F.

All day we have seen caribou — in small groups or medium herds — in fact, we woke to a bunch grazing right next to us again at our Caribou Gardens site. Many caribou are swimming the river in groups and one keeps coming up to look us over from the beach while we're skinny-dipping.

No people, no bush planes today. We have our best paddling day yet, making over 30 miles. Another fabulous sunset — half the sky is a sweeping salmon-colored cloud — bright gold around the sun — the wide-angle lens can't begin to take it in.

Cricket and Dave are exhausted as usual — no back rubs, no reading.

August 8

We wake to a steady patter of rain on the tent after the beautiful sunset last night — no fair! We try to out-sleep it, but to no avail as we finally arise, eat breakfast and pack in the rain. Even the mosquitoes are still active in all the wet.

The rain eases in the early afternoon, but the heavy steel-gray clouds follow us all day and evening. It's another long paddling day of over 30 miles — we pass the Anisak River and start looking for a campsite, rejecting five in the process, including a spot with huge fresh bear tracks.

By the time we find a suitable site (also with bear tracks, but smaller), it's after 10 PM. A fox follows us along the bank for over half a mile, just looking us over as we search for a campsite. We finally pick a sandy spot, not having found a grassy one. Very strange, but ever since we passed the Cutler River last evening, we have not seen a single caribou — as if they have an imaginary boundary! Again, no people, no bush planes today.

We made up another verse to go with the old Air Force song — this one's about the Cessna 185 that brought us in.

Don't give me a 185,
You're lucky to get there alive.
She'll bounce and she'll quiver,
And just quit in the river,
Don't give me a 185 — No!

David's hands have broken out, itching and hurting all day. I treated them with Bactine on the skin and gave him an anti-biotic internally. Saw our first trees today — a small grove of twelve-foot cottonwoods on the north shore toward evening.

August 9

We wake late, with full sun on the tent, drying things out so we can shake out the sand and start fairly clean. David's hands still look the same so we stop anti-biotic treatment with the thought that it might be a reaction, since we've been treating his thumb for a week. His stomach is upset after breakfast, but returns to normal with an hour of paddling.

The Folbot develops a small leak — about two gallons an hour — right at the stern wear point. I put on a vulcanizing patch during lunch, which seems to do the trick.

Again, we don't see a caribou all day. Also, no people, no bush planes. Generally, we have a north wind — it wants to blow us off the river on the north legs of the hairpin turns. We pick a south shore campsite and are immediately greeted by a fox, which sniffs the tent, kayaks and almost us as we are assembling camp! The fox just sits and watches from various vantages, then takes a ten-foot leap over the creek and is gone.

August 10

We're seeing more and more trees now — all cottonwoods, all near the river and all under 15 feet tall. A golden eagle soars majestically along our route, stopping just a moment on its nest atop the cliffs north of Isaoktuvik Creek.

From our campsite of last night to the start of the Grand Canyon of the Noatak, we've noticed a strange noise on the surface of the water — like CO_2 bubbles when a soft drink has been opened. Under close inspection, you can actually see tiny bubbles rising, but not obvious on the surface. This occurs for perhaps a couple of hundred yards, then again a mile or so later. There must be some kind of gas being released through the river bottom.

We've also encountered quicksand at a number of places on the trip, usually where a small creek joins the river. The sand nearby may be very firm, and then all of a sudden the whole surface is quivery and liquid-like. Boots tend to disappear quickly and it can be a tough retrieval if the fit is loose. We've noticed also, from their tracks, that bears never walk in the quicksand!

David's hands continue broken out — itching and tender — and now Cricket's left hand appears to be starting the same thing. We pass a dead caribou on the north bank — the first we have seen since we started. In fact, it's the first dead animal of any kind that we've seen.

We paddle most of the way through the Grand Canyon, which so far isn't much like a canyon at all. Rumors of rapids here appear unfounded, as we have not encountered anything better than a Class I. This has been the most favorable day for paddling yet, with a warm sun and a very slight breeze that seems to be *following* us, of all things.

Clothes have seemed unnecessary, and we paddle in the buff most of the day. As the afternoon wears on, we are startled by the sound of an aircraft engine at low altitude — the first we have heard in almost a week. The bush plane zooms low over our heads, the pilot does a double take, and banks around for another look. The smiling passengers are all waving and, not embarrassed in the least, we wave back.

Camp is pitched at the junction of the Kaluktavik River (east shore) and Noatak (north shore) after making close to forty miles. I soak David's hands in Epsom salts and warm water but it doesn't help. At bedtime we try Tenactin cream, but I doubt that it will help either. The bumps appear to be an allergic reaction.

August 11

An 11 AM start is the best we can do again though we hoped to be earlier. A low-wing, single-engine plane goes over very high and heading north about noon. We leave the Grand Canyon with no sign of a real rapid. Along the way, a loon swims ahead of us, diving and surfacing only for a second or two, each time squawking more excitedly between dives when she sees us closer. Finally she flies off in disgust.

We stop on a beach with small fine gravel to bathe and eat lunch. We've just stripped down when we're joined by a female red fox. More curious than any we've seen, she comes within a few feet of each of us, inspecting us and all of our gear several times before sauntering off down the shore. The sun is warm and the rock finding is good — all told, we relax for two hours.

So far, no medication seems to have worked on David's hands. Cricket points out that it's the left hand that is worse on David and that the same hand has started bothering her. We decide that the ailment must be sun poisoning, since we generally paddle west and the sun always stays to the south (our left) in a medium-low arc from east to west. We apply plenty of sunscreen lotion and cover-up with hats and clothing whenever possible today. For the first night in a good while, David's hands don't hurt at bedtime and Cricket's rash seems to have subsided.

Cricket and a red fox check each other out. Apparently both curious and fearless, foxes would often come into camp, sniffing our equipment and looking us over.

We enter Noatak Canyon late in the afternoon with good Class II rapids. It's such a beautiful place that we decide to stop early and camp here (7 PM). We pitch the tent by a singing creek and climb the hills behind us to watch the river and sunset. Just before we leave, two Inuits in a longboat with outboard motor pass by heading up river — probably hunting caribou.

For the first time, stars can be seen (two of them!) at night, since we are in the canyon. We saw our first conifers today when we stopped for lunch. The cherries for the gorp were not pitted, so we carried them separately — this made for great diversion, shooting cherry pits at each other down the river! Joe and Cliff will be finding pits in their boats for years to come.

August 12

We can't help lingering a little longer than we had planned, the canyon is so beautiful. Just as we are loading the boats, a bush plane flies low over our site and dips its wings.

Dave's hands are definitely improved — Cricket's hand is OK. We apply sunscreen generously.

As we round the first bend past the campsite, we see a mud slide at work. Globs of mud and rock, pieces of turf, small trees just keep coming down the mountainside. Maybe there's a lake above with a wall beginning to give way. I just checked the map — there is a big lake up there!

A brief afternoon rain shower and windstorm appear, complete with rainbow. We pass the junction of the Kelly River in late afternoon, where a US Geological Survey team has an encampment of large white tents.

Just below the Kelly, several Inuit families have set up a hunting and fishing camp. Here we enter the huge maze of islands that is characteristic of the river all the way to its mouth, as it empties into the Arctic Ocean.

We look at several possible campsites, one with bear tracks of a mother and two cubs. We choose another that has several sets of very large bear tracks. David finds a neat circular root (a dead one) that we build a fire in — it burns all evening. The night is slightly dimmer, but still light right on through 'til morning. The quarter moon is bright (for the first time) just before setting beyond Asik Mountain. David catches a beautiful five-pound Char at midnight. Two meteors flare briefly in the southwest sky.

August 13

As usual, we sleep late. The nocturnal fishing efforts have pushed departure back a bit more and we're off at 12 noon. After the activity yesterday above the Kelly River we feel as if we're really in the wilds again.

Then late in the afternoon we meet a party of eight Germans in six boats, four of them Metzelers like ours. They started at the Cutler River seven days ago, so have been about a day ahead of us for the past week, until now. They must have paralleled us for a while through one set of island channels, then come together at the tip of a large island. They will finish at Noatak where a plane will meet them.

We play tag with the group for three hours through the islands, burning up the miles in the process. Finally, the Germans take the right side of an island and we take the left. Twenty minutes later, we find that we have come out a quarter mile downriver from Noatak. We can see the town, but have islands and a heavy current between it and us. We've decided not to stop at Noatak anyway — it's evening and we really don't have the desire to do anything or buy anything there.

Perhaps two miles below the village of Noatak, the river is bordered by ice cliffs that continue for another quarter mile. The current has cut into the tundra in a wide curve, eroding soil and banks as high as 25 feet, exposing solid ice in the permafrost layer. Chunks of turf and mud keep falling into the river as we paddle past. A cold wind blows from the ice and the whole thing has a medicinal smell - like a billion Band-Aids, as Cricket points out. We pass a tree every once in a while whose leaves have turned golden, reminding us that it's already half-past August, nearly a quarter 'til fall.

Paddling another five miles or so, we make camp on the downstream tip of a pleasant island. The two stars appear again, even though we're not in the canyon. The nights are just slightly dimmer. David fishes. As always, we enjoy a cheery campfire. We're now committed to the ocean crossing by kayak.

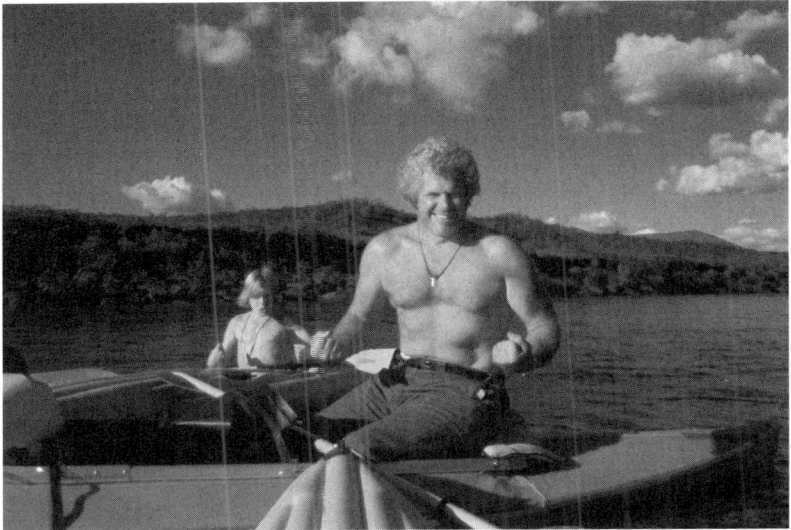

Feeling our muscles after two weeks on the Noatak, trying to average thirty miles a day against headwinds and crosswinds.

August 14

We wake to a warm sun on the tent and are on the water by 10:55 AM. We go "flashing" by an Inuit family that has set up a fishing camp. When asked, they reply that the fishing is good, so it must be *really* good!

We hear the sound of an outboard behind us and soon a longboat with three persons aboard comes into view. We recognize John (Jan's John), his brother Doug, and friend George. They give us Sweetie-pies and oranges and we give them some beef jerky. We decline the offer of a ride, they assure us that our boats will do fine on the ocean crossing, and will look for us in Kotzebue tomorrow night.

As we leave the maze of islands, the river widens and deepens and the current drops to almost nothing. We pick up a crosswind and every mile is hard fought. From the Nauyoaruk bend to the mouth of Lower Noatak Canyon is agony. We're so exhausted that we stop and dig into the main food bag for more beef jerky. Though we had hoped to cover a greater distance, we stop at 9 PM and camp on the south shore at the entrance to Lower Noatak Canyon. A beautiful sunset, but clouds are moving in quickly — temperature is dropping — tomorrow may not bring favorable weather for the ocean crossing.

August 15

Wow! We're packed and underway by 10 AM. We head into the canyon, which is beautiful, but everything from here out is pure, tough work — no current to help out. A light rain falls sporadically, then in the afternoon the sun breaks through and the day grudgingly clears.

Each leg of the river — and there are only four of them left today — is a major one, taking hours to paddle. The river is so wide, it is difficult to gage your progress — two to three miles across between banks in this area. We've packed double lunches and extra jerky, for we know this will be our longest paddling day.

Backs ache, arms ache, fannies ache. We've been paddling for eleven hours, the last hour and a half alongside Kinuk Island, the final piece of the Noatak Delta. The temptation to stop and camp is overwhelming.

But at 10 PM we pass the downstream tip of Kinuk Island and enter the Arctic Ocean. A spectacular sunset — like fire embers all the way across the sky — has been underway to our right for almost an hour. The lights of Kotzebue twinkle on the horizon, barely visible ten miles distant. The ocean is like a mirror — not a breath of wind stirs. No matter how we feel, this is the time to go.

A mile out, an Inuit family slows their outboard beside us and a young man offers us a ride. With aching muscles and conflicting feelings, we decline.

Halfway across, we finish the jerky and gorp. All around us is silence except for the dip of paddles in the water. The sunset is now blood red behind the mountains and on the water, surrounded by a bright gold. Seals break the surface of the color-drenched sea to pause and look at us, turning their heads from one side to the other, then diving again.

Cricket and Dave's kayaks and their wakes register black against the rich reflection of color. Cricket sings to help take our minds off the physical exhaustion — John Denver, Jim Croce, Simon and Garfunkel, Barbra Streisand. It's dark now, except for the sliver of light at the horizon — it's hard to see each other's shapes, even a couple of boat lengths away.

We pass close to a seemingly abandoned small boat, only to startle two sleeping Inuits who are tending one end of a salmon net. Ten minutes later, we pass the boat at the opposite end of the net.

The patch of clear sky shrinks to nothing at the horizon and a layer of clouds and mist hugs the water, moving ever nearer to us from the open ocean to the west. The lights of Kotzebue gleam closer and we begin to make out the shapes of buildings behind the glow. It's midnight, we've been paddling close to 14 hours, but now the end is within our grasp.

At 12:15 AM, we slide quietly out of the darkness and nudge the shore at the foot of Mission Street. No wave laps the beach — the ocean is still a black sheet of obsidian.

But Kotzebue is alive and hopping. An old Inuit weaves his way down the street and staggers toward home. Teenagers walk arm in arm and Hondas raise dust clouds on the gravel street. The noise and smell of gasoline engines seem strange to our senses.

It's been hours and hours since our last pee stop and now it's a screaming priority! Dave and I step behind a fishing boat while Cricket scurries around the corner of the nearest building.

Relieved, I head toward the construction trailer a quarter mile away, where the crew (Glen, Gary, Dick and Scott) is about to hit the sack. A friendly greeting, and they pull on their boots again, pile into the truck and head for the water. Boats, gear and people are whisked aboard in moments and we're back at the trailer for hot soup, roast beef sandwiches and hot showers. We manage to chat a bit, then curl up on the floor at 2:30 AM.

We're awakened at 7 AM by the crew piling out for breakfast. The morning is a shuffle of gear from river bags to airline bags and washing of clothes. Weim Airlines is booked full on today's flight, but we find space on the earlier Great Northern flight at 2:15 PM. It's then a last minute scramble to clean, dry and pack the boats. While I'm dismantling them, one of the Inuits working on the apartment building comments on our trip and I recognize him as the man who offered us a ride as we were starting our crossing last night. A huge handsome Inuit working with him looks exactly like the chief in *One Flew Over the Cuckoo's Nest.*

Before leaving Kotzebue, we again run into Doug and George who, with John, had made the crossing the day before us in John's 23-foot longboat. They had run through four and five-foot seas the whole way, taking on a good bit of water, even in the big boat. With conditions like that, and depending where the wind was, we could have taken six or eight hours for the crossing rather than two. We definitely went at the right moment. And we did the whole 430 miles ourselves!

Tying up loose ends in Kotzebue, I stop and pay Baker Aviation $504 for the Noatak bush flight. Jan bids us goodbye, Cricket gives her a hand-made shark's tooth necklace and we're winging toward Anchorage, two hours away. The Electra we're on is mostly a freight plane and all the passengers squeeze into 16 or 18 seats behind the bulkhead.

We land in Anchorage in a steady drizzle of rain and call old friends from the Chattooga — who are in the midst of enjoying a hot shower — to pick us up. Kathy Miller and Bob Bauknight have just returned from a backpacking trip to Mt. McKinley. We all go out to a late but delicious dinner at Elevation 92. Then a big surprise — Joe Terrell is in from King Cove, has tracked us down, and appears in time for dessert. We retrace the Noatak in vivid detail for him.

August 17

The morning sun streaming in through Kathy and Bob's windows has begun to restore energy to our tired bodies as we roll out of our sleeping bags. Though we're unaware of it at the moment, our day is destined to become even better.

Kathy rushes into the room. "Mount McKinley is crystal clear at both ends! This only happens a few times a year."

Bob joins in. "You won't believe your luck. John McCabe just flew into town last night." John is a skilled bush pilot and a close friend of Kathy and Bob. "I'll give him a call if you like. I bet he'll fly you out to McKinley for just the price of the plane rental."

And so we scramble out to the local airstrip at 10 AM, pile into a fast new six-place Piper and head for McKinley. John is an experienced pilot in many types of aircraft (land, float and chopper) and has grown up flying this area as a native. He's happy to fly us today for the $80/hour rental fee. Ten minutes out he gives me the controls at 3000 feet. I hold a line for the large glacier that flows directly toward us and climb to 5000 feet. As the massive peaks loom closer, John takes over again and I pick up my camera.

We fly low up the glacier, following its curves between jagged rock towers, and peering into crevasses and gleaming blue ice holes. At the head of the glacier — and we've been climbing all the way — John stands the Cessna on a wingtip for a 360° turn, gaining more altitude and checking for hidden peaks that might block our exit route. The path is clear, and we fly right through the narrow gap in the mountain. More impressive peaks — one just off our left wingtip — and then we're descending into the valley to skip over lakes, marshes, streams and woods. It's still an extremely high visibility day and almost no turbulence over the mountains.

Later we return to John's place on Willow Creek for an exciting air-boat ride — the boats can run atop almost no water over gravel shallows, low logs and whatnot — but what a noise! I would really have been pissed if I had met one of those coming up the Noatak.

We visit again with Joe and his sons, Joe-Joe and Jamie, driving up to Angel Pass to watch the sun set beyond Anchorage. Joe barely gets the boys on the evening flight to Atlanta to meet their mother. The next morning we all fly out, heading back to the places where others expect us to appear.

~

Many years have now passed since that early morning when, exhausted, we pulled our kayaks from the water on Kotzebue's shores. As we re-entered our familiar, modern world that August long ago, we had questions even then. What would the trip mean in times to come? Would it fade from memory and lose significance as other rivers swirled through our lives?

It's now safe to say that our time on the Noatak was perhaps the purest wilderness experience of our lives. I know that a yearning for those uncomplicated days on top of the world still burns brightly within my heart, and the three of us often talk of that trip as we gaze upriver once more.

No doubt about it — the adventure was unique in that very few people have done or will do what we did. More precisely, taking the trip, self-guided, into one of the more remote areas of the world and covering, with the exception of the highest headwaters, the entire length of the Noatak. The few folks we did run into were all doing shorter portions of the river with planes meeting them. Traveling the entire length under our own muscle power, and especially those last sixty grueling miles, pushed us close to our physical limits.

It's perhaps a disappointment to the reader — though certainly not to us — that we did not have some disaster to overcome, such as a major injury, a wild animal attack, a wrecked boat or the loss of food and equipment. In fact, we never came close to tipping a boat. The Folbot, with all its weight, probably touched no more than five or six rocks — with the exception of landings — in the whole 430 miles. But a very precise course was necessary to accomplish this in the upper part of the river.

If we had capsized, our gear was all in waterproof, floatable bags, lashed to the Folbot. Our river experience was far beyond what was demanded. In the early days, there was a question of our physical ability to cover the required daily miles — this, in turn, tied in with how long our food would last — but we found that our endurance increased and our bodies toughened enough physically to meet the challenge.

If we had run long on time and short on food, we could have survived — berries and fish were plentiful and we had the means to bring down a caribou should it ever have reached that point. We had whistles to signal each other for help, and in the end, we could probably have stopped a bear had the situation become that extreme.

The only available U.S.G.S. maps were sectionals with a 1/250,000 scale and a 200 foot contour interval — making it much more difficult to read and identify features than on a 7-1/2 or 15 minute quad. Nevertheless, the sectionals were absolutely vital to keeping the trip on schedule and to the measurement of our paddling progress.

The weather smiled on us, we knew — when we really needed it calm or clear, there it was, just as we had hoped. Perhaps the Inuit good weather charm I had worn around my neck really worked.

A bad injury or illness would have been the worst thing to befall us. We had put together an excellent medical kit with inflatable splints and prescription drugs to cover a host of maladies. We knew how to lay out a ground signal for help and we had mirrors to flash a plane. But then — we went six days without even hearing a plane or seeing any sign of humans at one stretch. If evacuation had been critical, it would have meant leaving one of the inflatables and probably the camera gear, putting the incapacitated person in the Folbot ahead of the paddler and making use of the long daylight to paddle all night if necessary, with only short food and rest stops. Thankfully, this was never required.

But all this is not to say that the trip was a pushover. Far from it. It wasn't a float trip — it was a muscle trip. Each day demanded a great deal from both our minds and bodies, but each day also gave us back so much — the scenery, the wildlife encounters, the feeling for the vast country we were in and our relationship to it. And, perhaps most of all, the challenge, temptations and accomplishments of the final two days of the trip. Though time may have intervened, the lesson of challenge met and overcome will remain and always be an important part of our lives. The Inuit word Noatak — *from deep within* — continues to have a very special meaning for the three of us.

~

Arriving back in Georgia, we knew it was time to pay back a Noatak debt — but not a monetary one. The Alaska National Interest Lands Conservation Bill had been introduced in both the United States Senate and House of Representatives the previous year, and I had then testified before John Sieberling's House Subcommittee on Alaskan Lands when it held hearings in Atlanta. I spoke as an engineer, showing the Subcommittee how more than 60% of the lands considered as "mineral-rich" by the mining industry did not conflict with the lands that would be added to the National Park, Wildlife Refuge, Wilderness and Wild Rivers Systems. It was a challenging appearance for me as the Subcommittee members, particularly Alaska's Senator Ted Stevens, questioned many of my premises, making me feel as if I were in a court of law.

Now it was time to lean on U.S. Senator Sam Nunn (GA) and U.S. Representative Ed Jenkins (GA). I visited Senator Nunn in his Atlanta office, where he listened politely, but was more interested in how I was related to Emily Woodward,[43] whom he had known during World War II.

Cricket, David and I all went up to Rep. Jenkins office in Jasper, where we not only gave him supporting data for the Alaska Lands Bill, but a brief pictorial recap of our Noatak adventure. We kept the correspondence flowing to both Nunn and Jenkins, and received a personal letter from Jenkins telling us that he had voted for the Alaska Lands Bill on May 16, 1979 when it passed the U.S. House of Representatives.

The bill that later emerged from the Senate was much weaker than the House version, giving watered-down protection to smaller areas, despite the support of President Carter and Interior Secretary Andrus for the House version. Conservation leaders worked with Representatives Morris Udall and John Seiberling to draft a stronger compromise bill, but when it became clear that Ronald Reagan had won the 1980 election, President Carter had no choice but to sign the Alaska National Interest Lands Act, as it then stood, into law. Nevertheless, it was an historic moment when the Act became law on December 2, 1980, preserving 104.3 million acres of wild country.

[43] Emily Barnelia Woodward was my great aunt; a newspaper editor and owner, and a war correspondent in an era when these were almost exclusively the provinces of males. She was an author and a champion of civil rights and social justice long before it became a widespread movement, and was unwavering in her defense of free speech. It is not surprising that Senator Nunn remembered her. She died in 1970 and was honored as a "Georgia Woman of Achievement" in 2004.

Tandem Once More

Often, places that are closest to your heart have a profound effect on your future, many times in a manner that you don't recognize at the time. So it was for me with Cumberland Island, the southernmost of Georgia's coastal isles. Certainly not whitewater paddling territory, Cumberland would nevertheless provide a connection with an individual with whom I would paddle many rivers in years to come.

Claude Terry and Maggie Tucker introduced me to the live oaks, dunes, tidal creeks and twenty miles of uninhabited beach in the fall of 1971. Accessible then only by ferry from Fernandina Beach in northern Florida, Cumberland was nearing the climax of an intense struggle between advocates of development and those who would see the Island remain in its semi-wild state. We would come to know some of the major players on the environmental side — Carol Ruckdeschel, Sam Candler, David Brower — and see Cumberland become a National Seashore in 1972. We would add our own voices to the proposed NPS plan for the Island, an ever-changing plan that still generates controversy today. But the Island is a magnet. Every year, Cricket, Dave and I would throw together our camping gear and food, and find our way back to Cumberland.

Trish Severin and I met on Cumberland Island. Twice. The first time, she had come as the companion of one of my good paddling friends, Mark Warren. Nearly five years later, in May of 1979, she was unattached, backpacking Cumberland with a fellow Atlanta teacher, Karen Kievit.

Several weeks after leaving the island, Trish called me at home, asking if I would like to paddle or hike with her. A few days later we met to paddle the Yellow River, east of Atlanta, and I was impressed to see how well she handled her eighty-pound Blue Hole canoe from the solo center saddle. We went on to paddle together the Conasauga, Cartecay, Chestatee, Chattahoochee, Etowah, Toccoa, Talking Rock Creek and many more. Then came Alaska — the Tatshenshini and Alsek.

Trish Severin paddling her Blue Hole canoe solo on Georgia's Cartecay River, a month after we met; June, 1979.

A year after the narrow escapes on the Tatshenshini, Trish somehow managed to overlook my questionable judgment during that adventure and the two of us made a long-term commitment. We were married in the woods in front of our Lilburn, Georgia home, a handful of family and friends standing with us. The music of Paul Winter played in the background as we shared with others the words that the two of us had written.

Merging our outdoor experience and Trish's teaching background, we were soon into the business of experiential education. We would work with individuals, teaching canoeing or kayaking, or take a whole classroom of kids out for a week, combining environmental education with instruction in outdoor skills. The logistics of assembling equipment, lining up transportation, and creating worthwhile programs as we headed for river or mountains was a lot of work, but it was work that we loved.

I found Trish to be a catalyst for change and within a year of our marriage, we had sold the Lilburn home, left our jobs at Galloway School and Western Electric, and rented an old farmhouse in the North Carolina mountains. Before another year had passed, we had found land, started building our own home and brought Autumn, our first child, into the world. Over the next ten years, Autumn would be followed by three brothers, Forest, Rivers and Canyon.

When we left Atlanta in 1982, we sold or gave away much of what we owned, the intent being to simplify our lives and reduce our needs. As much as possible, we wanted the freedom of being able to choose our own path and make those choices without the encumbrances of modern American consumerism. Along with these changes came the deliberate choice of a healthier diet and a household without television.

From the time they were infants, outdoor adventures became a part of our children's lives, whether backpacking, bicycle touring or running a river. Even early birthdays were celebrated in the wild, Autumn's first being observed with an overnight camp at the sandy edge of the Chattooga where the river empties into Lake Tugaloo. When Rivers turned one, on an unusually mild January day, we bundled him up for a day of canoeing on the Little Tennessee River near home.

As each of our children became old enough to hold her or his head up (usually five or six months of age), we would tuck that child into a backpack, bike seat or canoe, often for weeks at a time. On our early trips, we would use cloth diapers exclusively, rinsing them out and hanging them to dry on bushes around our camp. Eventually, we switched to disposables in the wild country — carrying them out, of course — while continuing to use cloth at home.

～

When Autumn was not quite two, Trish and I planned a backpacking trip in the Olympics of Washington State. Our flight from Atlanta to Seattle had been reserved weeks ahead, our trail days planned, camping gear fine tuned, and backpacks ready to check on board. Two days before we left, the latest issue of *Backpacker* arrived in the mail.

"Hey, look at this article!" as Trish handed me the magazine.

"Beautiful country," I replied. "I'll read it later."

"No! Read it now. It's a ten-day canoe trip in British Columbia. We could do it instead of this backpacking trip."

My jaw dropped. "You're kidding, I hope. Everything is set for the Olympic Peninsula and we're leaving the day after tomorrow." But it was

Trish, her mind going a mile a minute in a new direction. I knew she wasn't kidding.

"Look, it could be a great trip. We fly to Seattle as planned, rent a car and drive the 500 miles north to the Bowron Lakes. I'll check on renting a canoe there, and if it's a go, we start switching our camping gear from backpacks to waterproof river bags. I'll call Ross and see if he and Karen can go with us." Ross Brown, a long-time friend of Trish's, was a NOLS (National Outdoor Leadership School) instructor and he and his wife Karen had a sea kayak of their own.

Sure, I thought. Karen is six months pregnant with their first child and we're giving them a whole two days of notice to get it together. Not a snowball's chance in hell they could go. I was wrong, of course.

Three days later, on September 3, 1985, the five of us are sacked out in a tiny cabin in the Caribou Range, resting for our morning departure. Rain pours down on the cedar shake roof all night long.

By morning the rain has subsided, but dark clouds hang low. Karen and Ross are packing gear into the center hatch of their tandem sea kayak while we load our sleek eighteen foot rented lake canoe, carefully leaving Autumn's seat loose in case of a capsize.

By the time we depart on our seventy-two mile circuit of lakes, rivers and portages, the sun has broken through and the clouds are scudding for the horizon. We quickly cross the north end of Bowron Lake and unload for the mile and a half portage to Kibbee Lake. Portages with a wee one are a challenge, as Trish takes a load while Autumn toddles behind, then stays with her at the end of the portage trail.

The paddle across Kibbee is only a smooth, sunny mile and goes quickly — the next grunting portage, a mile and a quarter. We're feeling the effects of our overloaded foot travel, and make camp less than two miles into Indianpoint Lake.

Morning rain catches us in the middle of cooking a pancake breakfast. We pack up a wet camp, Indianpoint Lake glides under us much too soon and we find ourselves at the third portage trail, a mile to the head of Isaac Lake. The rain follows us as we make the multiple foot trips once more. The toughest portages are now behind us and we're looking at thirty miles of open water ahead.

A wind is rising and whipping the surface of the lake into a frenzy. Steady, hard rain continues to fall. Soaked right through our rain gear and badly chilled despite the strenuous exercise, we hug the north shore and finally give it up seven miles into Isaac. We set up camp at the mouth of Wolverine Creek, which we see rising significantly in the hours following our arrival.

As the rain soaks our camp, the five of us huddle around a small fire, partially protected by a tarp, trying to absorb a bit of warmth. We each hold a piece of Autumn's clothing over the flames on a stick, attempting to dry her limited wardrobe as best we can.

All night, and throughout the next day the rain and wind continue. Isaac Lake resembles a storm-tossed ocean, the wind blowing the tops right out of the five-foot waves. One of our two days' emergency food supplies is eaten as we use the time to discuss alternative plans beside the fire. Karen and Ross will wait out the weather and paddle on, even if we don't, figuring that they can make up a portion of their lost time in the sea kayak, by far the fastest craft on the lake.

Shortage of food is not yet a concern, but could become one. For us, the most pressing question is whether we can keep Autumn dry and comfortable as, even being as careful as we can, her fleece clothing is still getting wet right through her full rain suit. At this point, with only about a sixth of the trip distance behind us, it would make sense for us to reverse our direction if we need to escape the weather. The discouraging part of that plan is the fact that we would have to retrace almost four portage miles with our canoe and supplies. The four remaining portages are relatively short compared to what we've already done.

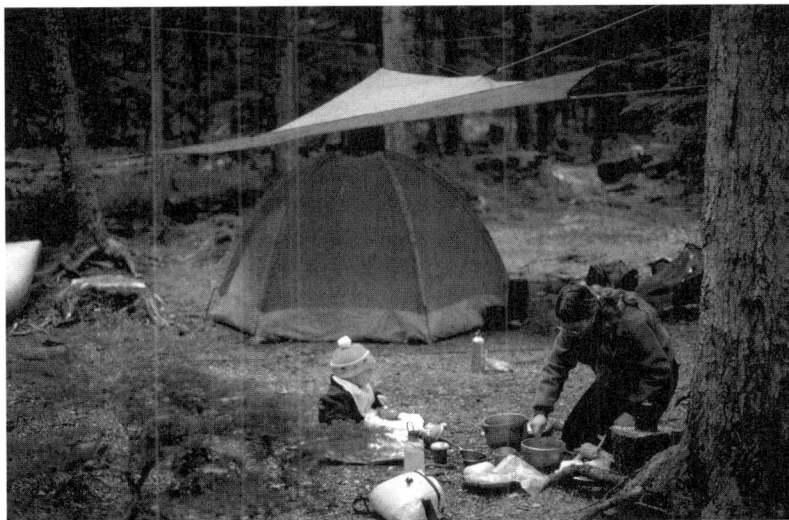

Bowron Lakes, British Columbia. Trish works on dinner as Autumn (not quite two) watches. A severe wind and rain storm kept us pinned down for two days, felling a large fir tree only feet from our tent.

At dusk, the storm takes a more ominous turn. The wind velocity has noticeably increased and has a voice of its own. We can hear "tongues" of wind racing down the ridges above us with a force that is flattening trees in their path. They fall like dominoes, often ten or twelve in series, one crash rapidly followed by another. Becoming increasingly uneasy, we count hundreds of crashes in an hour.

"Do you think any of the trees here in our camp could come down?" a concerned Trish asks.

I try to reassure her. "I don't think so. The dead trees have been cut out near our camp and they'd be the ones most likely to fall."

I rig our lightweight tarp over the tent and rain fly, trying to add a third layer of protection from the foul weather. Autumn is the only sound sleeper in our tent tonight, trusting her parents implicitly, as only a two-year-old can do. Trish and I toss fitfully, listening to the trees crashing as the wind roars down Wolverine Creek from the north.

In Edgar Allen Poe style, the storm chooses the black of night to hurl its worst at us. We hear it coming, but the warning offers no escape. As the violent river of wind envelopes our tiny camp, a tree trunk explodes no more than thirty feet from our tent. I reach for Trish, and together we try to shield Autumn as we wait out the longest four seconds of our lives. With the impact, our tent jumps and the earth moves beneath us as if it were liquid. I shine a light out of the tent door and see nothing but branches.

"We're out of here!" shouts Trish as she scoops Autumn into her arms and bolts for the edge of the lake. I follow as quickly as I can gather the tent and sleeping bags into a bundle that can be carried. A sixty-foot Douglas fir lies between our tent and the spot where Karen and Ross were sleeping, pinning one edge of our tarp to the ground. I shiver as I think of the probable results had the tree fallen a degree or two to either side of the spot it actually hit.

The other four are already on the rocky beach, Autumn no doubt wondering what in the world her parents are doing, dragging her around in the middle of the night like this. I re-erect our tent at the wind-swept edge of the lake, we climb in to escape the ever-present rain, and try to find depressions between the rocks for our hips and shoulders.

Morning arrives at last and we drag our aching bodies out of the tent once more. The rain has stopped, but a stiff wind — no comparison to last night's blow — is still kicking up whitecaps on the lake. We inspect the fallen tree we so narrowly escaped and breathe a silent thanks. The campfire is resurrected and a few pieces of Autumn's clothing are dried completely. After some initial hesitation, Trish and I decide to paddle on, keeping our small group together.

A stiff wind, and the possibility of a mid-lake capsize, dictate that we hug the east shore of Isaac Lake, which has turned in a southerly direction after passing Wolverine Creek. We're physically drained from the previous night and camp only nine miles farther down Isaac, at the mouth of an unnamed creek. The wind is easing up, the sky beginning to clear, but the temperature is plummeting. We spend a frigid night snuggled together.

Nevertheless, we meet the next day with energy, paddle the remaining fifteen miles of Isaac Lake, run the exit chute into the Isaac River, and make two relatively short portages. The halfway point of our trip finds us setting up camp at a beautiful spot on the edge of the river. Sunshine streams down through the treetops to turn the river mist into a luminous cloud and we take a short hike upriver to see the thirty-five foot waterfall we had portaged an hour earlier.

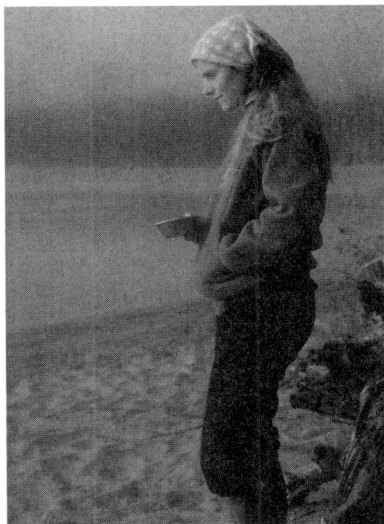

Left, Karen and Ross Brown back their sea kayak away from shore as Trish, Autumn and I prepare to board our canoe for another day on the seventy-mile circuit of lakes and rivers that make up the Bowron Lakes Provincial Park. Right, Trish enjoys the serenity that followed us after the stormy start of our canoe trip.

It is now autumn in the North Country. There is no doubt whatsoever as the air is calm, the sun pleasantly warm and the nights have a sharp bite to them. We glide smoothly along Lanezi, Sandy and the Spectacle Lakes, snow-capped peaks rising from the Mowdish, and Quesnel Ranges. A string of mergansers dives, one by one, from a log as we pass. Sand beaches are a delight for Autumn. She stuffs herself with blueberries from the bushes that surround our camps. Loons serenade us far into the evening. We are paid back in exquisite currency for the pounding we took at Wolverine Creek.

～

As the children arrived one after another over the next eight years, new family adventures would continue to take us far from the southern Appalachians. Our Isuzu Trooper, looking like a gypsy wagon with boats, bikes and child's bike trailer hanging all over the top and rear, made several trips west before we finally gave in to the need for a van. We would take week-long bike trips, camping along the Oregon Coast, Montana's Yaak River, or the Snowy Range in Wyoming. Interspersed with these were short river runs, where the kids could be involved.

One of our more ambitious trips took us to the other side of the world. In late January of 1988, Trish, Autumn, Forest and I left the mountains of North Carolina to bicycle New Zealand's South Island for three months. I would pull a Burley child trailer to accommodate the kids, who were four, and one-and-a-half at the time. We would camp and cook en route, brave the wind and rain of a hurricane fringe, and make many friends as we traveled.

While laying over in the town of Wanaka for a few days of rest, I noticed a hand-written sign on the door of an outdoor shop. There would be a river kayaking class the following day for beginners. I tracked down Chris, the instructor, told him I would love to get in a kayak again, and asked if he needed help with the class. Apparently my protestation of experience didn't convince him and he said the only way I could get in a kayak was to sign up for the course. So I did.

We paddled the Motatapu River that day and had many swimmers and loose boats. By the time I had finished a day of picking up people and pieces, and giving kayaking advice, Chris insisted on refunding my fee for the course. We all enjoyed cups of steaming tea, made with freshly picked mint, that his companion Margaret had waiting for us at the take-out. Chris asked if I would guide a raft on the Clutha River for him two days later.

I agreed to do it. He had two raft loads of teenagers, but only one guide (himself) — I'm not sure what he would have done if I hadn't shown up. The river drained Lake Clutha and was a fast-moving, high volume run, Class III+ with some rapids bordering on IV. I went over the basic paddling commands at the put-in and we were off like a stone from a slingshot. The rafts were professional grade sixteen-footers, the kids responded well and our lines were accurate. As we blasted through a large wave at the tail of the second rapid, an enthusiastic girl turned and asked,

"What's the next one like?"

"I've no idea — never been on this river before," I shot back. She looked as if she were about to be sick.

I added enough explanation to keep the group from thinking they were on a captain-less ship, and the rest of the day went well, as did the remainder of our family bicycling trip.

~

It was on one of our western odysseys that we discovered the Gates of Lodore section of the Green River in Colorado and Utah. Being "purists" from a canoeing and kayaking standpoint, we had never seriously considered rafting. But with a young family, even though our kids were being introduced to our traditional watercraft at an early age, our mind-set was about to change.

"If we had our own raft and rowing rig," we were thinking, "We could take our whole bunch for a week on the Green River next fall. I wonder if we could get a permit?" As it turned out, we were able to obtain both raft and permit that year, and headed west once again, this time in late September.

What follows is my journal account of that first trip on the Green, written at the time. Canyon was not yet born.

Lodore to Dinosaur — September, 1991

We made camp by the Green River to begin thinking whitewater and to await Cricket's arrival. On our way by the NPS River Office, we find out that the flow is 1300 to 1400 cfs, not 800 cfs as we were led to believe — we're not yet sure whether this is good or bad news. Autumn, Forest and Rivers made our first campfire and became our fire specialists for the rest of the trip. Cricket surprised us and zipped into camp in time for dinner after driving eleven hours from Santa Fe with only a brief rest. It's great to have her here so soon.

As the campground gradually begins to fill, three men pull into a site near us and begin unpacking river bags. Trish goes over to talk and I join them about twenty minutes later just in time to catch tales of heavy water, plowing into unavoidable rocks, and getting thrown out of the raft — they've just finished the trip we're about to do.

About an hour later, Trish approaches me in the dark and says, "There is no way the kids and I are going to run that stretch of river! Those men are experienced — both on the Green and other rivers — and they had a lot of problems."

I think to myself, experience and skill do not necessarily equate, and I counter with, 'Two factors I noticed which indicate questionable judgment — they were pulling firewood on an inner tube tied to their raft (a loss of steerage) and they had quite a supply of beer on the river (including a good bit left over)."

Even so, Mom's apprehension has spilled over to the kids and they all express negative thoughts about running the river. I don't sleep well that night, and the thought of one of the kids being tossed out in a large rapid haunts my dreams.

Sunday morning and it's our launch day. I flag down the ranger circling through camp and ask him about the river flow.

"Oh, it's running 1,800 cfs — always does — Flaming Gorge has to release enough to take care of irrigation rights downstream." One more opinion to put in the grinder.

After discussing our options, including splitting up, we decide to head for Gates of Lodore, talk to the ranger there, and evaluate the situation again. We gas up in Maybell and make Lodore by noon. A group from Boulder is preparing for their launch the following day. They assure us that the kids can walk around any difficult rapids and that the higher water level should help.

Our consensus is to go ahead as planned, putting in together here at Lodore, but a certain tension still remains. Despite many long family trips in the wilderness, and years of paddling whitewater rivers, none of us have run the Green before and this will be our first experience with guiding a heavily loaded raft on a multi-day river trip. How well will kayaking and canoeing skills transfer to rafting?

Dark clouds seem to boil right out of the high red-walled chasm that forms Gates of Lodore and we're drenched in a gusty rain squall as we scramble to assemble the raft and frame, and to pack and load gear. I slip with a load and fall prostrate in the mud. A few minutes later, Rivers does the same and ends up sitting in the river — not a happy prospect for a 2-1/2 year old when dry clothing is limited. Trish and I explode at each other and embarrass ourselves in front of the Boulder folks.

We've used up far too much of the afternoon but at last we're ready. Despite — or perhaps because of — our frayed nerves, the Boulder folks have stayed close, lending a hand here and there. One of them, Philip, catches me alone and slips a small animal bone into my palm. "Keep this always with you on the river — don't lose it — no one will swim, you'll enjoy the river and the weather will smile."

I thank him and tuck the bone safely into my paddling shorts, where it will remain for the rest of the trip. The weather has already begun to smile as the late afternoon sun paints warm colors on the canyon walls. But with October only a day away, the daylight will not last long and we must be off. I hand my camera to RW, one of the Boulder oarsmen, and he takes a picture of us — afloat at last!

The put-in fades into the distance as the oars dip and we slide silently toward the mouth of the canyon. From high on an eastern slope, a photographer waves and takes our picture. "He's from *National Geographic*,"

Trish says, "I saw him get a shot of the Isuzu Trooper while it was still loaded like a gypsy wagon."

There will be no rapids this afternoon as we pull into shore an hour later, now well into the canyon. We set our camp not far from the ruins of the old Wade & Curtis cabin; dinner is finished in the dark. As soon as dishes are done, we turn in for sleep — tomorrow will be a demanding day and the one just past has had its own share of stress.

Morning is chilly, but the myriad faces of early light draw our eyes to the beauty above and around us. In the low-use season — which we're now in — river runners are allowed to burn driftwood and the morning fire feels great. A large pan is used to contain the fire; and ashes, as well as dishwater, are strained and carried out. All human waste is taken with us as well.

We notice that the release from Flaming Gorge is not constant and the river has dropped about six inches overnight. But it's now on the rise and by mid-morning, as we take to the current again, we're riding a crest. I feel good about the way the raft has handled so far, but today I know the raft and oarsman will be put to the test.

Our first encounter will be with Upper Disaster Falls, where the No-Name was broken in two and lost on Powell's 1869 exploratory expedition. A scant four miles below our camp, we carefully watch for the islands and steep canyon wall on river left that will mark our approach to this rapid. Even so, I almost put the raft right into it and only a hard minute of back-ferrying pulls us away from the brink.

On land once more, the six of us follow the shore for the next half-mile to Lower Disaster Falls, scouting the continuous rapid as best we can, our view being partially blocked by another island. Autumn, Forest and Rivers strip to their skin and enjoy playing in an eddy at a sandy beach while Cricket and I make our way back to the raft. As we approach the main chute of Upper Disaster, our velocity increases, position is perfect, and the broad hole is punched with little difficulty. The next half-mile demands a number of moves, but there is plenty of time for each and Cricket and I decide that 1800 cfs must be an ideal water level for this rapid. We spin happily into the kids' eddy. In retrospect, I would certainly run it with all hands aboard.

A quick lunch and it's on to Triplet Falls. When you're in the right place in this rapid it looks easy, but it takes a strong ferry left to get there after S-turning through the upper part. If you miss the exit route, the main current will take you right into two room-sized boulders, almost assuring a flip or pin. The kids walk around, but I feel confident enough that I would probably take them through next time. Our run is uneventful.

The walking and scouting has slowed us down and shadows are creeping into the canyon. Hell's Half Mile still stands between us and camp, two miles away. Within ten minutes, we can hear the roar of the rapid and stop to scout. One look at the entrance and I motion the kids to walk — this one will have to wait until they are a good bit older.

A string of rocks — looking for all the world like huge teeth — block most of the river as it begins to drop steeply. An opening left of center marks the only possible route as half the flow seems to be rushing into this gap. In thirty feet, the river pours over a six-foot drop and into a violent back curl. The hole must be avoided with a quick and strong ferry to the right just after passing the entrance rocks.

I set up for the right hand move. The first stroke is good, but the second catches an underwater rock and pops the oar off of its pin. Before I can recover, the raft slants down the right shoulder of the drop, spins 180 degrees and hangs on the big boulder that the main tongue is pouring over. Cricket instinctively jumps to the right place and bounces the raft free as I jam the oar back into place. The rest of the run is full of challenges too, but none that match the first drop in excitement!

The "walk-around" almost matches the rapid in difficulty as the billy-goat trail soars high above the river with a sheer drop to the water's edge. Cricket ties off the raft and we both scramble back up the trail to help Trish with the kids. All in the raft again, we now relax and look forward to the Rippling Brook campsite twenty minutes ahead.

Camp is made at the lower site, a beautiful shaded area with a pebble beach and rocks convenient for sitting. Autumn, Forest and Rivers are immediately off to explore shallow caves near the sparkling stream that comes skipping out from between the western canyon walls. [In retrospect, Rippling Brook became our favorite site — calling us back in the years that would follow.]

Autumn and Forest take turns building, lighting and tending the morning and evening fires, a favorite chore. Our dinners are basic — lentils & rice, tortillas, spaghetti and the like — and most welcome. There are no leftovers! The sky is ablaze with constellations and paints the canyon with its own soft light through the clear night air.

Mornings are nippy (in the 40's), but quickly the sun brings its warmth to the day. From Rippling Brook, we slide into the fun rapids of Whirlpool Canyon, passing the impressive Steamboat Rock to arrive at Echo Park for lunch. The Yampa River joins the Green River now in the most spacious area we've seen since entering Gates of Lodore.

Our friends from Boulder catch us here, we exchange a few river experiences and they decide to eat lunch while they row. We suspect they want to make sure of first campsite choice at Jones Hole, where they'll spend three nights. We relax for an hour, fill water jugs and take to the river again. The next five miles are soon behind us as we pass the Boulder folks making camp at Jones Hole I. Jones Hole III is our choice and we set up amid the luxury of picnic tables and outhouse. [Outhouses have since been removed since all waste is carried out with each rafting party.]

We spend two nights at this friendly area, enjoying dips in the crystal clear creek and hikes up the canyon to appreciate colorful vistas and pictographs from Anasazi times. Cricket and her lizard catcher are a hit with the kids as several individuals are looped and identified, then returned to their rocks. A gopher snake is taking in the morning sun and as it senses our presence, withdraws backward into its hole. Two garter snakes make it a three-snake day.

We get to know our neighbors better, too — they've made the Green River a tradition, usually planning two trips a year. Todd, RW, Bill and Philip have been running rivers for a good while, Kim has friends at the Nantahala Outdoor Center, and Lois refers to herself as an aging hippie.

On the second night, they plan a Mexican party, complete with a piñata containing play money, jewels and condoms! Cricket and I arrive in time for the campfire, which is a fun round of stories, songs and jokes — Philip is just starting an animated take-off of one of Robert Service's poems as we find a spot near the crackling flames. Lois interjects lively comments and emphasis throughout. Cricket lends her captivating voice to several songs, tells an off-color joke that has the group almost rolling into the fire, and I contribute a rendition of the *Eddystone Light*.

With only seven miles to our next camp, we take our time packing and loading next morning and make a late start on the river. We pay for it, as a fierce wind comes up after lunch and at times actually blows us upriver. We swing the bow downriver, and Cricket and I take turns pitting our best strokes against the wind. At last we make camp at Island Park, a more exposed location than any we have camped at yet. The wind does not abate, adding another dimension to the chore of setting up tents and cooking dinner. Sunset is beautiful, but we sleep fitfully as the tents at times seem close to taking flight.

Our last day on the river dawns calm and we try for an early start to avoid afternoon headwinds in Split Mountain Canyon and to give Cricket more time for her drive to Santa Fe. The rapids in Split Mountain seem no more intimidating than on our evening run last summer — perhaps at a higher water level they've got more bite. Even SOB, with its many moves, goes by smoothly.

The bone Philip had given me at the put-in still remains in my pocket and the river experience has gone just as he predicted. Perhaps the spirit of that small animal still watches the Canyon of Lodore!

～

We returned to the Green several times over the years, depending on our luck in the permit lottery. Our most frequent companions were close friends from Georgia, longtime river runners Andrea and Bill Timpone and their children, Connor and Mickey. Our Green River trips were always off-season so that we could spend more time in the canyon, but early October often brought cold weather challenges. We once headed for Hell's Half Mile through a morning of snow flurries.

Coming ashore at Jones Holes on the Green River in September of 1998. Rear, left to right; Forest, Trish, Doug, Canyon. Front; Rivers and Autumn.

In late September of 2001, two weeks after the events that stood our country on its head, we were putting our raft into the river at Gates of Lodore once again. Besides our family, several good friends would accompany us in a second raft — Ed Pontbriand, Erin Brown and Carol Brown, Erin's mother. The weather was mellow, and the solitude just what we needed.

Ed had been the district ranger in charge of this park (Dinosaur National Monument) prior to his present assignment in the North Cascades and knew the river and surrounding country as few do. But when I would look to him for a decision, or even an opinion, on the choice of a camp or the running of a rapid, he would always defer with, "It's your choice, your trip — I'm happy with whatever you decide." But his knowledge and presence made the trip run like a well-oiled clock.

Canyon would make his first run of the Green at the age of seven months, sampling the sand at each campsite! As the kids grew older, they would take their turns on the oars, even in the most difficult rapids and on other rivers, such as Montana's Flathead.

~

Our outdoor education and skills programs continued for a year after Trish and I moved to the mountains, but our market was in Atlanta, not rural North Carolina. The long distance business proved impractical, and with the arrival of our first child and the demands of building a home with our own hands, we ceased operation completely. Living frugally, we were still able to make ends meet and enjoy the freedom of family time on river and trail. Our time was our own, and we could step into the moment whenever the opportunity arose.

Then, as Autumn approached the age at which children in this society are required to attend school, we realized that a huge change to our family lifestyle was looming on the horizon. Trish had taught in Atlanta, both in the public and private systems, and knew the shortcomings of most public schools. A private school with a progressive educational direction did not exist where we now lived, even if we could have afforded it, which of course we could not.

"What about homeschooling?" we kept asking ourselves as the time for decision grew closer. We knew that some families in our area already were teaching their own children, but by and large, the concept was still in its infancy. North Carolina law gave families the freedom to approach homeschooling in many ways, and we decided to give it a try. We felt that it would improve our children's quality of education, as well as providing the flexibility to travel when the time was right for the most meaningful educational experiences of all.

Over the years, homeschooling has proved to be the right path for all of our kids, and in the process, we've tried to give a bit of ourselves back to the larger homeschooling community. At the time we started our children on the path of self-education, there was a scattering of local homeschooling support groups across North Carolina, and one statewide group. Since most of these organizations were concerned not only with homeschooling, but also with relatively narrow religious, political and moral issues, we felt the need for more open support groups. As a result, we (but largely Trish) created two organizations, one locally and one statewide, that welcomed all homeschooling families regardless of their viewpoints on life's other issues.

Homeschooling has obviously worked for our family, but has it really worked for the kids individually? Suppose they wanted to switch back to a more traditional path of education — namely college — after having been on a path of self-directed learning? Our kids thus far have chosen college, have been accepted at all of the schools to which they applied, and have been awarded academic scholarships at the schools they finally selected.

So homeschooling became the key to our appearing in out-of-the-way places at times of our own choosing. And those appearances, in turn, became the basis of not only our children's education, but Trish's and mine as well. Sure, we ran rivers in Costa Rica, Chile and New Zealand, but we also rode the chicken buses through Guatemala and Peru, camping, washing our clothes in a bucket, and playing soccer with the local kids. We lived and ate with Mayan families in the mountains of Guatemala and learned a little of how our lifestyle impacts theirs. Our children saw a reason for learning another language and still correspond with friends made during these travels.

~

I could be a bit pushy with my own kids when it came to running whitewater. David will likely never forget the first time I dragged him down Section IV of the Chattooga, the two of us paddling kayaks. He was a nervous sixteen at the time, trying to listen to my advice and then follow my line through all of the big ones. That day he did well, and his love of the sport grew along with his skill. He is known as "Woody" to his buddies.

He used to meet friends of mine on the river and hear, "Oh, you're Doug Woodward's son?"

Years later, he regularly kayaks such vertical runs as Overflow Creek, Tallulah Gorge and the West Prong. I meet friends of his at the river, but now they say, "Oh, you're Woody's dad?"

I kayaked the Nantahala with Forest and talked him into running the Falls at age six. A capsize in the hole scared him so badly that it probably set his paddling back by a couple of years.

Nowadays, Forest and Rivers often run the tough stuff with David. I don't. Sometimes I might rationalize that they have boats and equipment that were never available to me, but I know better. Their skills have gone far beyond my own.

Cricket was drawn to live in the West by childhood trips to Arizona, Colorado and Wyoming, now spending her outdoor time climbing rocks, riding horses and paddling on occasion. Autumn's energy is directed toward issues of social justice, but she still finds time to kayak the rivers of Montana during the spring run-off. Canyon enjoys our North Carolina rivers, paddling hard to catch his older brothers.

Trish and I? Do we really paddle tandem? Hardly. Trish still avoids the closed-in feeling and likes to be in control, enjoying rivers in a lightweight solo open canoe, while I paddle a high-volume creek kayak.

Our tandem effort comes in raising a family and helping each child form values that will mean something as they travel on without us. We're proud of the skills our children have learned, their creativity and their accomplishments. We could care less about their pursuit of careers or wealth. We hope that they have learned by now, wherever their rivers may take them, that every individual in this world — regardless of what life has dealt that person — has dignity and is worthy of respect and friendship.

Island In Time

"Three-five-zero, this is Steeck on McGregor. Medical emergency on the river at Buckner Hole. Injuries and apparent drowning. Need immediate response."

The lazy summer afternoon along the remote Stehekin River was suddenly shattered as Park Service radios up and down the valley came alive. The powerful repeater atop McGregor Mountain in the North Cascades sent the conversation on to the NPS Comcenter in Marblemount. A tense operator would monitor events to see if outside medical help would need to be called in.

There were, of course, rangers on call in the valley. "Steeck, three-five-zero on McGregor. We're on our way, Chuck. Eight minutes from you. Do you have any more details? How many involved?"

"It was the ranch raft trip, Greg. A fisherman just ran in from the river so I haven't been there yet. A boy injured and a girl unconscious, not breathing — there was a catch in Chuck's voice — I think the girl could be Chelsea."

"Oh my God."

~

There is often a very thin line between adventure and tragedy. Setting out that afternoon in two paddle-rafts were a handful of guests from the Stehekin Valley Ranch and a few valley residents filling in the empty spots. Moderate rapids, water battles between rafts and breathtaking views of the snow-capped Cascades promised an experience to cherish in memory. Today, there would be something else.

From the normal put-in, a mile above the ranch, to the point where it loses itself in Lake Chelan, the Stehekin River is considered a Class II run for rafts and kayaks. The frigid water temperature and frequent sweepers create hazards of their own, however. As the river passes Buckner Orchard, it narrows, piling into an imposing rock buttress on river right, splitting the main current and forcing a significant portion of it into the mouth of Blackberry Creek. Violent, rapidly spinning eddies are the result. And for several years prior to this day, floating trees caught by the buttress had been building into a fearsome strainer.

Minutes before Chuck Steeck's urgent call for help, the two rafts had been navigating this stretch of the Stehekin. Steve Farmer, an off-duty ranger for the National Park, held his raft left and neatly caught the eddy below the point of rock. The guide in the second raft was not so precise, allowing it to spin, broach and flip as he and his crew rode the current directly into the strainer.

There was momentary panic as the icy water closed over the heads of the paddlers. Several flushed past the strainer and were pulled ashore by the crew of the first raft. Ten-year-old Reed Courtney was caught in the jumble of logs and broke an arm as he fought to keep from being sucked under water. A daring assist by several others helped him reach the shore. "Not something I want to go through again!" exclaimed one paddler as two nurses from the first raft arrived with Steve Farmer to take a look at Reed's arm.

"Where is the little girl?" suddenly screamed a woman who had crawled out on the rock. No one had seen Chelsea, Reed's twelve-year-old sister, since the capsize. Steve knew she hadn't washed down to his raft and quickly scanned the strainer. A small bit of color showed beneath the surface — too far beneath the surface.

It took Steve only a moment to size up the situation, and he knew the odds of reaching Chelsea, let alone freeing and recovering her, were problematic at best. At the same time, too quickly for word thoughts, his mind grasped the enormity of the tragedy to the to this small community. This was Chelsea Courtney, the oldest girl in her family's generation of siblings and cousins in the valley. A gentle person, always ready with a smile and a kind word for friend and stranger alike. A leader, particularly for the younger children, as she spent many hours helping them with their school work. And an athlete, who could hold her own on the basketball court with the toughest of her male cousins. The loss to her family, and to this tightly knit settlement, would be incalculable.

Steve Farmer is a tall man. My six-foot frame has to look up when I speak with him. In any other circumstance you would be called a fool to risk your life in such a high velocity strainer, but Steve knew what he had to do and didn't hesitate. On his first attempt, he made contact with Chelsea's body, but couldn't dislodge her. With a good grip on a tree that was part of the jumble, he filled his lungs, stretched his full length, and kicked Chelsea with both feet as hard as he could. She floated free and was quickly hauled in by a chain of folks trying to choke back their tears.

The two nurses, guests from the Stehekin Valley Ranch, started CPR immediately while others tried to warm her as best they could. "Come back. Come back. Chelsea, come back to us," was the silent prayer of those who watched her lifeless form. Chelsea had been under water too long. Nevertheless, you have to keep trying.

Within minutes of that first urgent call, word spread quickly through the small community, many of whom monitor the Park radio frequency. It had been confirmed that, indeed, it was Chelsea who had been pulled unconscious from the river. There was a feeling of helplessness. Most could only wait.

Others did what they could, some heading for Chelsea and Reed's house to be with their mother, Liz Courtney. Liz's heart was tied in knots and she was in her own world as she paced back and forth, praying for a miracle. Meanwhile, the Park had called for a helicopter with an EMT aboard.

The floatplane was in from Chelan, waiting at the Stehekin dock for several downlake passengers to board. A ranger ran down the ramp.

"Nick, we've got an emergency and need you to hold the plane for us. It'll be Liz, Reed and Robbie [Chelsea's aunt] — and maybe Chelsea, depending how quickly that chopper gets here. Folks, I'm sorry but you'll need to make other arrangements for leaving Stehekin."

Back on the riverbank the two nurses continued to work in a steady professional rhythm, never pausing but taking turns, one administering CPR while the other kept a constant watch for the return of Chelsea's vital signs.

There was a slight but unmistakable movement in Chelsea's body. The nurses' eyes met as the same question sprang into both of their minds. Was that a postmortem spasm or a sign of returning life? One nurse held her cheek close to Chelsea's mouth and nostrils.

"She's beginning to breathe on her own," she whispered.

"And her pulse is returning!" exclaimed the other.

"Steve, can you ferry us to the Orchard side? I think I hear the helicopter." By now, Park personnel had arrived and Chelsea was getting oxygen assistance to aid her breathing.

The miracle was real. The frigid glacial water — often prolonging the life functions of drowning victims — and the quick action of those at the scene had pulled Chelsea back from the brink. She continued to respond and was transferred to the waiting helicopter. More frustration for Liz, who had intended to fly with her.

"Sorry, ma'am. I only have room for the patient and the EMT." It was the pilot speaking.

Tom Courtney, Chelsea and Reed's dad, was on his tug in Lake Chelan, bringing the barge on its long uplake run to Stehekin. He heard the familiar drone of the floatplane, a DeHaviland Beaver, as it headed downlake for Chelan. But it suddenly banked overhead, powered back into the wind, and glided onto the lake near the tug. Tom knew it had to be bad news.

Family tragedies were not new to the Courtneys. Tom's brother Gordon, in his teens, had drowned at Logger's Point on the lake years before. And his father, Ray, had been killed in a fall from a precipice near Hillguard Pass as he attempted to untangle a horse that had slipped from the trail.

A dark icy cloud of dread gripped Tom's heart during the minutes it took the plane to taxi close to the tug. Nick, the pilot, stepping from the Beaver's pontoon to pull the plane close to the tug, quickly told Tom all he knew — that Chelsea had been pulled from the river, that she had apparently been revived by the timely action of those on the scene, and was now being flown to the hospital under the care of an EMT. Tom sent the barge on its way with his assistant, climbed into the Beaver, and headed to Chelan with Nick and the others. From there, it was a tense forty-minute drive to the hospital in Wenatchee. Reed, who would be the last to complain, sat almost unnoticed in the back, still in his wet river clothes, his injured arm held against his ribs.

Even as the community waited for further word, Chelsea was being checked out, and Reed's arm set and put in a cast. The news had gone from "the worst" to "very encouraging." Beyond all hope, Chelsea had returned. Stehekin breathed a collective prayer of thanks and relief.

When I later asked Chelsea about that day, she replied with a smile, "I don't remember anything about it." Reed, who was conscious through the whole terrifying sequence of events, was not so fortunate. He can still recall the pain and uncertainty of those hours.

~

Residents of communities that grow up in a river valley are usually dominated by that river. Stehekin is no exception. Fed by the glaciers of the North Cascades, Agnes, Doubtful, Basin, Park and other creeks gather together to form the Stehekin River which in turn fills 1500-foot deep Lake Chelan. In late spring, melting snow can swell the river to ten or fifteen times its winter volume, sending water over the valley road and close to homes. Uprooted trees being swept down the river can end up in strange places, sometimes causing the river to change course and cut new channels.

The worst flooding, however, has come from torrential rains. In October of 2003, a record flood, which blew right off the scale of the flow gauge, rampaged through the valley. Many dwellings received water damage and Postmaster Al White's home ended up in the river, twisted and splintered beyond repair. Only a handful of residents live out of reach of the river's wrath.

Lying at the head of Lake Chelan near the center of Washington State, the community of Stehekin is surrounded by the North Cascades National Park. You may come by boat, floatplane, or foot. If you're brave enough to attempt a landing between the steep walled sides of the valley, you can even fly in with your own plane. But you won't drive to Stehekin. The nearest road ends more than thirty miles from the community along the south shore of the fiord-like lake. Don't expect a grocery store, television or telephone service. Leave your cell phone behind; it won't connect. Stehekin is not for everyone.

But for a few fiercely independent individuals, Stehekin is the only place. They accept, even relish, the challenge of carving out a secure homestead amid the uncertainties of isolated mountain life. Secure, of course, is relative. When you have bear and cougar for neighbors, and Mother Nature always looking over your shoulder, ready to unleash flood, fire or avalanche, security takes on a new meaning.

You know how many cords of firewood will take you through fall, winter and spring, and that fir will keep your fire burning through the night. Your groceries and mail will come in from Chelan on the *Lady of the Lake*, three days a week in winter. By late November or early December, you will be pulling those groceries in by sled.

A local road, which never came close to connecting with the outside world, briefly ran nearly twenty miles in the valley, from the boat landing to the start of the climb to Horseshoe Basin, back in the era of up-valley mining. Avalanches each winter made it impractical to keep the last two miles of this road free of boulders, tree jumbles and other debris and it was not long in returning to a natural state. A fall flood in 1995 chopped off two more miles between Glory Mountain and Cottonwood. Then the big one in 2003 ate away sections of the road all the way down to Six

Mile, isolating the Stehekin Valley Ranch for a time. Portions of the road were rerouted so that there was again access to the ranch, but it's likely that Mother Nature will continue to rule the upper valley.

Tom Courtney will bring your vehicle to the valley by barge. He'll supply your gasoline the same way. You can drive anywhere in the valley that the road remains, but you'd better be your own auto mechanic.

Part of a disappearing breed nationally, the one-room schoolhouse in Stehekin remains alive and well. A log structure of pleasing appearance, its entrance hall displays photos of two generations of Stehekin log schoolhouses which preceded it. "One room schoolhouse" is a misnomer — "one classroom schoolhouse" would be a more descriptive term. With its own library, a small gymnasium, computer stations in several areas, an early learning room and a kitchen that doubles as a photo darkroom, the facilities are anything but "backwoods."

Despite snows that regularly reach a depth of five feet or more in January, classwork goes on around the crackling woodstove of the schoolhouse as it does on any other school day. "Snow days" are unknown in Stehekin — an aberration for the outside world to wrestle with. Cross-country skis protrude from mounds of snow close to the covered entranceway. In milder weather, those spots will be filled with bicycles.

The school serves students from kindergarten through eighth grade and schoolmaster Ron Scutt is approaching the end of his third decade at the Stehekin School. Honored by the State of Washington for his out-standing teaching, creative works of his students adorn the classroom walls. Each school year culminates with the publishing of a newspaper, *The Way Through* (the Native American meaning of the word "Stehekin"), filled with photos and writing by the students. Having known some of his students for the full eight school years, Ron's heart follows each of them as they leave. Graduation is a time of special recognition for the one or two students who reach the end of their Stehekin schooling each June. When kindergarten age children enroll, Ron's wife Kim comes in to teach and bring the early learning room to life.

Roughly a third of the year-round population of Stehekin work for the National Park, or are the families of those who do. Some of these Park employees have been so captured by the magic of people and place in this community that they have bought land and built homes with the intention of staying on. But not all who want to can find private land, for it is scarce and very expensive when available. At one time the Park was actively trying to buy up the remaining private parcels and still holds life estates, which chip away at the private land base when the owner dies.

Other residents have deep roots in Stehekin, often reaching back to their parents' or grandparents' generations, and provide a living history for those who take time to listen. In summer, and at other times, many folks come whose families have lived in and had an impact on Stehekin in the past. The Buckner sisters, Irene, Hobbie and Bucky, grew up with the Orchard property as their home. Long married and living elsewhere, they still return at times throughout the year to enjoy Stehekin with their families.

But today one cannot envision Stehekin without thinking of the Courtney family. Five brothers and their cousin, and particularly their wives, combine skills that allow the Valley to function. Whether it be heavy construction, a hearty array of food at the bakery, saving a life with EMT training, a multi-day pack trip through breath-taking scenery, flying the float plane, serving a sumptuous dinner at the ranch, or just getting something to work that no one else could, the Courtneys can do it.

Jim, Tom, Mark, Cragg and Cliff, all sons of Esther and Ray Courtney, grew up in a small cabin at Nine Mile where the Stehekin Valley Ranch now welcomes guests. "Formal education" ended with graduation from Stehekin School. Yet each of these individuals deserves to carry a Ph.D. in practical wilderness skills behind his name. Now their twelve children, the fourth Valley generation of Courtneys, are rapidly becoming as competent as their parents. Cousin Mike Barnhart, son of June Courtney, and his wife Nancy are superb photographers, offering Stehekin photo workshops, publishing books and calendars, and often hanging shows of their work, both within and outside the valley.

Despite the feeling that you've stepped back in time when you come ashore in Stehekin, technology has made itself felt here. Electricity appeared, not without opposition, several decades ago, first with Art Peterson's hydro venture near what is now the Park maintenance area and later with the PUD's (Public Utility District's) construction of a 200-KW hydro plant on Company Creek. Those facilities eventually dimmed the kerosene lamps of Stehekin, although most residents still keep them within easy reach.

With the electricity came many possibilities. One of these even provided an opportunity to draw the community together. A 16mm movie projector was obtained and movies could be brought uplake for special showings. But with the coming of the VCR, this social event gradually disappeared.

At this writing, a proposal for a telephone system in the valley has generated terrific controversy. It appears that a majority of residents are stubbornly set against it, while a few others are trying every means to bring it into being. There is little doubt that it would change the character of life in Stehekin; but strangely enough, many of the telephone opponents are already connected to the Internet in their homes through a satellite system. Where once a trip was made to a neighbor's house to ask a question or relay some special piece of information over a cup of tea, now that same question or information appears impassively on a computer screen.

Yet some remain true to the way of life that worked so well in the old days. Mark Courtney and his wife Monica live in the last inhabited cabin as you travel up the Valley. They heat and cook with wood and have a long snowy trek to their cabin in wintertime. Mark is a skilled carpenter with EMT certification, as well as an expert archer and bow-maker. No PUD lines run to their home. A small creek behind their home provides both water and minimal electric power through a homemade generator. They've raised two children, Jake and Mistaya, and helped them choose the best of both worlds.

Jake and Reed are part of the fourth generation of Stehekin Courtneys who are fast becoming adults. The two cousins now fly their own airplane in and out of Stehekin. But once, when Jake was younger, he brought home a Gameboy. Mark watched him play for half an hour, then walked over, picked it up, opened the wood stove and tossed it in.

～

The summer of 1976 found me on the highway, heading west out of Atlanta, trying to escape the memories of a lost love. I had picked the North Cascades as my destination, trusting that the wild natural beauty there would fill my empty heart. Just as wilderness had always healed me in the past, it helped once more. I entered the infant National Park from the west side, climbing, mostly cross-country, to a spot just below the toe of Quien Sabe Glacier. There I spent much of a week socked in by rain, listening to the roar of avalanches hidden in the mist, and holding tea parties for the marmots and picas. On a gloriously clear final day, I crossed the glacier above me and trekked to the top of Sahale Arm. As I gazed over the sea of snowy peaks on all sides, I had no idea that Stehekin lay hidden in the valley to the east, only twenty miles away.

～

Trish and I first came to Stehekin with three of our children (Canyon was not yet born) in the summer of 1990. We stayed in a tent cabin at the ranch and mainly hiked the trails to Horseshoe Basin, Agnes Gorge and Coon Lake, never really getting to know the folks that lived in the community. On that trip we met and chatted with Esther, Cliff and Kerry Courtney. We even talked ranch raft guide Dave Wilson into a late summer raft trip while I ran along by kayak.

Trish was born in Spokane, spending her first twenty years in Washington State and it has always been a magnet drawing her back. Our family had made a number of trips from our home in North

Carolina to backpack trails in the Olympics and Cascades, but one of her visions included having our children experience a period of living in the West. "How about Stehekin?" she suggested.

"Are you out of your mind?" I replied. "We could never afford to live there!"

"We won't go in the summer. It should be cheaper off-season. Let me scout it out."

She did. Camping at Purple Point and biking the Valley, Trish must have spoken with nearly every resident of Stehekin! There were several possibilities within our budget.

"I think we should stay at Wally's A-frame," was her conclusion. "He's an old-timer there and I really liked him."

It was a good choice. The cabin fit the family, the four kids sleeping upstairs in the loft while Trish and I had the downstairs bedroom. Wally lived in a smaller cabin right across the gravel road. He was well read in the science of astronomy and would also contribute gems of valley history now and again. We soon found that despite a seemingly gruff exterior, Wally's heart was pure gold. We drove his second truck, a thirty-year-old Ford, when we weren't on our bikes and when we would pass him on the road the kids would ask, "Was that the finger or the thumb?" as his hand shot into the air. Fortunately, with us, it was usually the thumb!

We had decided to stay in Stehekin the months of October and November. Almost as soon as we arrived, I was splitting firewood, huge rounds of old-growth fir that Wally had hauled in and had drying for two winters. The kids had always homeschooled, so we were flexible, but we all felt the Stehekin School would be a unique and stimulating experience for the boys; Autumn was already past the eighth grade. Schoolmaster Ron Scutt agreed that they could attend for the short time period, and so we increased the school enrollment from eight to eleven!

We met more folks at the end-of-season bakery picnic and soon came to know them all by sight. The Fall Festival, a late October community event, was great fun for kids young and old, and we began to feel as if we belonged in Stehekin.

It was sometime near the end of October, as we hiked the trail into Agnes Gorge, that I turned to Trish and said, "You know, I could live in Stehekin. I don't mean just these two months, but for a long time."

Did I really say those words, I thought? I, who had built our home by the waterfall in the secluded cove in the North Carolina mountains? I, who had vowed never to move again?

"I know," she replied. "But let's see how we make it through the winter first."

A decision had been made. The discussion would follow. Usually the other way around.

There was a mad scramble to surmount the obstacles that were suddenly rearing their heads. Wally's place was not available due to prior rental commitments. Where can we go? We have no vehicle. Can we find something in time to get it on Tom's barge since he only runs about once a month in the winter? If we find a place, will it be suitable for winter living? How much wood will I need to cut and split before the snow comes in earnest?

We had briefly met Berneita and Babe Miles a couple of weeks earlier as they were leaving the valley. Was their house at Six Mile available? Great! What about winter there? A larger woodstove is needed to heat the whole house? OK. Yes, I'll work on wood immediately to add to that already in the woodshed. Sure, we know it's a long walk from the house to a parking spot on the valley road, but I think we can handle it. Often cut off by flooding during spring run-off? We'll have friends ship our raft to us.

I went downlake twice, once for a truck and again for a woodstove. Both had to be in good shape, reasonably priced, and able to meet our specific needs. I had nearly given up on each trip, when a new ad would appear in the paper at the last possible moment. My quest for a truck took me to Entiat and the stove all the way to Spokane, but at last I had just what we needed.

Sometime during that hectic November, I had stopped by the home of Roberta and Don Pitts to let Roberta know of our plans, since the boys would be continuing at the Stehekin School. At that time, Don was still the Stehekin Postmaster and Roberta the superintendent of the Stehekin School District. Yes, tiny Stehekin has its very own! I recall Roberta's words of advice on hearing that we would be staying the winter.

"You know that as a family, especially with four children, you are an asset to the Valley. It's often a struggle, since there is so little private land and so few places to rent, to keep the necessary number of folks here to make Stehekin a thriving community."

"But let me tell you something else. You will be watched, by everyone, to see how you meet the task of living through a Stehekin winter. Not that folks won't help you if you really need it. Anyone will. But things will go wrong. It will be difficult, particularly living that far from the valley road and in an area that floods during spring run-off. You may handle it or you may not."

The winter did present its challenges. The alternator on the truck died. The wrong one came up on the boat from Chelan. We charged the spare battery at the workshop and sledded batteries back and forth between the shop and the valley road to keep the truck running until the correct alternator arrived. Working with near-frozen fingers, I would drop parts into the snow and spend ten minutes searching for them. The water heater element burnt out and we were without hot water for three days until a replacement arrived on the boat.

By January there was five feet of snow on the ground and keeping a path shoveled to the woodshed and workshop was demanding. Our route over the little bridge and out to the valley road (on top of the snow) had to be continually tramped down by snowshoe to keep it stable. Snow piling up below the eaves would block the first floor windows and require more shoveling. Meanwhile, the kids were having a ball sledding off the workshop roof! Rene and Jim invited us to their mid-winter potluck and fireworks spectacular, a full moon reflecting from the river and the surrounding snowy landscape.

"Park under that tall fir tree at the end of your road when you walk in," Wally advised. "There'll be less snow there." He was right. And each time he plowed the valley road, Cragg Courtney would carefully clear our little parking spot under the towering fir.

Once, when I was out of the valley, Trish had driven about a mile down the road from our snow trail when the truck quit and would not restart. She hiked home. A day later, the truck mysteriously appeared in its accustomed parking spot, in good running order. The guardian angels of the valley had worked their magic for us.

So winter passed and the floods of spring appeared. Icy water poured out of the woods and spread across McGregor Meadow, blocking our route to the valley road for several weeks. We tried wading the first time, but with a strong current and thigh-deep water, it took too long and our legs had little feeling left by the time we reached the road. I strung 450 feet of rope between trees, which gave us just the span we needed to ferry ourselves in and out using our raft. There were other flood channels we had to wade through, but at this river level they were manageable on foot. Later we would see the river rise to the point where we could do nothing but sit tight on our island until it subsided.

Indeed, we did survive that first year. In fact, we thrived on it. So much so, that our original "two months" became four years. But, as often happens in Stehekin, families with teen-age children have needs that cannot easily be met in an isolated community. So, with mixed emotions, we too, reached that point in our lives where we bid a sad farewell to our Stehekin friends and returned to our familiar mountain cove in North Carolina.

~

As I wrestle with thoughts that can never quite do justice to this place and its people, I am once more in Stehekin, paying more attention to the scene outside of this tiny cabin than to the words I have just written. A cold, early spring drizzle has fallen for the past two days. But now a brilliant blue morning reveals the mountains in all directions painted with a glistening mantle of fresh snow. A hundred feet away, the river rumbles peacefully over a small drop. Last year it was shaving the near bank. Now it has piled a huge gravel bar in that spot and moved itself to a far channel. Where will it be when I next return? Totally unpredictable, it has a will of its own. The river rules.

Rivers Woodward kayaking the Stehekin River above High Bridge, August, 2003.

Into The Mist

I never expected to arrive at this eddy so quickly. Sure, there are more rapids yet to run, but what a fascinating river lies behind me. As I gaze upstream to the day in 1944 when that first canoe came to take my heart away, I could not have imagined all the twists and turns that awaited me downriver.

There would be mellow, sunny days of gliding past cliffs and cow pastures; starry nights on a hundred river banks; logjams and waterfalls; deep pools and thundering rapids; rolls and swims; slalom gates and finish lines; rivers that beckoned and others that intimidated; friends with whom to share the river; ecstasy and tragedy.

But if I had to choose the one type of experience that has most satisfied my longing for rivers, there is little doubt that it would be the extended wilderness journey. Going into vast expanses of country where human beings are but minor players in the scheme of what's happening, and the outcome of the adventure is never assured, is healing to the soul. Those with whom you share such an experience will be close to your heart for the rest of your life.

Would I call myself a "cutting-edge" paddler? No. Not even at the peak of my river running days. It was not my paddling skill, but my love of the sport that I was able to pass on to others. To see one of my friends enthused about whitewater boating, to watch one of my Scouts turn in an inspired slalom performance, to realize that my children's boating skills have gone far beyond my own — these are the reasons for my river years.

Each river has etched herself into my memory, yet all rivers merge into one. There are reaches of incredible mystery, beauty and challenge that will stay alive as long as my own spirit lives. I have seen her in evening light and morning mist, peacefully approaching, my paddle at rest. I have watched her uncontrolled anger, as she tumbles boulders to rearrange her bed, sending me scurrying for a safe eddy. I would like to think that she might recognize my feelings, or would at least remember how she once bore me along in joy. But I know better.

Acknowledgments

Thoughts of writing this book had flitted in and out of my head for years, but it took a spark from a new friend to suddenly put the process in motion. Two years ago, I was camped with my family in a remote Baja cove, a spot made nearly inaccessible by the ravages of recent hurricanes. Around a cheery driftwood campfire, we exchanged tales with several other hardy souls who had braved the hair-raising descent to sea level. My stories tended to gravitate toward whitewater, producing a response from a young lady who had been a kayaking competitor and river guide in our home mountains of North Carolina. "You *must* put these stories into a book," Brooke Robertshaw implored, making me realize at last that someone else might enjoy my words. When we returned home, my kids kept the pressure on. The project was underway.

When I thought memoir, I visualized sitting down at the keyboard and writing down my memories, as many as I could recall. Then I realized how inadequate my own mind was for this task. To confirm dates of events, persons involved and other particulars was going to involve searching old newsletters, personal journals, and the Internet, along with tracking down folks who had shared the experience. Even my own memoirs were going to require research.

Reconnecting with paddling buddies, some of whom I hadn't seen or spoken with in years, took me back to the days of exploring unknown rivers, small trips, emerging races and a time when you knew the occupants of any vehicle with a boat racked overhead — and probably where they were headed. I would particularly like to thank, for the light that they have shed on rivers of the past; Jim Stuart, Charlie Walbridge, Claude Terry, Payson Kennedy, Barbara Brown, Ed Gertler, Buzz Williams and John Sweet. Lewis King, James Dickey's inspiration for the Lewis Medlock of *Deliverance* (played by Burt Reynolds in the film version), filled in several gaps in my account of the real-life canoe trip which spawned the idea for Dickey's novel.

Both former President Jimmy Carter and *Newsweek* Middle East Editor Christopher Dickey took time from their busy international schedules to review and comment on early manuscripts of *Wherever Waters Flow*. I am profoundly grateful.

Experienced authors often add suggestions that can make the birthing of a first book go smoothly. Such has been the case with contributions of expertise from John Lane, Ron Watters, Ana Maria Spagna, Linda Cooper, Katie Lee and Jim Holechek, all of whom have offered tips on publishing, content, and style.

A special thanks to Ruth Scales, Head of Technical Services for Hege Library at Guilford College, for taking the time to catalogue *Wherever Waters Flow* according to Library of Congress standards.

The events that take place at the beginning of the *Island in Time* chapter had a profound impact on my own psyche. Even though I was not present at the time they occurred on the Stehekin River, my love for both the people of the community and the river itself made them as real to me as if I had been there. A special thanks to Ranger Steve Farmer, one of the heroes of the Stehekin story, who shared the official reports of the rescue, as well as letters of thanks from individuals in the community. A grateful thanks to members of the Courtney family, Liz, Tom, Mark, Robbie and of course, Chelsea and Reed, for describing that difficult day with its intense feelings and agreeing to let me write about it. Mark Scherer and Ana Maria Spagna also supplied details which contributed to the accuracy of the account. My thanks to all of you.

As the book evolved, my wife, Trish and my children, Cricket, David, Autumn, Forest, Rivers and Canyon had to suffer through multiple readings of various versions. They all made comments for practical improvements in the kindest way possible. Forest somehow took time from a busy semester at UNC-Chapel Hill to completely edit the manuscript. Cricket performed a similar edit at her home in Oregon, along with the design of the book jacket. When I saw that design for the first time, I immediately called her. After fielding several minutes of my superlatives, she simply replied, "Hey Dad, that *is* what I do for a living." Later, she performed the equally gargantuan task of typesetting the text and photos to meet the formatting requirements of our printer.

No one knows better than Trish the patience it has taken to tolerate the schedule of an active father trying to become a working author. The month that she gave me for writing without interruption of telephone or Internet in our Stehekin, Washington hideaway was golden, as was the two weeks I spent writing and researching at the quiet and beautiful home of our good friends, Elena and Paul Carlson, in the nearby Cowee mountains of North Carolina. We have managed a number of family outdoor activities during the writing and publishing periods, but never enough. I will be in her debt for quite a while.

Do you paddle *white water*, *white-water*, or *whitewater*? I remember John Sweet, writer and champion C-1 competitor — before the days of Hearn and Lugbill — raising this same question in one of the early *American Whitewater Journals*. As I recall, he felt that the separate words referred more to the color of water as if it had been painted, and the hyphenated version was simply an intermediate stage of the evolution of the two words into one. He urged the adoption of whitewater as the preferred term for both rapids and the sport of paddling. I agree with his logic and have used the single word throughout this book.

While practicing engineering, I was frequently required to be a technical writer. At such times, I would take pains to strive for truth and clarity in my words. This may be an attainable goal in the supposedly objective world of engineering reports, but in other areas such a goal may remain as elusive and ephemeral as morning mist on the Chattooga River. I have learned in writing paddling articles that the reader who is familiar with some event that I've described may have had an entirely different take on the lesson learned, differ with me as to the details, or supply facts and insight of which I've been completely ignorant. I'm sure that that will be the case with many events in this book. To such friends and fellow paddlers of rivers past, your comments are welcome. I would enjoy hearing from you.

Photos:

Front Cover: Rodger Losier
Back Cover Flap of author: Forest Woodward
Back Cover Flap of The Sinks: unknown (author's camera)
Page 9, 215, 236: Lynn "Cricket" Woodward
Page 16, 161 of author, 260: Trish Severin
Page 29: Harvey Beeler
Page 55: Nancy Rayburn
Page 68 of Dave Kurtz: Tom Sargent
Page 163 of author and Claude Terry paddling: Payson Kennedy
All other photos by author, three with self-timer

About The Author

Known in the southern U.S. kayaking scene as one of its "Founding Fathers," Doug Woodward has been running rivers for nearly fifty years — as an instructor and companion to many boaters, a boat-builder, a founder of Southeastern Expeditions guide service, and an advocate for paddlers and our rivers.

He builds his stories like he builds his boats — with precision, loyalty to the content, and interwoven humor.

Wherever Waters Flow, reveals Doug's abiding love of rivers, one of the major threads running through his life. He pursues, however, other parallel dimensions, many of which have been as intense and enduring as whitewater paddling — defender of peace and social justice, self-education (homeschooling) advocate, family homestead creator, wilderness educator for young children, and writer and photographer for many publications in the United States and other countries.

Doug Woodward running Etowah Falls, north Georgia, May, 1980.

Index

Would you like another copy of *Wherever Waters Flow*?

We'd be glad to send additional copies! Just send a check or money order (payable to Headwaters Publishing) for:
$26.95 for each book,
$5.00 for packaging and postage of the first book,
$3.00 for packaging and postage of each additional book on the same order, to:

Headwaters Publishing
PO Box 494
Franklin, NC 28734

If you would like the book(s) autographed, please indicate this at the time of your order.

We're not Amazon or Barnes & Noble, just a tiny family business tucked away in the Southern Appalachians. We apologize for not dealing in plastic and electronic ordering, but we will do our best to get *Wherever Waters Flow* to you as quickly as we can.

I wish I could give a copy of *Wherever Waters Flow* to every person who would like to read it, but since our family lives on a small fixed income, I haven't yet found a way to make that dream happen.

If you have questions or would like to contact us, we're reachable via mail at the PO Box above, email: nakedkayaks@yahoo.com, and our website: www.headwaterspublishing.com.